I0156489

WHAT READERS ARE SAYING ABOUT

DISASTER ISLAND

"*Disaster Island* offers a fascinating, disturbing, and insightful look into how easily a child who is bullied, especially while going through puberty, can fall into making detrimental life choices when he lacks the much-needed attention and affection of those closest to him. I cried, I laughed, I loved every page, and I hurt for Kyle when he was at his most vulnerable."

— Tyler R. Tichelaar, PhD and Award-Winning Author of *Narrow Lives* and *The Best Place*

"Although written as fiction, this story portrays realistic situations surrounding bullying, abuse, and PTSD. It offers readers a fresh and relatable perspective and lights the way to a brighter future."

— Susan Friedman, CSP and International Best-Selling Author of *Riches in Niches: How to make it BIG in a small market*

"Compelling. By reading the story from the perspectives of the hero and his truest allies, one can finally experience how an otherwise happy person can be driven to feel alone. More importantly, we can see through James's writing how positive it is to listen more closely to those around us and how easy it is to become part of the cure."

— Patrick Snow, Publishing Coach and International Best-Selling Author of *Creating Your Own Destiny*

"Heartwarming. A positive and valuable lesson about trust and bonding."

— Paula Sullivan, Author of *Simply Being Happy*

"Disaster Island exposes the experience of being bullied. I didn't just sympathize with Kyle's pain and isolation as a victim, but felt it with him. This book exposes the ugliness of bullying and the resulting PTSD. It also gives hope for the possibility of happiness. I look forward to the sequels."

— Toni Keif, Author of *Old Baggage*

"There is a naivete that veils some in the middle class, including me—a 'growing wiser' age woman. Reading about Kyle in *Disaster Island*, in a middle-class Christian American family who suffered these 'things I did not know' has made me aware that none of us should hide from the realities of others. I loved the story, the writing, the message, the sense of desperation, and the caring. Through the author's wit, bad and good blended into a valuable lesson, not a scolding. I feel humbled and a bit embarrassed by my inexperience and blindness."

— Yvonne Mendenhall, MS Gerontology, Senior Resource Leader

A very intense and emotional story abouyt the life of a teenage boy that takes place in the 1970s. The author has a knack for using simple events to evoke quite powerful emotions.

— Aida Kozlowski, Avid reader

A very emotional and thought provoking read. The author captures the isolation and emotional duress of a young man in the most critical part of his sexual development. We learn to love and care deeply for young Kyle as he wades through a rollercoaster of PTSD. Can't wait to read book two and watch his further development. A raw and real story breaking the silence and bringing to light the troubles of our youth. Love LOVE LOVE!

— Corrine Farnham, Avid reader

BULLIES & ALLIES: BOOK 1

Kyle's life seemed simple until all his secret troubles collided on

DISASTER

ISLAND

A Story of Hope Amid Bullying, Abuse, and PTSD

JAMES F. JOHNSON

DISASTER ISLAND:

A Story of Hope Amid Bullying, Abuse, and PTSD

Published by:
Aviva Publishing
Lake Placid, NY
(518) 523-1320
www.AvivaPubs.com

James F. Johnson
Email: james@jamesfjohnson.com
Website:jamesfjohnson.com

ISBN: 9781944335892

Library of Congress Control Number:02017952870

Editing: Tyler Tichelaar, Superior Book Productions
Cover Designer: Nicole Gabriel, Angel Dog Productions
Interior Book Layout: James F Johnson
Author Photo: Robin Nellist

Every attempt has been made to source all quotes properly.

Printed in the United States of America
First Edition
2 4 6 8 10 12

For Angela.

You taught me to watch for the signs that someone I love is fading away, going invisible, and vanishing forever.

The bullies that we love can do the most
damage

The characters and Torano Island, along with all its street names, businesses, schools, and churches, are fictional.

FOREWARD

I have known Jim Johnson for twenty years, and during the last five of those years I have had the privilege of watching these terrific novels take shape and find their way onto the page. Jim's dedication to using his art to reach others who may be suffering the trauma of shame and abandonment, or the anguish that is the legacy of trauma, has been a process of great humility and courage. Nonetheless, you don't need a personal history of bullying to be deeply drawn into the world Jim has created.

These are novels that are enormously compelling. Not only does Jim know how to tell a powerful story full of sympathetic characters, who struggle bravely to find love and the essence of who they are, but he is clearly an author with a deep and sophisticated understanding of the legacy of trauma.

One of the things I admire so much about Jim's work is the humanity that is evidenced on every page, by which I mean a deep compassion for his characters and a sophisticated awareness of the myriad challenges that come with trauma. There is, as well, a powerful generosity and sensitivity to how much life asks from us.

First and foremost, however, these novels are great reads and difficult to put down. They offer a world that leaves us changed and somehow more human.

I hope you will find them as enticing and eye-opening as I have.

Trip Quillman

PART 1

Awakening into the Dream

St. Paul Train Station

Almost midnight, July 26, 1974

1

The End

*This passage is written by a Good Samaritan. An ally whom
I only knew for a few moments, but whose quick judgment and
willingness to get involved changed my life forever.*

By a Stranger in a Baseball Cap

He stood dead-still some twelve paces ahead, facin' away, toes over
the edge. I kept my distance. Didn't want to have to be no hero to rescue
him if he fell onto the tracks. A resting locomotive, a couple a platforms
away, thumped like a dinosaur's heartbeat, bringing the hum of life to
the whole place. And there he stood. Sort of out-a-place for this bad part
of town in the middle of the night. A little blue suitcase dangled from
one hand, a gym bag from the other. His grungy white T-shirt, un-tucked
in the back, looked like it'd been on him for days. His matted hair was
almost as white as my old man's, but he was a kid—a little one, maybe
a runaway—none of my business, I guess.

He stared straight ahead, but he didn't seem like he was lookin' at anything. I don't think he knew I was behind him. I couldn't take my eyes off him. Was he waitin' for a train? Or had one left him there?

About the time I thought he'd fallen asleep standin' up, he flinched and looked over his right shoulder, slow-like. I saw enough face to know he couldn't have been more than twelve. Probably still didn't know I was behind him to the left. What the hell was he lookin' at? Maybe he was crazy and seeing things—again, none of my business.

Soon enough, he went back to starin' forward. This time, I watched his head slowly scope the scene like he was looking over an ocean. He looked down at his feet like the tide was rollin' in on him. Damned if he didn't look like he was about to step into it.

A horn blew from the north. Its echo broke me outa my stare. I turned to watch the bright headlight comin' fast out of the night. Felt the platform rumble under my feet. I winced at the massive, steely howl. WoooWAAAH! WoooWAAAH!

It came in hot and fast, maybe doing thirty. A white pigeon or bird of some kind flew off the track and almost hit him in the head. The horn blew again, like it was shoutin' *NOOOOOOO!*

"SAVE HIM!" screamed a woman. I leapt for the boy. Why'd I have to be so damn far back? He couldn't a heard me comin', but right when I reached, he jumped. It had to be Sweet Jesus himself that guided my hand to his elbow because my grip barely made it in time. Dropped me to my knees. The headlight flew past—then the engine—then another engine. I'd stopped his jump, but it wasn't pretty. He hit the pavement with a bad thump. Pretty sure his head was gonna be hurtin' for a while after that. My old knees sure were.

The whistle from the third or fourth engine scolded him, WooWAAAAAAAH! A blast of warm air nearly blew my hat off. He didn't look grateful. I was mad. A line of freight cars followed the engines, hooked up like links in a falling anchor chain.

"It's a God-damned good thing that woman yelled for me to save you kid!" I angrily yelled over the rolling wheels. "You're lucky I did! Ya gotta be more careful around trains. Ya *hear* me?"

He nodded and closed his eyes.

"Huh!" I calmed down a bit and looked around the platform for the woman who'd yelled.

"Well, that's odd" is all I could say. "I was sure I heard someone yell '*Save him*!'" But there wasn't no one—nowhere—in any direction. We were alone. The boy and me. I looked back down at him. He was glarin' straight into my eyes. He was alive, alright…just didn't look like he wanted to be. I had one last question for him.

"Just how did you get here, anyway?"

Five Weeks Prior

Torano Island, Washington State

June 22, 1974, Summer Vacation

2

The Crash

How did I get there? Good question. This bittersweet story follows me as I transform from being a cute little stinker to a PTSD-driven suicidal lost boy in one short summer—a summer that may have been the darkest cloud of my life, but with the brightest silver lining. The summer that almost took my life, but in the end, did the opposite. It saved me from living under the ever-darkening control of the shadows of my past.

At first, I seemed to have everything the American Dream had to offer a boy. But a month before my fourteenth birthday, an accident—the final straw in a long, long line of secret woes—shook the truth for me about that Great American Dream. The fantasy. The lie.

I learned that the Dream (there shall be peace on earth; hard work and honesty are always rewarded; friends are forever; and family is always on your side) was mostly in our heads, and that true evil really can lurk in the heart of any man regardless of the position a person holds; be it friend, family, or foe, the truth is that anyone can prove to be deadly crazy in the end.

As for the man on the train platform's question, "Just how did you get here, anyway?" that was a simple question with a long, complicated answer.

By Kyle Rickett

Saturday, the twenty-second of June, started as an especially picturesque summer's day, and even better, school was out. The morning had put a bounce in my step. Warm beams of sunlight streamed through the island's thick forest blanket. Seagulls, minding their daily business, socialized faintly in the distance overhead. What could go wrong today?

Connor and I, both thirteen, rode bikes leisurely in circles from ditch to ditch, crisscrossing the center of the rural street. We bantered and giggled as always. Around us, medium-sized, contemporary homes nestled comfortably behind trees, down long, gravel drives, a block from the Boutielle (we called it Bottle) Beach boat launch. A gentle breeze off Puget Sound added a saltwater essence to the sweet-and-sour blend of fresh aromas from evergreens and skunk cabbage. I inhaled deeply. I loved everything about living north of Seattle, at the fringe of the stunning San Juan Islands, in a place I saw as a summer paradise— Torano Island.

"Why aren't you cutting firewood with your dad?" Connor's thick brown hair bobbed and slapped against his dark-framed glasses as he rode—crisscrossing through the sunbeams. The chrome fenders and handlebars of his new bright-silver spyder bike flashed and twinkled.

"He had to work today." My tone had a sour edge. A month older but noticeably smaller than Connor, I still sounded younger, often chirpy. Some of the neighborhood men called me "half-pint," which got me laughing every time. Ribbing was the kind of attention that made me feel liked. My excitable personality and large, rattling, hand-me-down bicycle helped me establish a presence despite my smaller size. My bike was an older Newsboy Special in fire-engine red with chrome that didn't shine the way Connor's did. I'm told it was my nearly pure-white hair and sparkling blue eyes that glinted in the sunbeams.

"I thought your dad hated working on Saturdays."

"He does," I smirked, "but some stupid farmer's 'most important tractor' blah-blah-blah wouldn't start and he whined so Dad would open up the shop for him." Sticking out my tongue, I wiggled my head side-to-side.

Looking back, I can see that my attachment to my dad, John Rickett, was especially deep and pursuant. Family stories told that I'd begun life as a toddler, routinely craning from Mom's hip with both arms to reach instead for Daddy's neck, and I grew to be an adolescent who would listen for the starter motor in his pickup—from as far off as the Bottle Beach ballfield. That starter was my cue to throw down the mitt and run for the driveway. I'd ask if I could ride along while getting in the truck, and would be buckled before asking where we were even going.

"Well, you don't have to get 'huffy' about it," Connor teased. His new spyder bike was made by Huffy Bicycles, which had sparked his new catchphrase.

"Whatever, Mr. Pun-boy. But why couldn't his tractor break down on Monday?"

"That's a rude tractor."

I laughed, like I always did at my best friend's comments.

"At least we get to play today. Usually, you have to go out into the woods with him on Saturdays."

We traveled slowly, first turning left, then right, then faking right and going left, then passing each other closely with a comment like, "Nice to see you again," or "Did you miss me?"

"Yeah. It means Dad'll make me work extra hard next Saturday. But today," I raised an arm to my imaginary cavalry, pursed my lips, and impersonated a deep-voiced man, "today we *play!*"

"Charge!" Connor exuberantly hoisted a hand in the same way and laughed as my face cruised by.

My special talents

I've come to learn that I could draw Connor out of shyness better than anyone could. Connor bragged to others about being my best friend, but at the time, I didn't know that. Back then, I figured the boy played with me out of the convenience of living across the street. I always tried to be as funny as he was so he wouldn't lose interest in me. My self-image was low, and I was naïvely unaware, then, of my impact on others. I closely watched the faces of people I was with, nervously judging myself through their reactions. Apparently, my iridescent blue eyes shimmered with more intensity than I imagined they did. Without realizing it, my habit of staring into people's faces was received by them as flattering. Neighbors, who hired me to work around their animals and large yards, appreciated my enthusiastic eagerness to please, to learn skills, and to work hard with obvious pride for my pay. I wasn't faking it either. I think I also made it clear that, for whatever reason, I was genuinely concerned about people, even as a boy.

My secrets were personal. The neighbors, including Connor, didn't know the dark side to the Catholic schoolboy who lurked quietly behind my spark. I was a deeper thinker, and a more introspective prayer-warrior than many knew. I carefully projected myself as fearless. However, I was anything but. I worked tirelessly to try to make people—and God—accept me. It didn't work as well with God and Catholic school kids as I needed it to, but the neighbors responded quickly to my charms. They saw, and enjoyed, the sparkling munchkin who shot out of the house at three-forty-five every afternoon, running and jumping in play clothes, waving at them in their cars, or offering to mow lawns for seventy-five cents an hour. What free time I was able to find was usually spent across the street, where Connor's mother treated me as if I were as important to her as he was, routinely describing me as "a cute little shit that never slows down."

"You like chopping wood with your dad, don't you?" Connor and I passed again and headed into the shaded shoulders of the roadway.

"Yeah!" I grew a big smile. "I can carry as much as he can now."

"*No way*!" Connor knew that John Rickett had a reputation as a peculiarly strong and hardworking man.

"Yes, way! I can carry a full load, as much as my arms can hold." I hoped it mattered to my taller friend. "And I can walk faster and farther than him now—*with a full load*!"

"How can you walk faster than him? He's got long legs."

"'Cause when I walk…" I giggled, "I really run." Then I excitedly added, "Our last truck? I loaded more than half of it. *Half!* That makes me as strong as him! Huh? Huh?"

Connor paused for a second. "Okay—wow—you're right. Okay, I'll give you that."

I smiled and looked down at the ground for a second.

"Your arm-full's not as heavy as his," Connor pondered like an engineer working the math, "but it's as big a load as you can fit in your arms, just like he can carry a full load in his arms too." Then he skidded to a stop while I continued rolling. "So it's not exactly the same—but it's proportional. You're like an ant."

"An *ant*?" I laughed loudly. "You're crazy. Even your granny's stronger than an *ant*!"

"No, really. This make sense if you think about it. Mr. Scorsy said in science class that ants are the strongest creatures in the world. They can only carry a few fractions of an ounce, but it's like a million-billion times their own weight."

"A *million-billion*?" I truly believed Connor to be smarter than me, and so if he answered yes to this, then a million-billion it was.

"Well. I don't remember the exact number. But it's many times their own weight. Many."

"Okay." The honest admission bolstered my already high trust in my friend. "So, I'm *Atomic Ant,* strongest ant in the whole hill."

"Atomic *what*?"

I spun my pedals backward to make a ratcheting sound and kept the bike—and the joke—going. "I'm the strongest hell-of-an ant in the hell-hole of the whole hell-of-a hill!"

"You're such a dork," Connor teased.

"Am not. *You're* a dork."

"Am not." He laughed. "Why didn't your dad take you to work with him? I thought you went everywhere together."

"I don't know. He was gone before I got out of bed. If he needs my help, he'll call my mom. I can ride down there in less than fifteen minutes on my bike." Then I bit my lower lip while thinking, or more likely now plotting, to stay close to home in case Mom came looking.

I'm not important

Connor and I proudly sported similar outfits that day. In honor of summer, we'd decided over the phone, before meeting, to wear our shortest cutoff jeans so we could go swimming without having to change into suits if the opportunity presented itself. Both of us wore skin-tight undershirt tank tops. I had no shoes, but we both had on our coveted "puka shell" necklaces purchased together the previous summer, and then jokingly swapped so we could say we had given each other birthday gifts. On our left wrists, we wore oversized brown leather watchbands, the style that year. Gravity continually spun my watch face downward around my scrawny wrist.

"We should enter the milk carton boat races at Seafair this year," Connor suggested, referring to the annual summer festival in Seattle.

"Oh, that'd be cool!" I orbited my bike again, but this time tightly, teasingly edging close without touching. Then I moved out and began to arc back to do it again. "We could make our boat look like a pirate ship!"

"Do you think your dad would help us? He has all those big trucks and would know where to get enough milk cartons to make a boat with."

"No. We'd have to find some other way to get milk cartons."

"Why—"

"No!" I quickly interrupted. "We can't ask my dad!"

"But why not? You do stuff for him all the time. How come he doesn't ever help you with your projects?"

My handbrake squealed me to a stop behind Connor, and barely out of his sight.

"He never takes you shopping for that car you want either."

"He takes me places," I defended.

"Does he even know which car it is?"

"I don't know.... I think so."

"He takes you where *he* wants to go and *you* look for Hot Wheels when you're there."

"Hey! He's busy. His life is important. He has work, and he really, really needs my help for important stuff. Someday I'll find that car. I had it in my hand once...just didn't have the two-dollars to buy it that day."

"Oh, okay," Connor said awkwardly, no doubt detecting the displeasure in my voice. He sarcastically added, "But you know that *I* know which car it is, and I hope you find your 1967 Signet Gold Pontiac GTO Hot Wheels car someday." He smiled boastfully.

"My dad's important on the island..." I argued, not ready to give up the fight, even if Connor was conceding. My temper was starting to boil up a bit. I hated when it would do that, but I didn't always seem able to make it simmer down.

"Yeah, I know."

"No, really. He has the only truck and farm implement repair business on the whole island."

"Kyle, I already *know* that." Connor twisted to see my face.

"Good!" I had one leg on the ground. My oversized bike leaned so I could hook the other leg over the frame. I moved my arms so the bike bumped Connor's gently. "Stupid," I giggled. Sometimes humor worked to calm me down. Lucky for our fun morning, it worked this time.

"How come you think his stuff's important," Connor started again, "but he doesn't think yours is? You've wanted that car for a long time."

"He helped me rebuild a tractor last year."

"*Your* tractor?" he blurted back, almost scolding.

"No...it's his, but it was my idea."

"I'm not sure that's the same thing as him helping you with your projects."

"Well…*his is work*! Mine's kid stuff." I couldn't see Connor's point. To me, adult activities were important but kids' activities weren't. Even my poor grades went unchallenged by either parent. My kid issues just didn't matter to adults.

"I don't know…. I sometimes think it's rude that you are always helping him with things, but he never…." He hushed.

I was now giving him *the look* with wide eyes pressing invisible but detectible laser beams of energy toward him.

"Never mind. You're a nice guy, Kyle."

"I love you too, Connor." I turned the handlebars, kicked off, and perched back up on the saddle. I called upon a tad more humor and blew him a Hollywood kiss.

"Shut up, you homo!"

Race to the scene of the accident

"Let's get wet. Race you to Bottle Beach!" I egged. "Last one there's a *real* homo!"

The two bikes then rattled and shook as we put every muscle into pedaling them northbound and down the sloping grade of Bottle Beach road, toward the boat launch on Puget Sound. Connor, being the larger boy on the lighter bike, darted into the lead. Fenders rattled, chains whirred. His brown hair flowed behind.

"He-*heeeee*!" he shouted excitedly and glanced rearward.

I shifted gears, which gave Connor the cue he needed to speed up. My bike was a three-speed, and with the gravity of the slope, that meant I now had the momentum to really roll. Connor had no gears, so he tried to speed up the hard way, by pedaling faster. The last thing I wanted to turn into today was a homo, even though at that time in my life I didn't really know what the word meant, so I had to beat my buddy to the sand. Connor looked behind. My wide eyes were fixed securely on him, and I had a look of sheer determination on my red face as I bounced up and down on my pedals, almost ready to pass.

Connor stood up to pedal as fast as he could. Then something happened when I reached for the chrome bar at the back of Connor's banana seat to slow him down.

"Don't!" he screamed.

"Oh, shit!" I screamed back.

Perhaps it was the loose sand that we had traveled onto, but for one reason or another, the two bikes suddenly lost direction and balance.

"Oh, crap!" I shrieked, but there was nothing I could do.

For what felt like ten long seconds, gravity blended with momentum to throw both us boys into a tizzy. Handlebars yanked from my hands, and pedals vanished from beneath my feet. Something hit me hard in the crotch. My bike wiggled left and right, and the sound was an awful montage of squeaking and crashing steel. Gravel flew in every direction and pelted my bare legs like shrapnel from a grenade.

To this day, I still remember the cold unforgiving earth sliding across my face, and then I rolled once or maybe twice, finally coming to rest on my back, facing the crystal clear blue skies of summer. I didn't hear anything but the squeaking of a wheel that was slowly coming to a stop somewhere not far from my ears. I lay for a second, thinking about what had happened. With one hand, I gently felt around for damage and drew it back. Three fingertips dripped dark red blood. My heart sank.

I heard no response from the other victim. I lifted my head and saw Connor about two feet to my right, fixing crooked glasses back onto his nose. From my position beneath the wreckage, it almost looked like a single four-wheeled vehicle had collapsed. The scene around me began to turn bright white, as if a light bulb had been turned on. My face felt flush, and I became weak and nauseous. I lay back down on the cool sand, letting a few seconds slip by before opening my eyes. Connor stood above me, a concerned look on his face.

"Uh, oh! Kyle, you're bleeding bad. It's coming out of your shorts."

"Huh?" I scanned what I could. My own red, antique bicycle seat was in Connor's hand.

"I'm getting your mom!"

"No! Don't leave me here!"

"I have to!"

Connor ran off screaming, "Mrs. Rickett—Kyle's hurt! Kyle's hurt bad!"

3

The Echo

I call myself spiritual because of my unwavering conscious awareness of being a part of something bigger than myself. What makes me spiritual but not religious is that I don't need to grasp for human answers for unexplained events.

God, Allah, Santa Claus, the volcano...I don't need to pretend to know who drives miracles. I'm happy just knowing that when peculiar things happen, they seem guided by an overseeing force. For that, I'm both comforted and grateful.

It's time to introduce you to my next miracle, Tuck Taylor. I was about to discover that this crash was—for lack of a better word—designed to knock over the first domino and eventually topple the illusion that was slowly killing me. Unbeknown to me at the time, about 2,000 miles across the U.S., the person I wouldn't meet for a few more weeks was about to learn the same lesson about his illusions.

It seems my crash sent an echo and he heard it.

By Tuck Taylor

All I wanted was a few hours of sleep.

"Just a few fucking hours! Is that so much to ask?" It was noon in Texas and I had worked the night shift at a crisis clinic. I was a second-year psychology student doing a summer internship as a crisis-line volunteer for the midnight shift. I was also a hungry young man in need of money, so I worked as a short order breakfast cook in a pancake house from six till noon.

The two jobs worked in synch. First, I'd listen to hotline callers complain about relationships that they refused to leave. Then, I'd take out my frustrations on "normal people" in a hot kitchen. I wasn't mean to anyone, but I did like to rant and clank pots and pans. Workmates thought I was being funny—in a way I guess that's all I was doing—and joined in the fun with occasional hoots and pan clankings of their own. The down side to these two jobs was the hours. Between them, I worked from midnight to noon. If I could find any time to sleep, it was during the hottest and noisiest part of the day. This was not how I wanted to live, but I didn't see any other way.

To make things worse, I had just turned twenty-one and had spent the day before being celebrated by my...how should I say this...? *complicated*...best friend, Trenton, at a topless bar—which was funny because Trenton was gay, so he didn't enjoy my choice of party spots anywhere near as much as I did. Trenton himself was a kindhearted emotional person, but I was feeling left out from the direction his life was taking. I will admit that I fiendishly chose the location *because I knew he wouldn't like it.* I thought it was funny. Looking back now, I understand so much more about the trials of being a gay man in this world and I feel some real remorse that I kidded around with something that was so serious to my best friend. Maybe I was being a bit of an ass.

Trenton and I shared a two-bedroom apartment where his lifestyle progressively caused me increasing grief. Being gay in 1974 was an even more dangerous thing than it is now, and by association, I had as much skin in the game as he did. If people knew my roommate was gay, they would assume I was too, and then both of us could become targets for hate. True, I would have stood with him to the ends of the earth, but our friendship was getting more and more stressed as time passed, and I was beginning to worry it was going to end soon.

Trenton had been my best friend since childhood. I loved him. I didn't learn his secret until high school, but when I did, I wasn't completely surprised. I wasn't bothered by it either. He didn't change once I found out. I guess the difference for me was that I'd now become a part of his secret, which meant I had a new responsibility to learn how to help him safely maneuver our social lives. But all in all, Trenton and I were still the same two people we'd always been.

I took great pride in being supportive. Looking back now, I think my long-standing honor was beginning to matter more to me than it did to him. Because of it being *his* secret, his path was driving him in another direction with new friends who shared his interests and allowed him to flourish in his own way, while my path was rutted and stagnant. I'd pretty much left most of my friends in Minnesota and couldn't make any new ones in Texas because I was trying too hard not to let his gay world crash into my straight one. So I put a lot more energy into stretching out the last years of our relationship than he did. *Not knowing when to let go* might be a better way to state my relationship with him. So, since I was used to giving in to his lifestyle all the time, I guess I felt a tinge of revenge when on *my* birthday, *he* had to sit through *one* afternoon of boobs and G-strings with *me*.

But as annoying as all of this was, Trenton was usually out of the apartment on hot days. So, on this particular afternoon, I had the place to myself and I was so tired that, despite the sweaty heat, I finally fell asleep.

Crash

Until I heard a crash.

Every muscle in my body jolted. The bed shook. Words came to mind without anyone saying them.

Get ready.

A vision of a crystal blue sky flashed so quickly that it was gone as soon as my eyes could open.

Once opened, I covered them with both palms. The room was fine. The crash wasn't real.

"Shit. This means I'm finally crazy."

As I pondered the words "get ready" and the vision of the sparkling blue sky, I recalled them as two aspects of an intense series of dreams that had been dormant for three solid years.

The dreams were an integral and critical part of my past, and they had once provided me with great peace during a particularly dark time. The dark time, however, was something I tried not to think about anymore.

A sudden sense of dread befell me.

"Oh, God...'get ready' for *what*?" I whispered and wiped my forehead with one sweaty hand.

"Please, please, *please* don't let it be cancer again."

4

The Rescue

I needed saving, but I didn't know it yet. It was my best friend, Connor Mason, who first saw blood spilling into the gravel. I tried to keep him by my side, but he did the right thing and ran for Mom. At first, the panic in his voice seemed excessive, but I later discovered it was needed.

When trauma sets in, the person in pain is often the only one who can't feel it. Reacting, like Connor did, to help someone who's not asking, takes insight and honor. Hmm. Honor rhymes with Connor. How about that?

By Kyle Rickett

"Hurry!" Connor's distant yell was music to my ears.

Mom was no doubt struggling to keep up. Connor could run fast—which is why it was important for me to beat him on the bike. I pictured him running circles around her while she worked to keep up. The mental image was funny. I laughed. "Ow, ow, ow." It hurt.

He wasn't gone long. Or maybe I'd blacked out cold for a while.

"Mom!—*ooh!*" The shout sent a sting from head to toe, but at least I didn't cry like a baby.

"Oh, damn it, Kyle." She grimaced while catching her breath. "This is worse than I thought." She knelt down beside me. Her hair was wrapped by a light blue scarf, which told me she was probably scrubbing floors a few minutes ago. "It *figures* this would happen while your dad's in Seattle."

"I thought he was at the shop."

Mom never showed fear. She converted it too quickly into anger. Maybe yelling at scary situations gave her control or something. But angry or not, I was glad to have her at my side.

"He had to get parts." She angrily sighed as loudly as she could. "Oh, why did he have to leave when he did? Connor, help me get these bikes off him."

"Yes, ma'am." Connor lifted his bike first, then slowly dragged my heavier one away. A pedal knocked me hard in the knee, and a lightning bolt ripped a path of stinging heat from my chest to my right toe.

"OW!"

"I'm sorry! I'm sorry! I'm sorry!" Connor pleaded forgiveness.

"Oh, my God," Mom moaned. Her eyes followed the bloodied stem of my seat-post. "I've always hated this old bike. I *never* should have let you ride it."

"I *like* that bike." Through the ache, I forced out a defense for the family heirloom which was a critically important possession. My older brother, Daniel, was kept away by his truck route in those days, so riding his childhood bike helped me feel more connected with him—like I wasn't a late-life accident, but part of the whole family.

"How much pain are you in?"

"It's not bad if I don't move." I held a breath between sentences. "How bad does it look?"

"I can't tell, sweetheart. What do you think has been hurt?"

"I don't know, Mom. The pain is everywhere, front and back. Mostly on the right side. I'm not bleeding that bad, am I?"

"Yeah, honey, it's bad. You need stitches." She looked to Connor. "Stay here with him. I have to get my car."

More to Connor than meets the eye

"I'm so sorry, Kyle." Connor knelt down in Mom's spot while she hurried off, streaming a line of empty, rage-filled blaming comments about my dad not buying me a newer bicycle.

"Why? You didn't do anything." I exhaled only enough to make words. "This was an accident—I'll be fine in a couple hours."

"I don't care. I'm still sorry." His face reddened and he couldn't hold back. He started crying. "I hope your wiener's still there."

I chuckled, but it hurt. "Ow, OW! Don't make me laugh; it hurts!" In spite of his tears, I thought he was kidding.

"It's not funny!"

"I'm sure my wiener's still there."

"I'm serious! You always turn everything into a joke. Stop it!"

"Ow, Ow! C'mon, Connor. I said don't make me laugh."

"*Stop it!*" he persisted. "There's a lot of blood." He tried not to cry, but tears—real ones—cascaded both cheeks and his voice raised into anxiety. "Kyle! I *mean it*!" Now he, like Mom, was turning emotion into anger.

"Is it really that bad?" I started to believe him. This was serious. "Ow!" My whole right side stung when I tried lifting my head. By not moving, the pain settled down. At certain points, my brain sort of disconnected from it altogether, but it would only stay disconnected until I moved again.

I looked intently into Connor's face and saw more of what I didn't expect—real human compassion—aimed at *me*. How weird. As a child, I'd never seen that before. Friends were guys you rode bikes with, and who ran off when moms got mad. Connor had run *to* Mom, not from her. He even broke her loose from her obsessive cleaning—a feat in and of itself. A wave of warmth passed through me when I realized I wasn't looking into the eyes of a neighbor kid, but more into those of a concerned and true friend who was both protecting and comforting me. He cared. The child within me was baffled by the new, more adult emotional connection. Did I deserve this?

Connor, Merrick, and me

As Connor and I silently endured a traumatic moment together, my thoughts fell onto the last time we had done this. I'd seen Connor cry one other time. When we were eleven, his only brother, Merrick, was killed in Vietnam. It was sad for the island community, but it devastated Connor, who'd held 100 percent faith in Merrick's promise to come back alive. I remember feeling sorry for him, while being simultaneously grateful that my own brother had blown out his knee in a cross-country motorcycle crash when he was sixteen and couldn't be drafted. It hurt to watch Connor, but the guilt of being glad it wasn't my own brother's funeral confused me a bit. I'd done what I could for him, which wasn't much. I remained extra nice for a couple of weeks, and I made Connor the single focus of all my prayers for a good solid month—it was all I had to offer him.

But that was different. Back then, I was the one rising out of the silliness of play-time to comfort him. This time, it was Merrick's little brother who was staying close to *me*. In fact, he was even crying for me. Was this really on the same level of importance as a funeral?

"I'm sorry I said those things about you and your dad, Kyle. I feel bad now. You're a cool kid…my best friend! I shouldn't have—"

"Connor, don't." This was the first time since Merrick's funeral that I'd felt this close to him, but I was embarrassed by being on the receiving end. When his eyes flickered, I added, "This wasn't your fault."

"There's a lot of blood, Kyle."

"It doesn't hurt that much," I lied, "as long as I don't move."

"Don't *lie* to me!" Fear filled his outburst.

"Okay, okay. Sheesh!" I rolled my eyes sarcastically but swelled with a big wave of emotion at his concern.

"Don't *ever* lie to me…please." He calmed down but shook an annoyed head, adjusted his stance, grabbed my hand, and pressed a reassuring thigh against my arm, which brought me again to relive the mood at the funeral. I remembered doing exactly the same for him, holding his hand and pushing a compassionate leg against his. I still didn't get it, though. Did he feel that bad for *me* now? Like my brother had died?

I'll never forget the funeral. It was terrible and memorable at the same time. While Mom was seating me in the back with her and Dad, Mrs. Mason approached to ask if I would sit with the family. I agreed, but I hadn't grasped the honor of the request until the organ music started and Connor's hand squeezed mine. He sat like a cold mannequin throughout the ceremony, showing no emotion on his face, but discretely expressing it to me through his tightening grip. I felt like I was the most important person in the whole world at that moment.

Later, once the activities around Merrick's funeral were done, the community simply stopped talking about him. Perhaps it was meant as a courtesy to those who'd lost family, or it had something to do with the nation's squeamish attitudes about the war, but none of us kids or our parents talked about Merrick anymore. Even Connor went about his daily activities not mentioning having ever had a brother. That bothered me. Since the funeral, it was like none of it had ever happened and Merrick had never existed. It didn't seem fair to him. Merrick was a good guy. Rarely, though, Connor would confide in me—but no one else—that he still wore the dog tags under his shirt, and I often caught him fingering those tags. Even though he was behaving as the community expected, Merrick remained silently alive within him. I thought that was cool.

Will the closeness last?

But would this emotional moment go by the same rules? Were Connor and I once again in a private crevice in reality that only exists when "normal" can't? While we were here, one of us tending to the pain of the other, we were out of the public's eye, in that vortex we'd first visited at Merrick's funeral—a place where emotions between boys are allowed.

I knew our culture would make sure that we'd only stay there until I healed. We'd return to "play time" as if none of this had happened, and stay at an arm's length until one of us was to suffer another horrific loss. Is that how this works? If so, then I wanted to soak in the deeper friendship while it lasted. I was getting a chance to feel his attention the way I'd given it to him the last time we were in this space. If it was to be temporary, then I was going to focus and not miss a minute of it. This was a bad situation, but basking in our deepened connection almost made it good.

Connor craned our hands into his lap and rested them there. I didn't move again. Two of his fingers gently rubbed my wrist. I made sure to enjoy the kind touch while also wondering what hurt so bad in my shorts. I wanted to comfort him and say, "I'm going to be fine," but he had me wondering now whether I would be. I felt best while focusing on his face and keeping my legs tightly pressed together.

12:01 p.m.: Riding with Mom

Curled in the fetal position, head propped against the door, I rode on a spread of tattered towels that Mom had pulled from the rag bin. Heaven forbid my brush with death might stain a vinyl car seat or a clean bath towel. The scarf was gone too. And her blonde hair looked to have been brushed. There was no point in wondering how many minutes she'd spent primping and finding the rags she was okay with tossing out. I quietly kept my legs tightly together while clutching at the shorts.

"How come you wouldn't let Connor come with?" I finally asked.

"Now, why would I take a neighbor with me to the clinic?"

"A *neighbor*?" I indignantly asked.

"That's right. Connor is a neighbor."

"Mom, he's not 'a neighbor'; he's *my best friend*. Couldn't you see how upset he was?"

She huffed as if she disagreed that boys had feelings.

I huffed back in disgust at her huffing at me.

"What?" she blurted out.

"He's my *best friend*! I feel bad for him. He could have ridden in the backseat. He could have helped."

"Oh he's just a little boy!" she reiterated. "I don't need to take care of *him too* right now."

"Tuhhh! 'Just a little boy?'" I exhaled as loudly as I could, then turned sarcastic. "Mom! He's *thirteen*. He's potty-trained!"

"I don't need your little friends bothering me right now. So *drop* it, Kyle. I'm *your* mother. Not his."

"Tuhhh!" I repeated angrily.

12:09 p.m.: Arrival at the clinic

Nurse Kathy's jaw dropped when Mom helped me through the front door. The blood that had stained my legs, hands, shirt, and shorts now spattered Mom's sleeveless pullover top. The blood was black against the light blue of the fabric. We looked like bloody zombies with nicely brushed hair.

"Mrs. Rickett. Oh, my *God*!" She waved a panicked hand toward the hallway, "Bring him in. I'll go find Dr. Krieg."

5

The Unanswerable Question

As I witnessed my own emerging emotional connection with another boy (against my mother's opinion that boys had no emotional connection), the stranger in Texas was struggling to understand his emotional connection around his own childhood best friend.

By Tuck Taylor

An exhausted face stared at me from the mirror. His blue eyes were bloodshot and half-closed. "God, I hope I don't have cancer again."

I stuck out my tongue. "Blaaaah."

The lights were off so as to not add heat to the already sweltering room. Unflattering shadows darkened my cheeks to look even more war-torn. Older. Ancient. "So this is what I'm going to look like when I'm a hundred?" I shook my head. "Shit." I wiped my sweating face with a well-used hand towel. "It's what I look like *now*."

Why me and not him?

I've been obsessed with mirrors ever since my light brown hair all fell out at seventeen. Usually, I stare into them, grateful that my hair returned as thick as ever, but sometimes, it is more to try to figure out why I survived cancer at all. I'd died. For three minutes, I had walked in Heaven, but then I wasn't allowed to stay there. Why did they send me back? And was I finding the purpose they had for me? Or was I wasting my second chance away?

Still staring, I thought about Tommy, my former hospital roommate, who was younger than me and had a different kind of cancer. He died a few days before I did, but no one brought him back to life. Why? Why did "the other side" keep him? Was he just the victim of a bad doctor? Tommy was a good guy. Why had I lived for the next three years to find myself now standing at this mirror and asking why, when he didn't survive at all? His family cried just like mine did. Who makes these decisions?

I often had to work at not obsessing about it. I'd distract myself or just force my brain to not think about him. It would work until I'd have a rogue dream about Tommy, or I'd see a boy in a public place that reminded me of him, and damn if my heart wouldn't sink an inch as I'd once again feel some sort of strange guilt that I was alive and he wasn't.

Accepting the truth

Humidity made me claustrophobic. I had to focus constantly on not panicking. There was so little to like about Texas that if it hadn't been for Trenton, I probably would have moved on to a college out in California or up in Washington State. Someplace without humidity.

Trenton and I had traveled to Texas together. I used him as my excuse for being stuck there, saying that I stayed because *he* didn't want to leave. He had been a critical anchor during my cancer, and I still felt comfort by staying close to him. But somehow, that comfort was starting to flake away. At times, I felt he was losing interest in me. Some days, his cavalier attitude felt like he was shrugging me off. It made me mad at times, but he was *Trenton*, so I forgave him. Our history bound me. He'd always been an amazing friend, and I couldn't let go of that. I *wouldn't* let go of it. Since the cancer, friendship has consistently meant more to me than anything else in the world.

But also, I was a twenty-one-year-old man filled with vim and vigor. Honoring Trenton's secret gave me a warrior's sense of pride. I wasn't willing to back down. I was noble. Honorable. Being firm about my convictions and making a stance against public scrutiny proved I was a real man and a worthy friend. When we were in the presence of his friends, I took pleasure in being totally cool with who they were.

But Trenton didn't seem to need me to be like that. Looking back now I know I was too protective of him. Perhaps I felt indebted to him for standing by me when I felt singled-out and "different" because of my misfortune. I was viewing his lifestyle as something that made him different now and therefor in need of protecting in return. I now know that he saw himself as different too *but perfectly able to handle it himself.* I treated him like he was my smaller brother, but he really was a grown man. I was starting to wonder if this wasn't about *him.* Maybe I was really just selfishly dragging my childhood friendship too far into the adult world.

I gave a heavy sigh as I refocused on my dark eyes in the mirror, which looked like old, rugged black holes in a pasty, youthfully smooth, but grayish hued face. Trenton was becoming distant, and I needed to decide how deep my connection with him really needed to be. I stood up tall to look out the bathroom door at Texas through the window across the room.

"If Trenton doesn't need me, then why…exactly…am I *really* here?"

6

Some Backstories

The first hours of summer break started as a happy bike ride, but then became a painful incident. When Mom arrived, the incident progressed to an emergency transport. Now that transport had escalated to the status of a zombie in the hands of a medical staff. My head was spinning. How bad was this day going to get? (Spoiler alert: It was going to get a lot worse!)

It was time for me to accept the seriousness of everything, which is tough because that would mean accepting the need for help—and I don't accept help well. Some call it ego, but for me, it's more complicated than that.

Accepting a lending hand meant I would owe somebody, which meant I would have to trust that person's motives for helping me. There's the problem. In the Rickett family, the price for small favors was usually pretty high. The issue for me was not ego—but trust.

By Kyle Rickett

Surrounded by forest, the clinic was cool inside, mostly because of the park-like setting and morning shade from the east facing evergreen trees. Though the building was fairly new, it had been painted forest brown and green and built to look like a log house or a park ranger station. It would have been a relaxing place if it didn't smell like medicine. The odor didn't help my stomach any. I was already nauseous, but at the mere uttering of Dr. Krieg's name, I cringed even more.

"Oh no."

"What now?" Mom asked as if she were preoccupied.

"There's three doctors. How'd we get Krieg?"

"I don't care who's here as long as he's a doctor."

I cared. The three docs took turns being in the office on Saturdays. The odds were against Krieg being there this time, but this wasn't proving to be my lucky day.

"I miss Dr. Robby," I complained.

"I know." Mom shuffled along beside me, both of her hands gripping my left arm, doing what she could to help me to the tall, unoccupied reception desk. She leaned into it for stability while we waited for Kathy or Dr. Krieg to come get us. "You say that every time we come here."

"He used to give me suckers and make me laugh."

"I'll buy you a sucker on the way home." By her irritated tone, I knew this conversation was over.

The history of meeting Dr. Krieg: *Dr. Robby retired when I was six, selling his share of the clinic to a stranger with Arizona license plates, the mysterious Dr. Lee Krieg. My personal memories are vague, but thanks to family, I know the story. Mom told stories of how that sale marked the time when I suddenly became afraid of doctor visits. Lots of other kids didn't transfer from Dr. Robby to Krieg, but instead chose the other two doctors; however, like the asshole that he was, Krieg never accepted any blame for that. He dismissed the exodus by*

52

saying it was because "kids don't like change and too many parents let their kids rule the roost."

For me, it wasn't change I didn't like...it was him. Pure and simple. He made my skin crawl. I'd have left his care in a heartbeat also, but I didn't rule in my roost. My dad and Krieg had become friends after only my first visit. So like a trap, he was my doctor. Odd thing was, my dad didn't make friends easily. For some reason, Krieg pushed his way in despite Dad's reserved nature.

Krieg and Dad's business transaction—me

"Okay, go on back to room one. I'll meet you there in a minute," said Kathy, motioning frantically, pointing down the hall, and then disappearing again.

As Mom guided me past the empty Saturday lobby and down the long hallway, I thought about how complicated it was that Dad wouldn't let me switch doctors.

The history of my Dad and Doc Krieg's deal: *Krieg wouldn't take money from us because the very day he met me he became immediate friends with Dad. Right away, they struck a gentleman's deal in which Krieg would doctor Dad's son (me) in exchange for Dad maintaining Krieg's classic red Corvette. Apparently, the car and I were of equal value. The hook was that the car didn't seem to need as much maintenance as I did, so since day one, Dad had always felt indebted, like he always owed Krieg "a little more."*

So from then on, we, the family, were always on the hook to behave nice around Dr. Krieg, which meant that no matter how irritated I felt on this day, I would not be complaining about his cigarette-breath or mean sense of humor. The Corvette never complained about Dad, so I needed to return the favor.

If I ever did complain about Krieg, family complexity went through the roof. The fallout was always the same: First, Dad got quiet, and then, Mom got defensive. Then I'd feel bad for insulting Dad's only friend, and finally, someone outside of the circle, usually a cousin or my adult sister, would tell me how I needed to respect my parents and let the family calm back down. The trap was iron-clad. No way out for me.

"I'm sorry, Mom," I mumbled.

I felt sorry for my dad a lot, so I never wanted to upset him. He seemed lonely all the time. I knew this visit was going to add to his burden and make him believe that he owed Krieg even more, which could be why Mom was mad too. She was probably trying to figure out how to keep the whole thing from him. This office visit was my fault, and my only option now was to try to be as "non-wounded" as possible. I hoped stitches weren't expensive.

The history of Dad and Krieg's mysterious bond: *Somehow the doctor had related to Dad like no one could. Our stories of Krieg's gruffness didn't jive with Dad's experience of Krieg's generosity. Dad would defend him, saying that people didn't understand Krieg. When the two of them were alone, they must have talked about their World War II days, because somehow, Dad knew that Krieg had been in the same island battle as him. I guess the war was how they'd connected. Krieg made it into an even bigger deal when he told Dad about ending up as a Prisoner of War (POW) for a few months. Dad respected him for that, maybe even felt sorry for him. Of course, no evidence was ever shown to prove any of the stories, but no doctor would lie about something so serious just to get closer to a blond boy's dad...would he?*

Us Ricketts were at a loss to bond with Dad around his war days. None of us even knew which battles he'd been in because he never talked about the war. I knew two other guys my age whose World War II dads did the same thing. Men who'd served in offices told stories, but the guys who saw gunfire were closed off and quiet—or "stoic and strong" as their friends would say. Not many of us kids knew much about our fathers' battlefield experiences, so as far as I could tell,

Krieg's lack of proof was as normal as that of most other veterans.

Dad had a lot of tales about his childhood, but my family respectfully accepted his full eight-word military summary that he "went to war, came back, and married Mom" like it was a four-year long blink. If he did talk about his time on the islands, it was when he was alone with Krieg. Not with us. We had no choice but to respect that.

Krieg, the community's hero—or villain

Mom grunted. The hallway leading to room one had never seemed so long. I didn't weigh much, but she was practically trying to carry me, which is something she had quit doing when I was only four.

"Mom. I can walk on my own. I can lean against a wall now."

"We're almost there. I'm fine. Just don't let go of my hand."

My fingers, interlaced with hers, squeezed more tightly. As we passed the closed door of room two, my nausea peaked. It always did. The door was always closed and I always chose not to look at it.

My history in the clinic: Krieg's other heroic community service was to save the Island Voyager Scouts boys' troop. Back when he moved to the island, before the ink had dried on the clinic's sale, he'd gotten the other two doctors to agree that the office would be the troop's sponsor and central meeting location. He himself became the scout leader, claiming to have a soft spot for boys' troops because he'd been the "Desert Scout" leader in Arizona for his own kids—of which there were no photos on the walls. Thanks to his generosity, half-a-dozen boys, including myself, were able to keep learning how to tie knots and whittle totem animals in the lobby on Wednesday nights.

I started Voyager Scouts in 1966 when I was six, and I quit at nine after a particularly long troop campout in the San Juan Islands didn't go so well. That 1969 campout happens to be when my Kriegaphobia reached its violent peak. During those three years as a scout, I'd been having progressively worse memory voids, but I didn't think anything of them.

The phenomenon of memory voids: *To understand how I could not think of memory voids as problems, consider this: A memory void after a car accident would be a big deal. Friends would know about the car accident and would be supportive and compassionate. The memory void would be an openly discussed part of the accident. The victim might say, "I was in my car; then boom, it was a week later, and I was in the hospital," and everyone would accept that as a plausible situation. They'd know the exact amount of days or hours that couldn't be recalled. But for people who experience memory voids because they want to forget something they want kept secret, the phenomenon is different. They forget having forgotten. Instead of asking for help in cleaning up a mess, choosing to forget is a way of avoiding a mess they don't want anyone to know about. As long as no one pushes the issue or tries to force the victim to look at the memory void, the void itself is forgotten. It is an acceptable phenomenon, like a bad dream.*

From 1966 to 1969, no one knew about my memory voids until they had progressed to where they had become a problem—not for me, but for Mom.

My history with memory voids (known clinically as dissociative amnesia): *During the three years I was a Voyager, I had progressively become more and more difficult for Mom to deal with for two days every week. I'd become chronically agitated on Wednesdays and hard to awaken on Thursdays. I had asked a few times to quit Scouts, but Krieg was Dad's friend so I needed to go. Mom and Dad didn't seem to want to hear about why I hated the Scouts, so as time went on, they stopped asking how the sessions went.*

When the infamous campout happened in the summer of '69, I'd come back from it in such a bad mood that I barely spoke for three days afterward. I couldn't explain why because I honestly didn't know why. I didn't even remember the campout. That's when Mom had finally had enough and saw my *behaviors as* her *problem. She solved her issues with my behaviors by making me quit the troop so she wouldn't have to put up with my agitation or fight with me to get up for school on Thursdays. I didn't gripe. I was glad it was over.*

How I got my pills: *That was also when I got to the point that I couldn't go into the clinic building for anything as simple as a school physical without vomiting, so she solved her problem with my agitation by acquiring the first bottle of pills to calm me down. From that day forward; from nine years old to thirteen, I was given a single, small white pill one hour before every scheduled doctor's appointment. Then, forgetting what happened at the appointment was something I didn't need to explain. The pill itself may not have been strong enough to black me out, but it gave me an excuse for doing so.*

The history of Jack: *Those three years as a Voyager Scout were a wild time in my head. Memories of how the Voyager Scouts era came and went are, even today, fragmented and difficult for me to sort through. It was also a wild time on the island because it was exactly the same time that one of the Scouts vanished completely, creating a community mystery that lasted years.*

Jack was the oldest scout in the troop. He was almost as blond as I was, and he was a middle child of eight in a Catholic family whose dad had died. He was fourteen when he disappeared. People eventually decided he'd run away because of troubles at home. Some people—my mother and my sister to be exact—even made crass remarks that his running off was a blessing in disguise to his poor overburdened mother. That confused me. Where was their compassion for the boy who had vanished? And why was his mother glad he was gone?

The rest of the troop: *The most confusing scouting aspect—for me—wasn't Jack's disappearance, or the blank memories, or the pills, or the vomiting, but that after being a Voyager for three solid years, I didn't remember much about it. I even had a small box in one drawer containing a collection of whittled animals that I have no memory of making. I'd gained a deep-seated irritation for Krieg and even for the other Voyager boys, who, for some reason, avoided me as I did them in school hallways or island markets. Why?*

For the most part, we barely remembered each others' names. Jack, even though he'd vanished, was the only troop member I really remembered. I even used to have occasional nightmares about him calling out to me for help.

Krieg, the pediatrician

Once Mom and I were in an exam room and before Mom could even get me fully onto the examination table, Krieg appeared in the doorway.

"Marie!" He sounded surprised to see her.

"Oh, Lee!" she spun toward him. "Thank God you're here."

Krieg looked at the blood surrounding my groin and froze.

"Are you okay?" Mom asked him. I wondered the same thing.

"What the hell is going on here?" Krieg's voice was coarse and gruff. His question sounded like a demand. He was overweight and always looked worn-out. Something about his image obsessed me. At school, I drew pictures of him as a gorilla in an Island Voyager uniform with fangs and drool on his chin. Every time I picked up a pencil, crayon, or paintbrush, that gorilla was the image I wanted to express. My art grades were low because teachers were frustrated with my obsession, but I kept drawing. I called my fictitious creature Fang so no one would figure out it was Krieg.

Mom's anxiety-ridden rage

"Oh, that damned Connor knocked him down on his bike."

"*Mom*!—Ow. Ow," I protested. "That's *not what happened*."

"Well, I never had to take Fran in for stitches."

"Fran?" I clicked my tongue. "Uh!" I rolled my eyes theatrically. What did my *stupid* sister have to do with Connor's innocence? Fran was the eldest of us all, was on her second marriage, and had two daughters. How was this a fair comparison? I was sure now that Mom's fear-driven anger was making her crazy—her comments weren't making any sense.

"You and your brother are both like this. Daniel is just as reckless and clumsy." She turned her attention to Krieg. "I can't believe the dumb things boys do when they're not watched."

I might as well have had two moms. I'd gotten a kiss on the cheek from the warm one before running downstairs to get my bike. I had been her "special little sweetheart" all morning. Now, an hour later, I was a "reckless and clumsy boy." Well, luckily for her, if Connor's worries about my wiener being gone were valid, maybe I was now another daughter like she *really* wanted.

"However it happened," she ranted, "his bike was on top of you when I got there."

I rolled my eyes again. Now that she didn't need to be the strong one, she wasn't on my side anymore. She always needed someone to blame. Connor didn't deserve her rant, but she was going to keep it going anyway. I wished she'd have seen his concern—but then again, it wouldn't have mattered. Emotions seemed only real in girls. Even Warm-Mom had that opinion. According to the songs she'd sing, boys were made of nails, snails, and dismembered puppy-dog tails. You know—things found in garbage piles.

"Oh, so this happened while he was playing with Connor?" Krieg put on his white doctor coat.

"Yes."

"What about that third boy…your next-door neighbor?"

"What next-door neighbor?" Mom paused. "You mean *Chad*?"

"I think that's his name."

"Chad doesn't actually *live* there," she replied. "How do you know him?"

"He's in town now, Mom," I jumped in. "It's summer."

How *did* Dr. Krieg know Chad? The fifteen-year-old lived three cities away in Bellingham with his father, who was usually on the road distributing cigarettes for a tobacco company. During the past four or so years, however, whenever school was out, Chad stayed with his aunt and uncle next door to us. It seemed funny that he'd know Krieg.

"Well, either way, it was only the two boys," she summarized, "down on Bottle Beach. No Chad."

"Oh, okay." He looked at me with a curious brow. "It's Saturday. Where's your dad?"

"John?" Mom butted in. "He's on his way to Seattle. He doesn't know we're here."

"Is that so?" He stepped toward the door. "*Kath!*" He yelled into the hall. "Let's get his clothes off and see what we've got here."

My humiliation

"Bye, Mom!" I energetically blurted out.

"I'm not going anywhere, Kyle," she laughed.

"Mom—he's going to take my *clothes* off."

"Kyle, don't be silly. This is an emergency. You're bleeding. I don't think I should drop you off and go out for a *piece of pie!*"

"Yeah, but—" I actually thought her sarcastic going-out-for-pie reference was funny, but I was no longer in a mood to laugh.

"I'm your *mother*. I've seen you without clothes. You're in shock."

"Mom, I was a little baby back then." The moment the words flew out, I knew they were useless. Quietly, I droned, "Things look different now." Then I realized what she'd just accused me of, and in a burst of anger, I charged back, "And I am *not* in shock!"

"Don't you yell at me, young man!"

Oh. I was a young man when I was irritating her and a sweetheart when I behaved. She *did* want another daughter, didn't she?

"You're being silly…. I'm *staying*."

"Mom, please."

"Kyle!"

"Uuuuh!" I slapped both hands onto the table and gave up—but as loudly as I could. She was right about the emergency, and given the location of the gushing blood, my hope of not being stripped in front of her was pretty futile. Over the years, Mom was the one who had drilled it into me never to expose two things to anyone; emotion, and what *she* referred to as my dirty parts. I wasn't good at hiding emotion, but the dirty parts were well-concealed.

I once had asked Mom what puberty meant, and she'd told me to behave myself and talk nice. My own puberty, which was just beginning, was embarrassing for me, and we weren't allowed to talk about it. One day, on the last week of school, I'd found a brand new antiperspirant stick placed conspicuously on the sink of my bathroom. No one had said a word about it. I put it in the medicine cabinet. The next morning, it was sitting on my sink again but closer to the edge. I was humiliated by the message that I stunk and no one cared enough to tell me. I learned how to use it by reading the directions. Now, here I lay, about to be totally exposed in front of this person who couldn't even bring herself to discuss body odor with me.

Kathy's charm

Kathy finally arrived in the room. She was Krieg's opposite—young, maybe twenty-five or so, with a soft petite frame and nicely out-of-proportion large breasts—features that grabbed my attention in ways I knew not even to *hint* at in front of Mom. Unlike her boss, Kathy had a sweet voice and a kind face that made her a perfect nurse for frightened kids. She'd babysat Connor and me many times over the years before becoming a nurse. I liked her as much as I hated Krieg. I was thankful to have a friend enter the room—but I wished she hadn't been told to strip me.

Stripping my dignity

My mouth dried from nerves. They towered like giants. Kathy on my left and Dr. Krieg to the right, which is where I'd said the pain was. Both hovered over my bloody cutoffs, getting ready to do something I was trying to use my powerful mind to will them not to do.

My commanding thoughts couldn't stop them, though. And I couldn't talk Mom into looking away, so *I* had to. When Krieg said something about preparing the workspace, I turned my head toward the window at my right. The cold steel of metal scissors ran upward slowly along the outer edge of my right leg. It slid an inch, tugged, slid another inch, tugged again, then again, and continued this rhythm until it reached my hip. I closed my eyes and held a breath, then felt the tight garment release.

"Good," said the gruff old man. "Here." Every muscle in my body firmed as if bracing for a hit.

I refused to look, but apparently "here" meant the scissors had been handed over to Kathy. I wanted to say something like, "Please leave my underpants on." But who was going to care what I said? I was now Dr. Krieg's "workspace," and any distrust I felt for him, or inner feelings that might make me into a person again, were *my* problem to deal with. The tugs on my left leg were gentler. It took longer for the cold steel to make its way to the hip. Again, the tight wrap around my left leg sprung loose. I held another breath. They had cut both the shorts and the briefs together on each side.

"Keep going," he ordered. "Bloody old shirt too."

I shot a panicked glance toward Mom, who didn't say anything. Why my shirt too? Had I crash-landed into a dirty joke? I'd never known any kid to be stripped naked by his babysitter before, but I had heard plenty of boys nervously tell jokes about it—jokes that weren't real. They *weren't* real! How could this be happening to me? And even worse— why was this starting to feel like it might actually be a bad dream? I *told* jokes! I wasn't supposed to be in one!

My eyes closed tighter. Shallow breathing started to make me light-headed. The tank top sliced open quickly like a zipper; then Kathy cut the straps over my shoulders the way our butcher cut strings off skirt-steaks. Someone lifted the pieces off. It felt creepy. I couldn't think of a reason to cut it off me. Even pants-less cartoon animals were drawn with shirts so they weren't stark-naked in public.

Mom came around the table to help.

"Oh, for crying out loud," I whispered to myself as she took the shirt away. Why wouldn't she unleash all that angry anxiety onto *them* now? They were humiliating her son. Where was her anxious anger now? They deserved her wrath way more than Connor did.

"Thank you, Marie. That's a help." Krieg's gratefulness lacked sincerity.

"I'll take the pants too, if you want."

"Oh, for crying out loud!" I blurted out, loudly this time. My eyes rolled up behind their eyelids. I wanted to fly into outer space, which is something I did a lot. My nightly routine was to pretend my bed had a clear glass dome and lifted off out of my room so I could fly upward, into the darkness of space, where no one could find me. Space was the only peaceful place I knew. By lying perfectly still, I'd usually fall asleep right after reaching orbit.

There would be no falling asleep this time. The pants lifted off like a diaper. All eyes were on my newly developing dirty parts.

"That's huge!" gasped Mom.

"It's so long," added Kathy, "especially for such a little man."

I tightened my closed eyes even more. I'd *told* them I wasn't a baby anymore.

"It's okay, honey," comforted Mom. "You have a huge, long cut in your leg and that's all. But it's a good thing we got you here when we did because it's a pretty long gash."

"Especially for such a little guy," Kathy repeated.

"Oh," I laughed. "You were talking about the size of my *cut*?"

"Stop! Stop!" Both women shouted at me to quit laughing. Apparently, I gushed more blood when I did.

"I wish I could see it too." I lifted my head but saw nothing.

"Want me to take a picture for you?" asked Krieg.

First flashback

Screech! My levity skidded to a stop. I flashed a rogue image of a camera on a tripod, *in this very building*. In a burst of unexpected shame, I looked away from all three of them. I wished Mom had given me my pill. This place was scaring the hell out of me. What an asshole! Something about his offer hit me the wrong way. His off-color humor had always been one of the reasons I hated him. As he slid the shorts out from under me, I looked into the bright chrome lights above. The scene reminded me of the scary stories from TV where people were abducted by aliens. Maybe I *was* on a spaceship.

"Are you going to *probe* me now?" I sarcastically joked.

Kathy laughed by accident, then politely covered her mouth.

"Kyle, that's not funny." Mom took the pants and left my side. Blood wasn't considered a bio-hazard then, so she dug her fingers through the red pockets, making sure they were empty.

"You can throw them in there if you like." Kathy pointed to the stainless trash bin.

The foot-pedal clunked. The lid squeaked. Picturing a "huge" and "long" gash torn through my skin helped me to forget some of the embarrassment of being nude, making this situation a more legitimate medical emergency and less an adolescent boy's nervous babysitter-sex joke—until, that is, the sudden crash of the trash-lid slamming shut jolted me back into panic.

The naked-in-public dream

My clothes were now locked in a can. I was outside of that can, across town from my wardrobe, in a room filled with fully dressed people, one of whom was threatening to photograph me, and I had no way to get home. This was exactly like the many dreams I'd had of waking up naked at school, church, or at Voyager meetings. A creepy coincidence—*Krieg was usually in those dreams too*. This moment was equally as humiliating—but sickeningly real.

Or was it? Clinic visits were always dream-like.

I looked to my right again and tried to remember the pathway out the window and off to outer space. I then imagined closing myself into the protective steel of my own gold GTO and driving off too quickly to be caught. I imagined it was a spaceship disguised as a muscle-car, taking me off the earth where *no one* could touch me. I silently prayed a prayer I had prayed many times during my childhood. *Please, God, let this be a dream.* I repeated it several times in a chant. *It's a dream—it's a dream—it's a dream. Please, let it be a dream.*

7

The Admirer

I don't think my lifetime of feeling crazy and always half-dreaming was born into me. Also, my father's fragile temper and inability to talk about his battle experiences pointed to shell-shock (now called PTSD), which was wreaking its own havoc in my family. Some believe that children of parents with PTSD are prone to suffer with some form of it also. Is this genetic? Or is it because the families of shell-shocked victims are demolition derbies where one aggressive and damaged member crashes into and damages the rest of them? Families of PTSD sufferers can live on eggshells so delicate that the conditions of PTSD are passed on in the form of Complex-PTSD.

Tuck was starting to figure it out already, that in his own life, insanity was being brought home for him to deal with too.

By Tuck Taylor

The rattle of the apartment door broke my train of thought. Our apartment had two small bedrooms, but I wasn't in either of them. I was alone. Why stay in a bedroom when I have the whole place to myself? Clad only in a pair of white briefs and a thin layer of sweat, I was in the living room, lying on the sagging old brown couch Trenton's mother had sent to Texas with him. It was almost two o'clock in the afternoon and I couldn't sleep. I stared out the window nursing an uneasy dread in my chest. A dread I couldn't explain. I just wanted it to go away.

"Why are you up?" Trenton, a skinny, sort of hairy twenty-three-year-old, had come home in a loose-fitting white T-shirt, mid-length denim cutoffs and flip-flops. As he came into view, I saw he had a friend in tow.

"Hey, Tuck." Mark shyly waved a hand without lifting an arm any higher than waist level.

"Mark." I looked down the couch at my bare, sprawling legs. "Sorry; I'm not dressed…. I didn't know you were coming."

"Don't apologize. Mark thinks you look awesome." Trenton sarcastically laughed and threw a couch pillow at my face, which I caught after it hit me. "You grew up good." He teased some more. "You is a sexy man."

"Why are you here?" I asked through the pillow, ignoring his sarcasm.

"It's Saturday. We're heading to the beach. You should come."

"Yeah, Tuck," Mark interjected. "It would be fun."

I knew Mark had a thing for me. Trenton had introduced us a year before and made it clear to him that I was straight. But the nineteen-year-old, who was a little shorter than me and sported the same shade of light brown hair as mine, always, according to Trenton and a few others, brushed his hair just before he knew he was going to see me.

"I haven't slept in two days." I tossed the pillow back onto the floor and grunted as I sat up to make room on the couch.

"Whose fault is that, Mr. Couch Potato?" Trenton asked.

I flipped him off but didn't look at him. Mark chuckled quietly.

"You wouldn't have to get up right now if you'd have slept in your bed like you're supposed to," Trenton scolded. "This is a shared space, and now you're sharing your tighty-whities." He was a neat-freak. He picked up the pillow and placed it carefully against an arm on the couch, then patted it like he was telling it not to move from that spot.

"I think you look awesome in your whities," said Mark, laughing. "But you guys *are* the odd couple."

"If he wasn't so damn good-looking…" Trenton joked to Mark as he picked up my water glass from the floor beneath the couch and started carrying it to the kitchen, "I'd…uhhh!"

"You'd…uhhh…*what*?" I angrily retorted.

"Yeah. You'd what?" Mark asked. "He's too nice to kick out."

"Oh, how I know that. It's far too late for kicking anyone out…too much *love* between us." The water glass clinked in the sink. His voice echoed out from the kitchen "But I can sure as hell housebreak him."

Mark smiled at me like he was embarrassed at Trenton's arrogant humor.

"Just don't leave the door open." I shook my head in disgust. I really loved Trenton, but we were starting to bicker like this a lot. Speaking only loud enough for Mark to hear, I added, "This house pet might be ready to run away."

8

The Set-Up

There are no normal situations where a man is allowed to strip a boy and make jokes—but this was not a normal situation, and Krieg was not a man. This was a crisis, Krieg was a wolf dressed like a man, and I was in a cage with him. The rules of civility only apply during peace time. When a boy is bleeding to death, no one, anywhere, enforces those rules.

This wolf knew how to enjoy his opportunity to break the rules in front of my supposed protector—Mom. Maybe it was a thrill for him. Maybe it was part of a bigger plan to undermine what trust my mother and I had between us Who can really say now? Maybe he knew exactly how to make this crisis into a bigger deal so he could more easily get what he wanted. Crisis gave him control. I didn't want to trust him, but I had no choice. I had to choose to let him do things a person is never supposed to be allowed to do.

So instead, I escaped into the privacy of my brain. I'd had a lot of bad dreams, irrational fears, and blackouts, but this was going to be my first violently dissociative PTSD episode, which would prove to do its job perfectly to hide me when I couldn't run.

By Kyle Rickett

After my moment of angry silence, Dr. Krieg's leathery fingers started poking and tugging. I didn't like it, but when he grabbed my "dirty part" to move it out of the way, at least I could give Connor the good news that my wiener was still attached.

"Mom?" I nervously squeaked like my heart had taken a shot of caffeine. Krieg's grabbing hands were starting to panic me. Why wasn't he letting go?

"What do you need, honey?"

"Mom, don't let him…." I didn't know how to finish. I needed medical attention, but I didn't want Krieg's touch. "I don't know…. Just…don't let him—*OW!*"

Krieg's grip on my "thing" tightened. It hurt. Mom thought my shriek was from the wound, but I knew I was being sent a message to shut up or it would only keep getting worse.

"The doctor's here to help you." Mom fell for it.

"Ow, ow," I uttered again, but I didn't ask for more help. I had to hold my panic inside. I couldn't believe he was doing this to me right in front of my mom. I held my breath and looked at Krieg's face, which was cleverly searching the damaged area. The old doc's glasses had slid to the end of his big vein-cluttered nose.

"I think we're going to be all right." He eased his grip but kept tugging gently.

Both women sighed in relief and I let my lungs release. My stare froze on Krieg's old face. The pain proved I wasn't dreaming, but everything else was unreal.

The room moved slightly in a rhythmic circle and another fog of nausea quietly overcame my stomach. Again, I wished I was sedated on my pills, but I actually felt foggy like maybe I *was* on them. I blinked a few times quickly.

A tree began growing inside me. I looked around for branches. I'd had this nightmare before. I knew the trees were going to grow around my wrists, and down my throat. Panic attacked quickly, but I closed my eyes: *Oh, God, I hate this dream. Please let me wake up.* For a short and grateful second, I believed I was asleep—and alone—in bed.

"I can't tell if there's nerve damage yet, and it's in a tough place to stitch, but that worked in your favor, Marie. Keeping his legs together probably kept him alive." Krieg may have been making it sound worse than it was, for some reason, while he looked up at Mom. "It's a very bad cut to the top of the leg. Come over here and take a look."

Bringing mom into the dream

Take a look? Was he kidding?

"Let's not embarrass him," she resisted. "I can see from here, Lee."

Finally! My mother had *finally* stood up for me. She was back on my side again.

"Marie, you'll be caring for him at home. You need to see the damage." His gravelly tone gave an order, not a choice.

Mom didn't move a muscle for several seconds. For years, I'd listened to her talk tough about Krieg to my sister, calling him an "old fool" like he was a joke. But now, when I needed her bold anger, she instead went under some sort of a trance. Her snippy comments went silent. Whose side was she on *now*?

"Okay, I'll look," she droned meekly, and then to my utter amazement, she walked slowly up my left side and around my head to meet Krieg at the wound. I concentrated on her every step. She focused on Krieg's authoritative face. What the hell was wrong with her? Was my angry mother watching for his approval? Again, I wondered whose side she was taking.

Somehow, the feeling of being personally violated felt like it was something I'd had to deal with before, and so to avoid getting angry, which I didn't believe I was allowed to be, I just numbed inside from not knowing how I was supposed to feel when Krieg held my dirty parts away from my wound with one hand and kept pressure on the wound with the other. He moved aside so she could get in close, and all I did was shut my eyes to avoid memorizing an image of my mother's face in my crotch. I suppose any boy would be embarrassed to have his mother and doctor poking around in that area, but *why* was this so extra-terrifying to me? All I could feel at that moment was some strangely numbing humiliation because it was *him* directing her attention to that spot.

"You see there?" He let go enough for the wound to bleed a little. "It's about a half-inch deep, with torn muscle here…and here." He pressed the gauze back up to it. "Walking's going to hurt him from head to toe for a few weeks. That's why I wanted you to see it. So you'd know what kind of pain he'll be in." He let go of my dirty parts but kept pressure on the gash. "He ought to consider buying a seat for that bike of his. They're a lot more comfortable that way."

No one laughed.

Mom kept her visit by my side short. I peeked to see if she was gone. She looked toward my face. Our glances met, but we both looked away quickly. Krieg's eyes darted back and forth between us like he was watching a table-tennis match. When we wouldn't make contact, he almost looked happy about it. Mom stood up sharply and walked back to the foot of the bed. Hopefully, she was as humiliated as I was.

"Looks pretty bad," she muttered. "You can fix it though, right?"

"Of course I can!" he arrogantly responded.

Mom tightened her lips and shyly looked around the room.

Krieg's personality was as raspy as his voice and as dried out as his face. He joked a lot, but he never laughed. His wisecrack remarks left people off balance and guessing at when he was serious.

Bringing Kathy into the nightmare

"Let's get started." He pushed my knees together, probably to hold the wound shut, and turned his attention around to his silver trays of equipment.

"You hear that, sweetie?" Kathy leaned over my face to lay a tender hand on my forehead. "You're going to be okay."

I turned to smile politely at my babysitter friend, who was leaning over me. My eyes fell onto her blouse, now pulling away with gravity. "Oh, crap," I whispered. I accidentally saw the lacy edge of a bra and her cleavage, which I admit I had been admiring as of late. I checked Mom's face to make sure she hadn't caught me looking down Kathy's shirt. For me, this was a new obsession—of which I was ashamed and trying daily to control. I was a good Catholic boy—not a sex-fiend. But for the past few months, my eyes had been magnetically drawn to breasts. Before then, I hadn't even noticed women *had* them. The new obsession happened against my will. I never told anyone about it. What would a beautiful woman like this think about being ogled by a dumb little kid like me? I huffed a polite laugh, turned back to the window, and closed my eyes.

The doctor got up. I tried to follow his movements with one eye. A couple of drawers slid open and he picked out some shiny items. He sat back down, rested his heavy elbow on my right knee, and pressed.

"Ow, ow, ow," I squeaked.

"He's going to start bleeding pretty good now, Kath."

Her training kicked in, and she held a wad of gauze tightly against me. I tried to distract myself from the pain by thinking about something else. Maybe I could remember something funny, like the most recent joke I'd heard. But both her hands were between my legs and the lacey bra was the last image I'd seen, so guess what popped into my poor horny little mind?

"I'm going to numb that for you, champ." For the next few minutes, Krieg worked around Kathy's hands and cleaned the wound area with small patches of gauze while injecting short squirts of something. She let go and he went back to pressing into it. Soon enough, and to my joyous relief, the pain faded away.

"Okay, Kath, I need you to clean the blood off of him now while the cyclomethycaine sets in. I'll start stitching in five minutes. I'll clean this area here...." His eyes pointed at the greasy chair marks on my knees. "You do the rest." I knew that "the rest" was my dirty parts. I looked up at Kathy's face. Then at Mom, who continued staring at those parts.

"Mom?"

"Yeah, honey?"

"Can I clean my own blood off?"

"Ha!" she laughed. "I think the doctor and nurse should do that. Don't you?"

"Lee, why don't I do his legs?" Kathy chimed in, "or can we clean him off later?"

Complete control over everyone

"Oh!" Dr. Krieg looked squarely at Kathy, who now looked as scared as Mom had earlier. He sarcastically scolded, "You're a college-educated doctor now?"

She dropped her head.

"Marie?" Krieg turned to Mom. "You want to clean your son's private areas for him?" His emotionless voice sounded no different than usual.

I gasped. Was he serious?

"No, of course not." Mom sheepishly shook her head.

"My hands are busy keeping him from bleeding to death." Krieg looked back at Kathy with a scolding grimace. "Let's not kill him, okay? You're the nurse. Do as the doctor tells you."

"I'm sor-.... I'm sor-sorry, Doctor" stumbled from her nervous mouth. Then she apologized to me, "I'm sorry, Kyle. Dr. Krieg is right. I need to clean you up. I'll be quick. I'm a nurse now, not a babysitter. This is an emergency, so the rules are different. You're in trouble at the moment, and we're only here to help."

I'm the only one who saw Krieg smile at Kathy's remark that the rules were different now and we all had to do what the doctor ordered.

New rules

Out of those words, all I heard was, "the rules are different" and "I'm going to rub your naked body with my beautiful soft hands...." Not necessarily a word-for-word recap, but reality was turning out to be a fragile state of mind. An hour before, I'd learned that after an accident, two boys could show open compassion to each other without being scorned, and now, also due to an accident, all the rules of decency could be breached without any scolding. I closed my eyes and tried to leave the room again.

But maybe my previous moment of envisioning Kathy's cleavage wasn't the best choice of distraction. Also, some closed-off part of my brain suddenly awoke and knew I'd been naked in this clinic before. I felt a warm towel rubbing grease off my right thigh, and another towel, more softly, rubbing the left.

"Oh...dear," Kathy commented.

I knew why. I wasn't *that* numb. I could feel how my dirty parts responded to her touch. I looked over at Krieg's face.

"Well," he said casually, "no nerve damage." Then he locked eyes with me and winked.

He winked!

Driven out of my mind

What the hell did that mean? My blood chilled. Then, right before my eyes, he turned into Santa Claus. *Santa Claus*! Was I losing my freaking mind completely? He had made Kathy do this to me on purpose! I was sure of it. It was obvious—and somehow seemed exactly like something *he* would do—*wait*! *Why did I know that about him*?

I shook my spinning head to wake up. This had to be a dream. I looked again. He was Dr. Krieg now, but the confusion was overpowering. Maybe he was Santa in a doctor disguise—or vice-versa. I wasn't on my pills, but I felt like I was. The softer towel continued to clean around my excited sensitive area while Mom stared. I lost track of my age. I was seven years old. Maybe nine, but I wasn't sure where I was all of a sudden. Was this the tent from our campout? Or was I in room two, behind the door that's always closed? I tried focusing on figuring out my location on the earth. I could almost feel tree vines wrapping themselves around my wrists. My breathing increased as if I'd been locked in a cage with snakes.

For whatever reason, my arms lifted up over my head and grabbed the edge of the table to hang on. But then I put my wrists together so they could be tied. What was I doing? My mother was here. She should be helping me. As anxiety accelerated, I wished again for my pill. My mind wasn't in control. My body seemed to know this pose on its own. For some incomprehensible reason, I could almost hear my own internal voice screaming, *Look, Mom! Look at my wrists! You can see what he's doing. Help me!*

"It's show time," I heard, but I didn't know who said it. A flashbulb went off in my face. Was Krieg making good on his earlier threat? Was he taking a picture? Another flash blinded me. Then I heard boys laughing nervously. I completely lost all remaining sense of knowing where I was. I saw a tall, white-flocked Christmas tree, loaded with large wrapped gifts at its base. My nausea worsened. Where the hell was I?

Awakening into *a dream*

The tree vines grew so fast that I panicked. Up into my stomach and down through my throat they spread. The vines bound my feet and hands. This was not the first time I'd had what I've regrettably named the dreaded "tree dream," but I wasn't positive that *this* was a dream. For a split second, I was sure I had been physically tied up naked in this room before. Or was it Jack who had been tied up? Or was this the tent? I scanned for anything that could anchor me. I saw the clock: 12:34. Was this the moment it ended? Was my "normal" childhood—as I'd lived it— a sham? A lie?

The jig was up. It was over. I tried to use my best imaginative trick and placed myself into my super-safe gold GTO/spaceship, but when I did, I accidentally envisioned it crashing into an asteroid and bursting into flames. The infamous "tree dream" could now ravage my body as I lay helpless. That was my final conscious thought, because then, as if my batteries had given their last charge, I wandered into the blackness of sleep.

PART 2

Origins:

THE ROOT BEGINNINGS OF MY NERVOUS STOMACH

Three Years Prior

Torano Island

Mid-Winter Break, February 28, 1971

9

Scooter's Promise

The next seven chapters, 9-14 take place in the past to show what led up to this mess in Dr. Krieg's office. What I just described was my first violent dissociative PTSD episode, but it didn't happen in a vacuum. It never does. When people "freak out" over nothing, it's usually not over nothing. There's usually history—a buildup of a million "almost nothings" that witnesses don't know about. It's the last straw that breaks the camel's back, but the last straw is all the witnesses see.

*Almost everyone experiences trauma, which is the T in PTSD. Trauma causes stress, which is the S. So, most people experience TS at least a few times in life. It's when you add the P and the D that you create a lifelong situation. The P for "Post," which means the trauma is long past. The D stands for "Disorder," which is where it becomes a problem. Healthy Trauma Stress might result from the fear we have of getting back onto a horse a few minutes after being bucked off, or the nightmares we have on the night after a car accident. This becomes **Post-**Traumatic Stress **Disorder** when years later,* *that stress had been too big to deal with and has festered to become other symptoms. The "dissociative episode" is a current-day reaction to something that couldn't have been dealt with long ago. The disorder builds over time, adding more and more new symptoms until the victim feels permanently and uncontrollably broken.*

*With the next few chapters, I want to share with you the three years of **P**ost-**T**raumatic **S**tress that led up to this **D**isordered reaction. The nervous stomach was the first symptom. When nobody recognized it as a symptom, but let it go un-dealt-with, the nightmares came next. They began when I was ten, on a winter's night in 1971 with the first of many nightmares I've since called "the tree dreams." My then thirteen-year-old cousin Scooter, a self-appointed protector since my birth, was someone I could trust wholeheartedly. He was there with me that night. We boys had no idea what the dream meant, but as adults now looking back, he and I are both bothered by the obviousness of it.*

Scooter McBride, now a New York public defense lawyer, still looks out for me. Today, I get the sense that, because he saw himself as my guardian, our memories of this event bother him more than they do me. The big lug adds guilt and self-accusations to his version for failing to protect me. I hate it when he does that. Mean old Dr. Krieg and his wandering hands were the source of the dream. Scooter, who may have been twice my size, was still just a kid, and was soon to find out that he had problems of his own to deal with, and he was no match for that beast. None of this was his fault. But today, he feels remorse over something he's never had control over.

I'm going to honor his empathy for me by letting him air the story—through his own words—of the first night I ever reached out for help.

By Scott "Scooter" McBride

I was thirteen then and usually slept like a rock. But on Sunday, March 1, 1971, on Torano Island, Washington, a creepy late-night rainstorm gave me a sleep I'll never forget. We were visiting the Ricketts. Mom had driven my three brothers, Brian and Theo who were sixteen-year-old twins, Mikey who was nine, and thirteen-year-old me up from Portland for Mid-Winter Break. We made the rec room look like a sleeping lions' den the way we sprawled in sleeping bags across its floor. My three brothers were on my right, and my ten-year-old cousin, Kyle, was snoring on my left. I slept fine through the wind and rain, but at one o'clock, Kyle woke me up with his shaking and moaning. I listened for a minute. I didn't know what to do, but when he called my name—*my* name, *and no one else's*—I proudly pushed out of my sleeping bag and crawled over to him.

"Kyle!" His moans turned to screeches. The rain and wind gusts slammed the windows. His screaming spooked me, but the storm drowned him out and no one else woke up.

"Kyle!" I yelled straight into his face. Then I shook him, but the little shit fought me. Since both his arms were tucked in tight in his sleeping bag, he had to use his neck and forehead to push away from me.

"Jack?" His eyes finally sprung wide open. The streetlight shining in the window let me see his pupils grow, then shrink, then grow again. It was weird. He didn't even know who I was. It's like he was looking through me, not at me. He stopped breathing and stared like he was terrified.

"No! Christ, Kyle…I'm Scooter!"

His shivering got worse, but at least he quit fighting me. Wanting to be his big, tough rescuer, I hugged him tight and pulled his face into my chest, hoping he'd get the message that I was Scooter. A crack of thunder rumbled off in the distance as I squeezed him even tighter. I peeled the top of his sleeping bag down, releasing his trapped arms. The top button of his PJs popped open, exposing one little shoulder, cold to the touch but soaked with sweat. I thought he'd calm down now, but I was wrong.

His jaw shivered against my chest like he was freezing. Now he wasn't fighting against me, but his loose arms frantically grabbed at me like he was trying not to fall off a cliff, digging his fingertips into my back. Instinctively, I squeezed a bit tighter. My hug forced him to inhale through the cloth of my pajama top, which smelled like the cologne I'd asked my mother for and had gotten in my Christmas stocking that year. His pathetic squealing finally scared me shitless. If he hadn't calmed down when he did, I was going to run upstairs and get his mom.

"Scooter?" Something must have clicked with him. He settled down and muffled again into my pajama top. "Scooter?" Maybe my cologne helped jog his memory. "Is that really you?"

"Yeah." I exhaled a huge sigh of relief. "It's me. It's just a storm. We're okay. Really. You called my name," I boasted, "so I came right over."

"I'm so glad it's you-hoo-hooo." Another outburst scared me again.

I let him catch his breath for about a minute. I'd never seen him do such a thing. To me, he'd forever been small, but he'd *always* been happy—and brave. I was all about acting tough, but that naturally cheerful little shit—who could always keep up with me no matter how small he was—was my freaking hero.

I remember meeting him

I was bigger than most. Tall. Broad shouldered. My size intimidated other kids in those days. I talked tough and swore a lot, but the truth was that I was a gentle giant. From birth, my heart was softer than most would guess. Holding my panicked cousin on that night felt like an honor and brought back a good memory—my first one, actually—which was of the moment I'd met him.

I was only two years, eleven months old the first time I saw Kyle. They say that is about the age that cognitive memory begins. To this day, I don't know how accurate that memory is, but I know how it logged itself into my brain files. So, to me, the whole thing happened exactly how my brain's files tell me it did.

I was in a hospital. The sheets were stiff and the lights bright. My parents and Kyle's dad (my uncle John) had set me on a bed and were towering over me as they carefully put newborn Kyle onto my lap and took pictures. I distinctly recall looking up into their surrounding faces and asking them who he was. My mom said that he was my new cousin, and Auntie Marie's new baby. I asked what a cousin was and they said, "It's *like* a brother." Since my two older brothers had always treated me like a pet, I hoped this new little one would never do that to me.

But then I needed to know where he came from, and Mom's answer, "Obviously from Heaven," hit hard even at that age. At just short of three, I basically accepted everything I was told as truth. Years later, I learned why she'd said it. It was the same reason Auntie Marie wasn't on the bed that night. She had almost died giving birth and was in an operating room somewhere. Kyle would be the last child Auntie Marie could ever have. The reason my mom—her twin—said Kyle was from Heaven was because she had been praying so hard for a miracle that she actually believed God had intervened with a last-minute rescue so they both could live. I guess, to her, that meant this baby was somehow "a gift from Heaven." I didn't know any better, so I filed that information as truth.

Kyle's first two years were sickly ones, which made him into a long-time family worry. Whether that's my reason for being undyingly close to him for my whole life or not, I don't know. I just know that I've always loved him. I've always been closer to him than to either of my older brothers, or my eventual baby brother.

Kyle and I had a connection that rivaled natural brotherhood. Our moms were twins, and so were my older brothers. I could see the link they had as twins, but I couldn't comprehend it. I'd always pretended that Kyle and I shared the twin-bond too. It seemed special. I wanted it. My theory is that when the adults put him in my lap the way they did, he became the first person I'd met who was younger than me, and my little brain decided that I owned him. He was *my* baby cousin—my new twin. They'd given him to me because my twin-brothers weren't bonding with me. I'd been blessed with the chance to be the big brother now, and I was going to show the world how it was supposed to be done. I was going to be forever responsible for his safety.

Uncle John's a quiet man, but he's not cuddly, nor was he ready to take care of an infant. Even though Uncle John and Aunt Marie's daughter, my cousin Fran, was fourteen, the family didn't seem to want her to take care of Kyle either. Years later, I learned that—how shall I say this delicately?—*an ability to know right from wrong didn't seem to dwell within her heart.* Either they knew not to trust her with baby Kyle, or she flatly refused. The only Rickett left was Daniel, who was almost twelve and not ready for the responsibility. So, for whatever reason, I'm told that since we lived next door then, that we took Kyle home with us while Auntie Marie stayed hospitalized. For three solid weeks, Kyle slept in my room, in a large crib next to my bed. Mom slept in my bed with me. I'm sure this was all done so my dad could sleep at night, but I have no doubt my parents decided to tell me that we were using my room because I was his protector. I can't remember a time when I didn't believe I was.

We lived next door until I was nine when, in 1967, my dad, an auto mechanic, got a chance to manage a dealership garage in Portland, Oregon, so away we went. I was sad, but it helped that we visited several times a year on holidays and school breaks. Mom and Auntie Marie hated being apart as much as Kyle and I did, so we drove the I-5 corridor enough that, for both families, the four-hour trip just became a simple commute.

Nightmares

And so there in that dry room, surrounded by the scary thunderstorm, I tucked Kyle's hands back into the warm sleeping bag and held him to let him recuperate from some sort of a new night terror that I had apparently rescued him from. Even though I had become a larger-than-average macho thirteen-year-old, holding my smaller-than-average cousin once more felt nice. Real nice. I'm a protector by nature, and back then, I was planning my future as a policeman. I was routinely rescuing smaller kids from bigger ones and righteously telling bullies, "Pick on someone your own size." So, this nighttime rescue felt like it was just me being me.

"You were having a nightmare, Kyle," I explained as another rumble of thunder crashed in the distance. Another wind gust showered rain against the thin glass. "Probably because of the storm. But I promise you're okay now."

"Oh." He laid his head back onto my chest, "It was definitely a nightmare."

"What were you 'nightmaring' about?" I asked, "Snakes?"

"Trees."

"Huh?" I laughed again, "Trees?"

"Trees." He pulled away to sit on his own and do his best to laugh with me. "But they were really scary, Scooter." Jittering yellowy light streaming in through the violent storm gave his face, and the room, a ghostly feel.

"Why? Did they have machine guns?"

"No!" he chuckled. "They didn't have *machine guns*!" We could always make each other laugh. Both of us had definitely inherited our moms' senses of humor. "But they grew really, *really* fast."

"So?" I adjusted to sit cross-legged and rest both hands on my knees, palms up. He wriggled his arms back out of the sleeping bag and laid his hands in mine. He was calming down pretty good.

"*Really fast*, Scooter." He clutched my palms gently. "And Jack was there. But the trees killed him and then they came after me."

"Whoa. Is Jack that kid who ran away a few months ago?"

"I dream about him a lot. I always wake up hoping he's okay."

"You dream he got killed? Do you think he did?"

"I thiiiiiink..." Kyle wanted to believe something, so he just did. He was nine. "...he's okay. Maybe he's just lost."

"But...you really don't know." I checked to be sure.

"Hmm." He shrugged. "No one knows for sure, I guess."

"That's weird that you dream about him."

"I guess."

"What kind of trees were they?" I changed the subject.

"They scared me bad. They looked like Christmas trees."

"So?"

"I thought I was at the clinic in a Voyager Scout meeting."

"And that's scary?"

"Yeah, but I don't know why. I'm not a scout anymore."

"Why not?"

"Mom made me quit. But that's okay. Dr. Krieg was our scoutmaster, and I don't like him. He thinks he's funny, but he's not—"

"He thinks he's funny, but he's *snot*?'" I interrupted.

"He's definitely 'snot.'" He giggled. "And it was so boring I don't even remember what we did every week."

"How the *heck* do you not remember what you did every week?"

"I don't know." His voice went flat. "I just don't."

"Okay, well…." I dismissed his strange reaction. "Well, why is dreaming about trees *scary*?"

"I don't know. But in the dream, the Christmas trees at the clinic tied my hands together and then grew down my mouth…and up my butt." He squeezed both hands tightly. "And it hurt, really bad."

I giggled again. I was thirteen. Saying "butt" was *always* funny.

"It sounds so *stupid*!" He cleared his throat. "But it's scary, and I don't know why."

A wave of what felt like electric energy erupted from his hands and flowed through my bones, up toward my elbows. It felt good but sent a shiver through my shoulders and surprised me. It was part of the bond we had with each other. It changed my mood. It's like his spirit was so big it was traveling through me looking for comfort. I'd never heard of such a dumb dream, but somehow or another, with that energy flowing between us—even at that age I knew this was important to him.

"No, Kyle. It doesn't sound stupid. I think it's neat that you're such a nice guy that you worry about another kid enough to dream about him, and I'm sorry I laughed because you're right; it's scary."

"I love you, Scooter." Still wearing his sleeping bag from the chest down, Kyle leaned forward and again buried his head into me. "I'm glad you don't think it's stupid." The thunder sounded farther away now. It was leaving the island.

"Oh, my God," I muttered as his body trembled. The way he pressed in forced more hot energy through. "I'm always going to be here for you, Kyle. You hear me?"

He didn't talk again for a while, and he also didn't let go of my hands. I knew what needed to be done.

"Would you like me to sleep in your sleeping bag with you?" I asked.

"Yes!" he jolted back and let go. "I was hoping you'd say that. It'll be like when we were little."

"You're *still* little." I broke into quiet laughter.

"I know. And you're huge!"

The sleeping bag was tight, but we were okay. We were cozy and warm while we listened to the gushing water gurgling in the downspout outside our window. His breath smelled of the grape licorice I'd brought from Portland for him. I listened into the silence beyond the storm and made sure my three brothers were still asleep. They were. I wanted to go back to sleep myself because our moms were going to take us to Sunday morning Mass in a few hours—but I needed Kyle to fall asleep first.

"Did I thank you for the licorice?" he moaned groggily.

"About a hundred times."

Torano Island boat tour

The next morning, Cousin Daniel, Kyle's twenty-two-year-old brother, took us boating after church. The storm was finished and all that was left was a normal Pacific Northwest cold drizzle. That drizzle always brought all the smells of the Pacific's rich, green foliage to life and blended it with the salt water air. It gave a refreshing coolness to our faces. Daniel took the five of us younger boys on an all-day excursion in Uncle John's motorboat. We puttered around the islands, mooring at various docks and beaches, exploring the islands of Torano and nearby Camano. The small boat was laid out like a convertible car, with a steering wheel and seats for six. On the back was painted the name *Princess Marie* in red letters. By decree of Kyle's mom, the real Princess Marie, Kyle and Michael wore life jackets, or they weren't allowed to go. I wore one too so they'd feel less singled out. I was cool with that because I've always been confident in who I am. Comfortable in my own skin, as they say. My elder brothers' twin-bond typically had me feeling like their third wheel. I was obviously on *the other team* again, so by matter of practice I always made the best of it. The three of us young ones sat in the backseat and wore stocking caps because it was cold. My older brothers, who were sixteen, but acted like they wanted to be Daniel's age instead of mine, wore baseball caps to be sure they looked more grown up and cool in the front seat...*morons*.

My idiot brothers were totally into Daniel that day. Together, the three of them could be pranksters, and that day they seemed to be in an especially light-hearted mood. Warning lights were going off in my head. Daniel had just gotten a license to drive long-haul trucks, so this was their last chance to hang out with him before he took a "man's job" and drove off into the sunset.

But Daniel was a lost soul. You could see it in his eyes. He was never proud of working for his dad, rebuilding machinery. His sister, Fran, who went to beauty school, had constantly cut him down for not taking some of their dad's money to get an education, so he went to truck driving school, but *then* she bitched that truck-driving school was "hardly an education." The poor bastard couldn't win. No one really ever could win with Fran.

But for today, my attention was on Kyle and Mike, knowing that without a bodyguard, our testosterone-soaked elder brothers would ignore, or even torment them somehow. It would have been easy for Brian and Theo, and Cousin Daniel, to moor up on a beach, trick the little ones out of the boat, and take off for an hour leaving them terrified they'd been stranded, only to return and then make them beg for a ride back to the house. But the twins were on the lower end of average height—somewhere around five-seven, and I, as luck would have it had been blooming early, and was now about five eight-or nine; for thirteen, I was tall and girthy. I was the tallest boy in my class that year, and somehow, physically, I ended up being the tallest McBride boy on that boat too, and therefore, *no one was going to be left on an island for an hour*.

Licorice friendship

By noon, Daniel had tied the boat at the Torano Dock Shop, which sat on the north shore in a small, densely wooded cove. Boaters could moor there and buy fishing supplies, while cars coasted through the forest down the gravel hill from the highway. We noisy boys entered the old store in a mob, but we divided quickly into small search parties to invade candy shelves, sift through pop coolers, and browse comic books.

"Strawberry or grape?" I asked, while bent over the licorice display with Kyle crouching next to me, both of us still wearing our stocking caps and orange life jackets over winter coats. I recalled the warmth of his head pressed into my pajama top, and before Kyle could decide, I stood tall and announced to the other search parties, "I'm buying Kyle's!"

From the car magazines, Brian remarked, "You always buy Kyle's stuff. How much money you got anyway?"

"More than you assholes do! I can buy Mike's too. I don't throw my money away like you do. I save my allowance."

"Yippee!" Mike heard the offer, "Can I have a Marathon?"

"Yep. Grab one, little brother." I purposely sounded extra kind to make my elder brothers look like the selfish assholes I thought they were.

"Oh, boy!" Mike hooted. "Marathons are *expensive!*"

"Doesn't look like you're saving it now," commented Daniel. "Free food for everyone!"

The older boys laughed.

"Screw you guys. I'm only buying for the little ones."

"Grape!" announced Kyle.

"Good choice!" All my attention fell back onto him. "We'll share another whole package." I stuck my tongue out at the others, then turned back to Kyle, "Just you 'n' me." I grabbed a package of grape vines and a chocolate bar. "Let's go." We clomped across the creaky floor to the cash register where I plunked a dollar bill onto the wooden counter.

The magic of Kyle's spark

The nice gray-haired lady gave us back a couple of pennies, smiled, and said, "You boys be careful out there in that boat now. Last night's storm no doubt washed some logs into the tide." Everybody but Kyle ignored her. He nodded cheerfully.

"That's quite a smile you've got there, young man."

"Thank you, ma'am." As Kyle shyly responded, I saw his eyes sparkle at her the way they usually did toward me.

"Thanks, Scott," squealed Mike, who then grabbed his candy bar and ran back to the magazines with the older boys.

"Yeah, thanks, Scooter," Kyle chirped, his face glowing. Then he turned his attention back to the woman. "Bye, ma'am!" He waved cheerfully. "And we'll be careful in the boat. My brother's a good driver."

I chuckled and, for the first time, looked directly into the woman's eyes. She smiled. She wasn't just a gray-haired lady. She was a real person. I shook my head at Kyle's genuine politeness—and I think I learned a big lesson: Kids and grownups aren't so different. We all like to be smiled at.

"Yeah. Thank you very much, ma'am." I then waved too, but since I was older, I gave more of a mature salute and a gentler smile. "And don't worry. I always take good care of him." The wooden floor creaked beneath the shifting weight as I turned to leave.

We took off like gunshots out the front door, jumped off the old wooden steps into the muddy paths, and ran toward the boat.

I liked to joke with Kyle just to watch his freakishly blue eyes spark when his cheeks wrinkled for a laugh. I remember that I used to say, "Your laugh makes *me* laugh." Watching him with the store clerk made me realize that Kyle's ability to bring joy wasn't reserved just for me. It seemed he could make quick friends anywhere.

Kyle's weaknesses

My mom and Auntie Marie also knew how fast Kyle could draw people in. And from what I'd heard for years on my side of Mom's telephone conversations, Auntie Marie worried constantly. Kyle received more unsolicited attention from adults than the rest of us kids, and our moms didn't believe he had the drive, or the size, to protect himself.

Kyle looked like an even blonder version of our moms, except that his cheekbones were exaggerated like he was a caricature. His nearly white hair and sparkling blue eyes drew second glances pretty much everywhere. And finally, not only was Kyle small in stature, but he talked with a faint speech impediment, making him seem even more vulnerable. His "r's" and "l's" were challenged ever so slightly. He would say his own name with an "r" so smooth that it sounded like he was singing, "Kyhle Wrhickett." Despite his vulnerable size and attributes, I still wished I was his twin, and that we looked and sounded more alike. Even though I was fine with how I looked, it might have been fun to share a resemblance so it would be more obvious we were related.

Auntie Marie did things to keep him inconspicuous in public. It always pissed me off because his almost-white hair was so cool looking, but she would cut it short and even make him wear hats. *Hats!* Both moms lived by the opinion that he was a weak and vulnerable target. Though they went overboard with it, I didn't *completely* disagree. I guess that could be what drove my compulsion to devote my new macho strength to standing up and protecting the kid. He needed a football player like me to stand up for him, and he sure seemed to appreciate it.

Not going to burn in hell

"Why do you say swear words to your brothers?" Kyle asked. A few heavy, cold raindrops fell amid the misty drizzle. We ignored them. "Aren't you worried you're going to go to hell for swearing?"

I burst into laughter. We'd returned to the boat and were facing each other, lounging on the front seats while the rest of the brood had gone exploring the playground up on the hill. The small waves were nicely rhythmic, but every time one of us snapped bites of licorice whips in our teeth, the little boat jiggled a bit out of tempo.

"What's so funny?"

"I don't know. And I'm *not going to hell*." I giggled again and tapped his shoulder. "But it seems like *they* should." By this age, I'd abandoned any belief in hell, but I liked the insult value of it.

"Why should they go to hell?" Kyle asked, wide-eyed.

"I don't know. They're different than me somehow. That and…" I smiled fiendishly, "that and they're *assholes*."

We both laughed.

"You're nice to Mike."

"He's little. He needs defending." I poked him. "Like you."

"I do *not!*"

"Hey! I saved you from the scary trees, remember?" I slapped his arm.

"Oh, yeah," he laughed and tapped my shoulder in return.

We both snapped off more licorice while I admired the sparkle in his eyes. His hands and cheeks were pink from the cold drizzle and his nose was red but his smile bright. The cold meant nothing to us at that age. Raindrops were miniature explosions against the fiberglass hood and windshield. We continued to ignore them.

"I always wondered," I said, pointing to the bangs hanging in strings from under his cap. "Why is your hair so white?"

"How the *heck* am I supposed to know?" Kyle dropped his jaw and sprung his eyes open as wide as he could, while humorously raising palms face up, licorice whip and all.

"Oh, yeah," I laughed. "Well? Aren't you secretly a mad scientist who knows everything?"

"I wish!" He leaned back into his seat. "I'm no scientist."

"Oh," I joked, "but you *are* mad?"

"*Roar!*" He leaned in again and lifted his claws like a monster. "I'm completely *crazy!*" Then he whipped me with licorice. "Take *that,* human!"

"Ouch!" I exploded back with laughter, grabbed both of Kyle's hands, and moved to an inch from his bright eyes. "Not crazy…in-sa-a-a-a-ne!"

We roared monster sounds for a few seconds, then lounged back and snapped off more candy.

"I wish I *was* a mad scientist," he said, wriggling and tugging his coat's fur-lined hood up from its trap under the orange life vest and shrouding it over his head to protect himself from the rain. "Then I'd know how to make spring break last forever, and I'd still get smart." He pulled the two strings with a comical tug and the hood closed tightly around his little face. His gleaming smirk cracked me up again.

"Oh, cool," I played along. "You could invent a smart-shot. Just stick it in your arm and now you know math and geography and everything."

"I hope I get to go to college someday."

"What are you going to be when you grow up?" I slid my hood over my head as well.

"Probably a tractor mechanic."

"Why?" I curled a lip. Kyle had too much personality to be hidden under a farm machine.

"'Cause it's a good living that puts food on the table."

"You sound like your dad." I gently pushed him backward against his chest.

"That's 'cause it's what he always says," he replied, laughing. "I think it's what I'm supposed to be. Especially since Daniel didn't do it…I think I have to."

"A mad scientist can put food on the table too, you know. You should be what you want to be. Not what'cher dad says you have to be."

"Well…" he paused. "that's a long time from now I guess." He shrugged. "But whatever I do, I want to be really really, really, really smart." Then his hands became a plunger as he curled the entire purple whip into his mouth and laughed. The icy rain was increasing. It didn't matter. In fact, even through the wet skin of his cheeks, those eyes still sparkled like sunshine.

"You don't look too smart right now!" I teased. "That's gonna stain your teeth and lips and everything."

"Oh yeah? Watch *this*!" He grabbed for more licorice and looked up at the hillside. The other boys were running for the boat.

"Quick! We have to eat it all." I took the rest. We stuffed the entire package into our mouths as fast as we could and laughed hard.

Agent "Scooter" at your service, sir

By nightfall, the cold, fresh air and full day of freedom had worn us out. After my brothers fell asleep, I snuck back into Kyle's sleeping bag. His body heat felt cozy, like a fireplace. He giggled quietly and made a comment that at least the trees wouldn't get him again. He quietly offered another heartfelt thanks for rescuing him from the mess of vines that had been eating him up the night before. Somehow, I wondered if I wasn't the only boy who felt like an outsider in this family. Kyle made a lot of people feel appreciated, but his affection for me was unmatched by any other I'd witnessed. We weren't brothers, but we were twins, connected at the soul.

"Just doing my job, as always." I raked my fingers through his hair. "You're my favorite, you little shit. I like you more than my brothers."

"Do you love them?" he quietly asked. "I mean…'cuz they're your *brothers*."

"Yeah, I love them. I guess. But we're from different planets. They don't make me laugh like you do."

"I love you more than *my* brother too. You're a good protector. You *really did* save me from the trees."

"Agent Scooter McBride at your service, sir." I teased with pride. "Always have been. Always will be."

"We're a good team." He draped a tired arm over my waist and squeezed. "I promise to always be funny." He giggled sleepily.

I loved my siblings, but Kyle was different. He was more than a relative. He was my best friend and the only person alive that I truly trusted with all my heart. That was a distinction that would one day become intensely significant.

On this night, no nightmare trees were going to choke him or climb up his butt. And as I casually vowed to protect him for life and he jokingly promised to keep me laughing, neither of us had the tiniest grasp of the immense price our bond would one day cost both families.

10

Andreo's Betrayal

Scooter's protective nature couldn't do anything about my tension. It was too big for the both of us. The tree dream began during a time of secret stress for several island boys. I wasn't the only ten-year-old wrestling with demons then. Jack's disappearance had a mysterious twist; he became so deeply withdrawn before vanishing altogether that not everyone remembered the last time they'd seen him. It's like he faded away over time. He went invisible before he vanished completely. He'd become something none of us boys would talk about, but for some nervous reason, behind my closed lips, I couldn't forget him.

Many of the island boys were under private stress, and stressful times take tolls on friendships, often spawning frustration and betrayal between peers. The closer the friend, the more that betrayal hurts. But it seems like, in some fallout friendships, both sides of the alliance feel victimized. Without either side understanding why, both go into their futures resenting the other.

I feel it important to address my story's complexity. Complexity that itself became the villain I one day became unable to bear. As I've eluded to already, something so important that it deserves repeating is that adults with Complex-PTSD often have a final meltdown over something trivial. That last straw is the trigger, not the cause. But the victim—and the witnesses—overlook the back-breaking weight being carried daily below the surface until the final meltdown. The assumption then is that the person couldn't handle that last small ordeal, but the reality is that the person has been bearing a hundred small loads for so long that his proverbial back finally gives out from sheer exhaustion. He surrenders.

So, I have one more complicated friend to introduce to you in this story, and like Scooter, my Catholic school friend, Andreo, held my attention like a twin. As long as we were together we were invincible. Kids who bullied one of us were stood up to by both. We were strong together. We'd been best friends for about three years on the day that he changed his alliance and became the bully who hurt me the most. It would be years before I'd understand what had happened that day in 1971. I've often thanked God that I still had Scooter's long-distance friendship to get me through what happened locally when Andreo's "undying" friendship crashed and burned.

By Kyle Rickett

Sunday, March 7, 1971

Spring break had ended and Scooter had left. By lunch time, I missed him pretty bad, but Fran and her two small daughters had stopped over, and I used their visit as a distraction. Mom made tuna sandwiches and heated up some canned soup for all of us. I always loved kids, especially my nieces, so I had volunteered to feed the baby. I was having fun spooning food from a jar into one-year-old BJ's messy face, while I ate my own soup with the other hand and listened to five-year-old Jayne try to tell me a story about kindergarten. Unfortunately, she could be slightly difficult for me to understand and I was having trouble following her.

"Why aren't you paying more attention to Jayne?" Fran asked from the other side of the table. "She's talking directly to you."

I thought Fran was kidding, I looked directly at Jayne and said, "I'm listening. I just don't always understand everything you say. But I still get most of it. Kindergarten is fun. Right?"

"Oh, come on, Kyle; everyone else understands her."

"Fran," Mom jumped in, while Dad ignored the entire conversation, "she *is* a little hard to hear on the first try."

"Oh, she is *not*! If Kyle can understand that stupid boy he's befriending across the street, he could show the same respect to his own beautiful little niece."

"Connor's not stupid," I quietly defended as if she just didn't realize that about him. "He's shy; that's all. He's really smart. And he's nice."

"Whatever you need to tell yourself." Fran sighed heavily and dramatically. "It's just a good thing we all love you, Kyle, because you really aren't the best at making friends."

I couldn't absorb what I was hearing. Where had this attack come from? She'd always been critical of everyone except her own daughters, but this unprovoked attack felt more serious than usual. Was she right about me being too dumb to pick good friends? I looked over at Dad, who was focused on his soup, ignoring us as if sibling rivalry were just noise to him. Mom locked her gaze with mine and rolled her eyes like she was trying to convey a message to me that Fran wasn't worth engaging with. At least that's how I interpreted the eye roll.

"Just eat your soup, honey." Then Mom looked over at Fran and distracted her with a new topic. "So how is work?"

I don't know if that was the day when Fran became mean, or if ten was just the age when a guy like me could finally see that type of a mean streak in an adult. Maybe this was the first time Mom wasn't able to shield me from it. But I still remember to this day how defeated I felt by my sister's attack. It seemed so out of the blue. Ever since that moment, I began to see the erratic moods she could conjure up. Unfortunately, I also began to see that she always seemed to get away with them. Sometimes, her upward and downward mood swings were tied to events, but other times, as in this case, they never made sense. Nevertheless, with or without a reason, they always hurt. Really bad. Why did she call my friend stupid? Why did she tell me I wasn't being respectful to the daughter I was trying my best to understand? Why did Mom just change the subject? Mom saved me from more attack, and for that I felt supported, but I wished she would have gone to the next step and defended my friendship with Connor. Did she agree with Fran that I was too dumb to pick smart friends? Defending my friendship really would have meant a lot to me at that moment. It would have left no question in my offended mind as to whom she believed, Fran or me.

I didn't say much more. I let my soup sit. I stopped enjoying dinner. I focused intently on completing my commitment to feed little BJ, and I stopped looking at anyone around that table. When BJ acted like she wouldn't eat any more from the jar, I made up an excuse that I had to go to the bathroom. I went upstairs and stayed in the bathroom for as long as I could, imagining myself storming out of the house and never coming back. By the time I finally came downstairs, Fran was packing up to go home. Nothing more was said between Fran and me; it was as if I were now invisible in the room.

Connor and Andreo

At about two o'clock, I knocked on Connor's door. It was impossible to get Fran's insult out of my head, so when he came out to ride bikes with me I intentionally focused on looking for proof he wasn't stupid. I found plenty. In fact, I knew he read a lot of books, and I never thought that stupid people did that. I was sure I was right about him. He was smart. Just shy. And I reminded myself that Fran didn't even know Connor. She only knew him by sight and by name. She'd never talked to him. What in the world would make her tell me he was stupid?

Connor and I would eventually become legendary best friends, but in 1971, he and his older brother Merrick were still the new kids on the block. I liked Connor more and more every day, but he was a public schooler and I already had a long-time best friend at St. Tiberius Catholic Academy, Andreo. So Connor was my home-life friend and Andreo, my school friend and my *official* best friend.

Later that evening, the family telephone became mine to call Andreo with. He didn't live nearby. In fact, he didn't live in an actual house at all. His dad, an artist, had restored an older wooden yacht, a fifty-foot Chris Craft Constellation, where Andreo and his parents lived inexpensively in the Torano Island Marina, some seventeen miles north, on the tip of the island. I was intimidated by his exotic life, but Andreo bragged about it on some days, while on others, he complained about being isolated, only making part-time friends that he jokingly reported "moved in and out with the tide." I guess I was his one stable friend. We kept our bond active outside of school by talking on the phone in the evenings.

I don't remember the first time I met Andreo. Somehow, one day I just sort of realized he was my best friend and that I was hooked on him—infatuated with his boisterous energy and larger-than-life expressions. He was eleven, and the oldest and second-tallest boy in class, while at only ten, I was the youngest, and the shortest. He bragged about himself enough that I assumed he was better than me in almost every way. I was his sidekick. His follower.

A love song promise

"Spring break made me think," Andreo casually announced on the phone.

"What about?"

"I think I'm in love."

"Huh?"

"Yeah," he clarified. "For real."

"For real?" I asked, lying on my back across two kitchen chairs with my knee gently bumping the table. "With who?"

"I'm not sure. But the long break made me lonely."

"What?" I stopped bumping the table. "You can be in love with someone, *and not know who?*"

"It's not that weird, Kyle. Love is an emotion. It has a mind of its own." His answer was not an answer, but more of an avoidance. Nonetheless I felt stupid for asking.

I was a particularly young ten-year-old. Naïve. Andreo had always been the smarter of us—*or so I'd been convinced*—so, once again, I trusted that he was right and I was wrong. He was more credible because he was more interesting than me on many levels. Again—*or so I'd been convinced*—.

By blood, Andreo was full-up, olive-skinned Spaniard, but he was Texas-born and spoke with a faint drawl that became more obvious with excitement or fear. He was a talented pianist, and even though he wasn't athletic, he still carried himself with pride and passion. He was one of the three boys in class who was already starting to "change." He flaunted a light dusting of black fur over his upper lip and had long, thick, perfectly straight, jet-black hair, which was unusual among short-haired Catholic schoolboys; he often proclaimed himself a non-conformist. Apparently, another lucky attribute of the great Andreo Castro was that his parents supported his beatnik hair against the school's criticism. He was larger, older, and more boisterous, so I tried to make myself understand his new emotional phenomenon as best I could.

"I've been having those dreams lately."

"What dreams?" I asked.

"You know…those kinds that Dr. Krieg talked about when he came to school last month to give us Sex Ed."

"Really?" I sat alert in one of the chairs, put a hand to the phone, then whispered, "You mean *wet* dreams?" I looked toward the door. I couldn't let Mom hear this.

"Yeah," he replied calmly. "I've had like three now."

"Were they about a girl in our school?"

"I think so, yeah."

"You *think* so?" I nervously shifted my eyes toward the door. "Does your mom know?"

"Duh! She does my laundry, so why wouldn't she know?"

How could he not be embarrassed? Panic struck. If this happened to him, it might happen to me next. Fran had many times made it clear that I was a boy who could not control myself. If one of those dreams were to happen to me, and Mom were to tell her what she found in my sheets, which she *would*, Fran would humiliate me to death, publicly! In fact, she'd probably claim I was too dangerous to be around her daughters after that. Gads! My family had me by the gonads back then. I was ashamed of my own mind and body. Andreo was lucky to be an only child with no sisters to have to defend himself against. Life would basically *end* for me if I were in his shoes. I'd have no choice but to kill myself.

"And then all day long my stomach is full of butterflies." Andreo continued to speak openly, almost boastfully about his new feelings. "I'm definitely in love. I even wrote a song."

"You *did*? You mean…" I put a hand back against the receiver and whispered, "a *love* song?"

"Uh-huh. I'm going to play it for someone this week."

"That fast?" Oh, my God. How could he be acting so boldly without being punished? I'd be scorned to utter humiliation if I'd showed up at school with a *love song*. If this was how puberty affected him, what was I going to be in for when I got *my* mustache?

"My dad always says, 'Life is short.' And so I figure if I'm feeling like this, then I need to do something with it."

Those words kicked at my heart. He was so much luckier than me. My dad would never say anything that supportive.

"But you don't know *who*?" My voice raised an octave.

"Well," after a long silence, he half-disclosed, "I think I know."

"Who?"

"But I can't say yet."

"Oh." I winced from confusion. Andreo was happy to divulge private nocturnal accidents—but asking *who* the song was for was *over the line*? I was routinely told that I was too young to understand what my siblings were going through, so I was used to believing it to be the case at school too. I guess Andreo was just older and wiser, and I was, again, too young and dumb to understand.

Changing the subject shifted the stress. I didn't need Mom walking in and overhearing us talk about things I had no knowledge of: girls, and love, and *sticky sheets*. I needed familiar ground.

"I can't wait to see you at school tomorrow, Andreo."

He paused for a second or two. "Same here, Kyle...same here."

I smiled at how sincere that sounded. We talked for another ten minutes or so, giving me the chance to lighten the mood and share the fun I'd had with Scooter, and count how many packages of purple licorice I'd scored. We didn't revisit the love-song conversation at all. I thought maybe if I simply rode the topic out for the next few weeks, and continued to follow the story in digestible pieces, it would eventually make sense. Meanwhile, as uncomfortable as the subject was, at least I enjoyed being trusted.

Distant behavior

The next day at school, endowed with my best friend's personal confession, I felt mature and important. Andreo, like Scooter, being older and taller, made up for my disappointment at being a late-life accident who couldn't relate to my adult siblings. Maybe I was attracted to older friends because I was always yearning for the attention of my older family.

Scooter gave me a sense of deep comfort, while Andreo kept things exciting and edgy. I often fantasized that one day I'd impress him the way his artistic and bold stature had always impressed me.

Monday was the first day Andreo and I had seen each other in a week. I was shocked to see that his face bore three long, deep scratches along his left cheekbone that he'd neglected to mention on the phone. He didn't hide them, but he also didn't explain them, and I didn't ask. He didn't talk about the phone call or the song. In fact, he barely talked at all about anything. He was distracted, maybe even depressed. We often pushed up against each other or tugged one another around by an arm. But on this day, Andreo clung physically closer than usual, but he was also oddly quiet and emotionally distant.

Then, later that night, I was disappointed when his mom answered the phone, instead of him.

"Andreo ain't here, honey-bunch. He's outside, playin', um, baseball. Er...sump'n." I'd always liked her and her Southern drawl, which, since she'd lived most of her life in the South, was more pronounced than Andreo's. I thought she was funny too. A full-blooded Spaniard with a Texas drawl—you can't get odder than that.

I shrugged it off and hung up, but it nagged at me later. Andreo didn't *play* ball. Things didn't add up. I wondered if it was the new dreams that made him act differently. Or maybe the scars.

That night, I had a disturbing nightmare, probably triggered by Andreo's change in our connection. I walked into the school in the morning to find the halls filled with snakes. One fell from the ceiling onto my neck. I jumped awake. "Huh!"

"Oh, good, it was a dream," I muttered, face in hands. Then I prayed, "Dear Lord, please don't let there be snakes at school tomorrow. Amen."

As I lay still, trying to fall back asleep, I contemplated the increasing tension I was feeling due to all the boys growing taller than me, my fear of the often-angry Sister Jeanette and my increasingly difficult time with staying focused in the classroom enough to achieve decent grades. Not long before this night, I'd even awoken in the classroom one afternoon during my last class, having absolutely no idea where I had been for over an hour. While I tried to pass that off as just a daydream, it was pretty frightening.

Adolescent (but oddly abusive, sex talk

The next morning, Tuesday, just after arriving to the church to get ready for morning Mass, Andreo and his carpool arrived also. I was already seated, and as always, I perked up and waved with a big grin as they followed the rules and filed into the pew, single file, in the order of arrival. Andreo was now only a few bodies away to my left. He nodded back, but only half-smiled, like he wasn't in a good mood. As Mass started, I felt like I had the energy to really get into it. Music was important to Andreo, so I wanted to cheer him up and impress him with my own skills. I added umph to my usual extra effort and added a higher volume to my singing with each hymn. After the final note of the final hymn, I caught Andreo staring at me. After Mass, we were herded to school, again in single file, where we were able to talk.

"Hey, you never made any faces at me today."

"So?" he responded.

"You were first in the communion line today. You usually turn around and make faces."

"Sorry," he droned flatly. "Your singin' put me in a bad mood. I have a lot on my mind. You're lucky your cousin spent the week with you, 'cause you had a way better vacation than I did."

"What happened to make it bad?" I spoke softly. Gravity had drained my cheerful ego down into my gut at his comment that my singing had put him in a bad mood.

"Oh, noth'n I guess." He casually slid a finger along one of the scars on his face. I don't think he realized he'd done it. "We sh'go sit down."

"Okay." I smiled politely and cleared my throat, still embarrassed that I'd caused him to be in a bad mood.

My eyes, which he was staring into, must have twinkled as I tried to make it up to him because something about me drove a small spark of smile on one corner of his mouth. But he turned and walked away briskly. I didn't take it personally. Andreo had been moody a lot ever since his growth spurt had begun.

At first recess, we snuck off as usual into the taller grass on the outskirts of the playground, out of sight and mind of the other kids. This was something Andreo had been doing with me since we'd met. Without my noticing, he was, in various ways, isolating me apart from the class. I now know that narcissists are known for this technique. At the time, I just thought we were such good friends that he was all I needed for a social life.

We were barely settled when Andreo, now in a new and unusually unruly mood, asked some intrusive questions.

"Why don't you like talking about sex?"

"What do you mean?" My eyes widened.

"On the phone the other day, you let me tell you all about my feelings, but you wouldn't tell me anything about yourself. You just talked about licorice."

"Well…I don't really *have* any of those…feelings," I lied. I had been inexplicably drawn to the lovely face of a new girl in class, Marlene, but I wasn't ready to disclose that to *anyone*. In fact, she rode the church van with Andreo, so I was a little afraid that hers was the face he'd been kissing in his sleep. I didn't want to start tension over her.

"It's like you think people don't really do it." He sounded almost taunting when he blurted out, "I bet you can't even say the word 'sex.'"

"I don't want to." My heart pumped with adrenaline.

"Sex, sex, sex, *sex*!"

"Stop it! We're not allowed to talk about it."

"I can talk about anything I want to."

"I don't want to talk about it."

"You know your parents do it, don't you?" He blatantly ignored my resistance.

"They do not!"

"I can hear my folks doin' it in the boat sometimes."

"That's gross!"

"You're so naïve." He laughed with an unusually angry overtone.

"What does naïve mean?" Acid from my throat coated my tongue— the familiar taste of frustration.

"It means I'm older than you, and I understand things you don't. Trust me; your parents *do it*."

I closed down, feeling small and insulted, while he intently monitored the various expressions he'd been able to invoke in me.

"You don't have any hair in your pants yet, do you?" he chuckled, watching my eyes widen again. I'd never been dragged into any conversation like this before. Who was this guy becoming?

"We should go play tetherball. There's a pole open." I wanted him to stop. I got up to look over the tall grass at the playground. But before stumbling off, I was pulled back down. I let him do it because he was my friend.

"You don't have to be so afraid to talk about stuff like this. It's all natural and normal. You should just open up."

"Why?" I stared, waiting for a scolding to end. "I'm not *allowed* to talk about it."

"Says who?"

"I don't know. I'm just not allowed."

"I heard Dr. Krieg is going to show movies in sixth grade." He kept a lock on my eyes. "A kid on the bus told me how it works. He's going to come to the school and spend an hour with the boys only, like he did this year…but next year, he's going to show us movies about showering, and he's going tell us *how* intercourse works."

"Stop it."

"Why are you so scared of sex?"

"I don't know. I really don't like talking about it…and I already know how to shower. I don't need to see a stupid movie about it, and I don't want Dr. Krieg to show me *any movies—EVER!*" A knot was growing in my throat. Who were the movies *of?* Blood drained from my face. A sharp pain cut into one wrist.

"You should come home with me from school some night. I know where my dad hides his dirty magazines."

I bit at my lip without an answer for him.

"I'll find out from my mom what day you can come home with me next week."

"Okay," I obediently answered. I wasn't sure I wanted to, but the idea of viewing a few pictures sounded kind of interesting—as long as we didn't have to *talk* about them.

"Okay." Andreo's mood changed again. He relaxed, shook his head like he'd been joking, and let me off the hook. "Let's go play tetherball."

We didn't talk again during the two hours between first recess and lunch, but I kept feeling that I was being watched. Sure enough, each time I'd look over, I'd catch him staring. Each time, he'd quickly look away.

He was quiet at the lunch table but smiled at everything I said. I ate faster than he did, so I was excused first.

Ten minutes later, when he didn't materialize on the playground, I snuck into the building and found him in the sixth grade classroom plunking notes on the piano with Tanya, a sixth grader he'd befriended, who was now sitting beside the piano on a box of textbooks. My first thought was that he was warming up to play his song for her.

Indecent liberties

"Kyle!" He looked startled when he saw me.

"Should I leave?"

"No!" He blurted out and held up a hand. "Don't go. I'm glad you found me."

"Were you lost?" I giggled.

"I have something important to tell you."

"Why's Tanya here?" It seemed odd. Genders and kids from other grades weren't supposed to mix. But I guess Andreo *was* a non-conformist.

"I know I made you squirm earlier. But I didn't expect you to be so stubborn. I still have something to tell you." He paused but kept his eyes locked onto mine. "Tanya's here to support me."

"Support you?"

"It's important. I told you I didn't have as good a week as you did. In fact, it was horrible, and it changed me."

"It changed you?"

"You're my best friend, so…I need to tell you about it."

"Okay." I sat on the piano bench with him and gently pressed on a few black keys. The best-friend referral made me smile.

"It all started on Tuesday last week; I was swimmin' at the Community Club." He was nervous. His Texan accent started to leak out. "I was all alone, 'til an older kid came into the pool with me, and started makin' friends real fast."

"That's good. Right?"

"No. He was makin' friends *too* fast."

"Who was he?"

"I didn't know him. He don't go to our school." He looked hard over at Tanya, who nodded. He continued, "I got kinda' suspicious 'n'tried to get out, but he grabbed me from behind and pulled me under. I nearly drowned. That's how I got these scratches."

"He tried to *drown* you?"

"Yup."

"For *real*?"

Andreo shrugged and nodded.

"How'd you get away?" I asked.

"He let me go at the last second. I swam for the ladder. But he followed me and grabbed m'wrist and wouldn't let go."

"Really? What did he want?"

"Well…don't never tell my parents, okay?" Andreo's face hovered close. His eyes intently scanned every minute expression. "He held me hard against the ladder…n'pulled off m'swimsuit."

My blood froze. A flash of Jack's face came and went.

"Kyle, this is important. Yer ma' best friend. I need yer' support."

My mind went blank. I shook my head like I'd been given a dose of electric current. A vision of the tree dream flashed through my mind. A sharp pain shot through my rectum and one wrist. I don't remember how I responded beyond that.

Memory voids and not paying attention

The rest of the school day got lost into my wandering mind. The whole experience became another in a long string of blank voids in memory. My next conscious moment came twenty minutes later when, apparently, Sister Jeanette had singled me out. My response, "I'm sorry…what was the question?" made the twenty-three other fifth-graders laugh.

That night, the phone call happened on schedule, but it felt cold. I had already pushed Andreo's attempted story out of recall, and I had no memory of further conversations from the rest of the day.

"So, when are you going to play that song for someone?"

"What song?" he asked coldly.

"You wrote a love song."

"No, I didn't. Only an idiot would think I'd write a love song."

"But you—"

"You misunderstood me!" he boldly accused. "As usual!"

If smart, talented Andreo told me I'd misunderstood, then it must have been true. But how could I have possibly slipped up on something so important?

A slap in the face

The next morning, once again first in the classroom, I met up with him.

"Andreo! Look what I can do." I was planning a funny face.

"Get away from me, *you homo!*"

"No way, partner!" I bantered back, hovering two pencils out from my belt, pretending to be a character from a cheesy Western movie about to perform a quick-draw.

"I said, *get the hell away from me!*"

My eyes opened wide. Then from beyond my peripheral vision, Andreo's open hand flew in like a locomotive and slapped me hard enough to jolt the pencils from my grip and onto the floor.

I recovered my stance and tried to return the slap, but Andreo had early-puberty-advantage and was taller, heavier, and exponentially stronger. He was also prepared and, evidently, quite pissed. He grabbed my scrawny wrist mid-swing, stopping the slap before it could happen, and twisted.

"Ow! Ow! Ow!"

"Pussy!" he yelled back.

"Why are you doing this?"

"Because you're a homo!"

By end of the day, Andreo had gotten three other boys to start calling me "Homo" instead of my name. It was a word I'd not heard, and I had no idea what it meant. I went home in a fog. I didn't make my phone call that night. I didn't know how long he'd be mad.

It would be a few weeks before I'd learn two things: Without offering explanation, the Torano Island Community Pool instituted a new policy forbidding minors from swimming in the absence of a lifeguard, and my mysterious name-change at school had become permanent. After Andreo had somehow managed systematically to isolate me from the other students over the course of three years, cutting me out completely was the easiest thing in the world for him to do now. The nickname stuck, and with the whole class—but I would never be told *why*.

I went to bed that night and had the tree dream again, but this time, with a sharp knife's edge pain in my stomach. The dream and the pain were two things for me to learn to manage for many more years.

11

Connor's Friendship

Some people call what Andreo was doing to me, "Mobbing" or "Mob Bullying." It's the act of singling out one person from a group and using tricks, such as name-calling, framing, or telling rumors and lies about that individual to get the rest of the group to join into the bullying. It isolates the victim, and it gives great power to the person who initiated the mob, making the odds "everybody against one." The mob may be made up of people who don't realize they're in one. They're just blindly following the rumors and responding with their friends.

Lucky for me, sometimes problems have ways of balancing themselves out. As Andreo left my life, and started a mob at school, a new kid, Connor Mason, entered at home.

By Connor Mason

It was scary moving away from my friends, but my mother couldn't take any more Michigan winters. Dad found a job building 747s in Everett, Washington, and so we relocated to a place near there called Torano Island. I was ten. My brother, Merrick, was more upset, because he was a high school senior and wanted to graduate with his friends. But Merrick was an amazing brother who put his misery aside and became my best friend. The move brought us closer. I hoped our brotherhood friendship would last forever.

I met Kyle while the movers unloaded our stuff. At first, I thought he was funny-looking, small with nearly pure white hair. I made teasing elf jokes about him to Merrick, but I quickly regretted them when Kyle snuck me away, loaned me a bike, and took me to Bottle Beach to show me his best fishing spot. By the end of the first day, I'd already started counting my lucky stars that we'd moved across the street. Right from the start, I thought of him as one of the coolest kids I'd ever met.

I was normally a wallflower, who disappeared into learning about the world through books. Kyle drew me out of that. Throughout my school years, that happy, kindhearted kid changed my adolescent life in so many positive ways that I ultimately grew to be a better adult. For that, I'll always be grateful.

12

Shifting Alliances

I didn't see myself like Connor saw me. Between Andreo's unexplained betrayal, my confusing isolation at school, and my family's constant correcting of my thoughts and mistakes, I honestly believed I needed to prove myself worthy every day. In order to be lovable, I had to behave perfectly. Any mistake could bring the wrath of the world's hatred down upon me. I liked Connor, but I didn't notice his attention to me was as intense as it was. I was lucky to have his friendship, but to me, friendship was a moment-by-moment balancing act. It could be lost much more quickly than gained. I focused mostly on keeping my problems to myself so he wouldn't realize I wasn't worth his time.

By Kyle Rickett

By Sunday night, May 30, 1971, two months had passed since Andreo's slap had isolated me out as a freak. By now, every single person in my school called me "Homo," and I still didn't know what it meant. Sundays were the end of my peaceful weekends and were the most difficult nights for sleep. As soon as I'd lose consciousness, school and all its cruelty was to be the next waking event each Monday. Sunday nights, for me, were weekly visits to the purgatory before the hell.

I tossed and turned. In order to avoid thinking about school, I focused on the new kid across the street, Connor, who was turning out to be pretty cool. Not at all stupid like Fran seemed to think. I had loaned him Fran's old bike on the day he moved in so we could ride around while the movers unpacked his. In March, we'd ridden our bikes to the dime store on the other side of the island bridge, and we had each purchased a copy of issue number one in a new comic book series called Disaster Island, featuring the tough skinned, mystery-busting Inspector Carlen. We'd begun a friendship around bikes and the ritual of riding to the dime store on the first of each month so we could collect every issue together, then read it aloud in turns in his bedroom. Since the next day was Monday, the first of June, we had plans to take off after school to get issue number four. But first I had to find a way to fall asleep, survive my nightmares, and then endure my sentence at school. Andreo's mysterious slap across my face still hurt, emotionally that is. It still made absolutely no sense to me. I was nervous about Monday, so I did as I'd always been taught by family and church; I prayed for forgiveness and rescue.

"Dear God, everyone hates me. I'm so, so, so sorry for doing whatever it was I did to Andreo. Please forgive me for it and protect me at school tomorrow. I promise, I didn't mean to hurt anyone."

Earlier that day, I'd asked Mom to let me go to public school the following year with Connor, but she laughed like I'd asked her to let me vacation on the moon. She told me that it was only four more years, and that whatever was making me unhappy, I should just ignore because it would only be worse in a public school.

Just four more years might as well have been eternity.

"Dear God." I tossed left to face the window and clock. Ten o'clock was approaching. The moon had lit the trees to a surreal glow. My lifetime of hypervigilance was coming into full swing, and even the smallest of problems began to feel life-threatening. The longer the night lingered, the bigger my small problems became. "Mom won't help me. The nuns won't either. Someone stole all my pencils out of my desk Friday, and I'm going to be in so much trouble when I don't have one tomorrow. I'm scared to ask Mom for a new one. Please, please, please send a pencil to me somehow. And send someone to help me be happy again, if it's not too much to ask."

I churned uneasily, wondering whether Sister Jeanette would drag me to the front of the room by an earlobe for not having a writing piece. The nuns did that a lot to us kids. Mom kept me in that school because it was "love-based," but to me, the nuns' version of love was difficult to understand. Their anger didn't always seem to need a valid reason, and trying to figure out what I'd done to turn my classmates into an angry mob was becoming an endless obsession.

As I fell asleep that night, I felt a flutter in my chest and saw the flash of what appeared to be a dove fly from my heart and into the sky.

13

Ronnie's Dove

Though my story of the bike accident and the visit to Dr. Krieg weren't going to take place for three more years, this flashback to 1971 is when Complex-PTSD rescued me from going insane by compartmentalizing my brain and sealing away the moments of unbearable stress. Those moments didn't go away; they hid behind doors. What would happen in 1974, on Krieg's table, is that the energy of my stress levels was going to match the energy of the 1971 stress that originally built the doors—which, unfortunately, was going to reopen those doors and flood my consciousness with the past as if three years had never happened.

Complex-PTSD is not the only force that can transcend time and distance. So can a child's prayers of desperation. In 1971, at precisely the same moment that I released my dove and a prayer for rescue, a woman I wouldn't meet for several years, Ronnie Taylor-Donovan, found herself in a bizarre dream about her younger brother, Tuck. If you believe in the mystical powers of prayer or intention, then you must believe that it knows no limits, including those of time, space, and distance. It turns out I was not alone in distress. Without knowing it, I was one of three people sharing a moment of total despair, and for some inexplicable reason, all three of us were simultaneously visited by an iconic white dove.

By Ronnie Taylor-Donovan

A beautiful, shimmering white dove landed on my Washington, DC kitchen windowsill between the two scented candles I'd been lighting each day, hoping so much to attract a miracle so desperately needed. It stood still for such a long moment. It comforted me, which was good because my aching heart needed comforting. I'd been a nervous wreck for days. It stared and tipped its cute little head from side-to-side until I had finally calmed myself down enough to smile. Just then, a strange thought came to me—like words.

He's important.

"I know that," I answered.

I'll take him now. The dove's eyes sparkled harmoniously with the words, and then his gaze darted past me toward my small living room, where a hospital bed had magically appeared. Tucker, who was seventeen years old at that time, stood next to it in his favorite Minnesota Twins jacket. My heart sank. His light brown, wavy hair, once again thick and long, flowed from beneath his favorite Twins baseball cap. He didn't look directly at me, but his normally self-assured, adorable smirk had tamed to a surreally tranquil smile. My little brother was beautiful again. As he passed by, I sighed at the stunning joy on his face. He walked to the window and met the dove. Both then quietly lifted and hovered.

We're strong together, said the dove. It flapped its wings in a beautiful rhythm and turned away.

"I'm okay now." Tuck smiled and turned with the dove. The two then flew westward into the afternoon sun. My sinking heart broke into a burning ache.

"Oh, Tuck!" I awoke. My eyes were filled with tears. "Please, don't go. Not now." I sobbed quietly as memories flashed of the day he was born, and how I used to make him laugh by blowing on his tummy. In only seconds, I relived his first steps, his first bike, our first family photo, and my first hug from him after he had survived a horrible car accident at seven. He couldn't endure all that just to die now, could he? This was so unfair! I spent the next hour trying to fall back asleep, hoping that the dove was only another tormenting dream, stemming from the sorrow of watching my special brother—and my family—suffer for so many months. But then the telephone cut through my prayers like an ugly chainsaw.

"Oh, God, *no!*"

"Honey?" Don groggily moaned. Michelle fussed in her crib next to our bed.

I scooped up the phone. "Mom?" I already knew it was her.

"Yes, honey, it's me."

"What's happening? Something's wrong; *I know it.*"

"All his alarms went off." Sobbing had put a thick layer of sadness in her voice. "His blood pressure dropped to nothing. We don't know what's happening. They rushed in and took him…. No one's told us anything for over an hour."

"Was he awake?"

"No." Her breath trembled. "He's been asleep since Sunday afternoon. He said goodbye, but I refused to say it back. I'm so sorry I did that now. Oh, my God, honey…I'm so scared!" A few more shaky breaths broke her sentence. Then she asked that awful question that no one had an answer for: "I don't get it. My mother had cancer for two years before she got to this point. He's only had it a few months. How did he get so sick so fast?"

"Mom, I'll catch a flight first thing in the morning." I was tearing up, but not crying yet. "There's one that lands in Minneapolis at noon. I'll be on it."

14

My Plea for Trust

The mind of a child is strong. It learns by watching and mimicking. I needed to learn how to process thoughts and intentions, so I watched how other people did it. In Catholic school, we were taught that God communicated through the use of doves. After seeing that dove fly out of my heart as I was about to doze off, an idea hit me.

By Kyle Rickett

I needed to pray one last time before fading off completely. Not believing God could hear me, I suddenly had the idea to attach a verbal message to that dove. I imagined myself whispering into its ear. If the Catholics are right and doves are messengers, then I hoped my imaginary dove would fly all the way to God and deliver my prayer personally.

"Please forgive me for being bad. I just want people to like me. Please, God. Please teach me how to be good so people will like me."

I didn't know what else to say. As I pretended to release the dove, I exhaled in defeat. It was a stupid prayer, but it was the best I could do.

"I just want to die. I'm sorry. I wish I was strong. But I'm not."

As it flew off, I shouted one last request. "Please make me strong."

15

The Place Without Shadows

The irrational fear of abandonment steals the peace from millions. So does the fear of success or failure, or the fear of losing their homes and ending up on the street. Fear certainly steals my peace. I've lived my every moment in constant dread that my secrets will one day betray me. I'm not so different from the countless others who live in daily fear of shame, but most people don't realize how silly their fears are, nor do most people remember the moment the fear became a part of them. I've become an enigma by the fact that I remember exactly when it all started for me. 1971. On that auspicious night on Torano Island, the seed of suicide was planted in my brain. I began a lifetime of considering death as a solution from pain. On that night, I also began a three-year-long prayer for strength through a dove. No more middle ground. Give me strength or give me death.

On that same night, in Washington, DC, Ronnie received a dove's message about strength. Our entanglement reached a third participant when her younger brother, Tucker James Taylor, "Tuck," died in St. Paul, Minnesota—but only for three minutes. He was faced with death, but was given a message instead. A message of strength—from a dove! Of course, it was coincidence, but looking back, Ronnie, Tuck, and I have no explanation for the fact that our entanglement around life and death began on the same night through a similar white dove—real or imagined.

That dove would periodically visit each of us for the next three years. It began on the night death called upon a boy (Tuck). It revisited in the summer of 1974 when death would call upon another boy (me) as I finally stepped off the train platform and gave up on the very prayer that started it all, making it seem that the future bond between the lot of us had been forged at a place we had all visited: the blurred edge of surrender between life and death.

By Tuck Taylor

I awoke feeling good. No pain. No weakness. I saw light up ahead and kept walking forward through the earthen tunnel. A few other people—strangers I didn't need to know—walked silently with me. We emerged from the passageway into the grassy field. I never looked around to see my fellow travelers, but I knew they were there.

Together, we entered into the bright green field of grass. I saw more people coming toward us from the fruit trees up ahead. As a photography buff, I searched for the light source, but there wasn't one. There were no shadows—anywhere. How strange. No place on earth is without shadows. But this place had none. Not even under the fruit trees, or shading the hills, valleys, or divots in the lawn. It was as if the grounds themselves *were* the light source.

Everything appeared to be perfect. Every blade of grass the same vibrant shade of chlorophyll-rich green, and each exactly the same height. But the lawn, as flawless as it was, showed no evidence of having been mowed by machine. I'd never seen anything so perfect.

A slow-moving, glistening blue river flowed gently to my right, dividing the field in half with grass and more fruit trees on the other side. The sky was a shimmering deep blue. I saw through it, all the way to eternity. Occasionally, it sparkled.

Coming toward us were people dressed formally, but from different places and times in history. A small cluster of women with parasols, in fluffy, floor-length summer dresses, looking as if they had stepped out of a Monet painting, met up with a man walking to my right. A gentleman in a top hat came to meet a woman on my left.

They greeted my fellow travelers as family and longtime friends. Without hearing a voice, I detected the words, *There's no one coming for you this time*. But then, as if on cue, a pure white dove flew gracefully from the west side of the river, over me, and toward the tunnel entrance. As it passed overhead, its eyes twinkled and a warm surge of life filled my heart.

Show me trust, it transmitted to me. Then added, *and I'll make you strong*. Finally, I sensed the unspoken words, *now go back*.

I returned to the tunnel.

PART 3

Lost Trust:

MY WITHDRAWAL FROM THE REAL WORLD

Return to 1974

Back to 1974

In the Clinic with Kyle

First Saturday of Summer Break, June 22, 1974

16

Swirling Memories

Memories are a tad unpredictable. They come back to us sometimes uninvited. They can seem so real we have to shake our heads to try to clear them away. They knock us off balance.

By Kyle Rickett

At that moment, I didn't know what year I was in. Still passed out on Krieg's table, I could almost hear myself moaning out loud. I wanted to scream again at my mom, "Connor's my best friend," but her voice, calling him a mere *neighbor's kid*, seemed louder than mine.

Scooter, whom I trusted, snuck into my sleeping bag to rescue my sense of being alone, but just as he started to protect me, he turned into Andreo and betrayed my trust by calling me a homo

Somehow, I gained the clarity to wonder if I was awake or asleep, and I tried with all my might to force open my eyes to see where I was.

All these faces of friends and enemies, and all these years of prayers and defeat, were tumbling about in my brain in a disorganized scatter. I felt sadness, confusion, fear.

Even today, sleep, for me, can often be like this.

17

The Confession

Tuck and I were apparently going down similar paths. Our states of mind were entering the same types of confusion. Dreams were pestering us both. Friendships were going into limbo. And an unresolved past was catching up to both of us.

By Tuck Taylor

As the day progressed, I did end up going to the beach with Trenton and Mark. It made more sense to hang with friends than to go back to sleep since it was Saturday, my night off from the crisis clinic. I knew I still had to get up for work at five to make Sunday morning pancakes, but if I could get home by midnight, I'd be fine. At first, I didn't want to go, but Trenton reminded me that I was becoming anti-social by lying around the apartment. So, I forced myself to get out and meet the guys. I know they were officially Trenton's friends, but they were the only social life I had outside of work.

Loneliness is a powerful force in one's mind. I don't know if loneliness was to blame, or if this would have happened eventually, but Mark took me aside and started a conversation I'd have never allowed anyone to have with me before then.

"How come you don't date?" He sat next to me on the beach, both of us in shorts and flip-flops, knees up, fingers in the sand. This was pretty normal for he and I to break away like this. Mark and I were both part of Trenton's inner circle, but, like me, Mark wasn't a partier like the rest of Trenton's friends. His hobbies included cooking and writing poetry late at night. He tagged along and enjoyed himself, but often retreated a bit. He liked being with his friends. But he just wasn't as loose and playful as the rest of them. Somehow, he, like me, seemed to be a little bit alone, even when with friends.

"I haven't found anyone."

"Bullshit." He gently disagreed. In some ways, Mark was too gentle and cute to swear. It made me smile a bit whenever he did. "Trenton says you're a psychology major."

"So?"

"So, I sure hope you know yourself better than that."

"Is your degree in psychology too?" I asked smirking.

"Business."

"So…mind your own *business* then." I smiled.

"I know, I know." Mark chuckled softly. "But it doesn't take a shrink to see a certain…chronic loneliness…in your face."

"I've had girlfriends. They're hard work."

"Had. You've *had* girlfriends."

"Come on; I have friends all over the place. I'm here now, aren't I?" I waved my hands at the seven guys who had met us there and were now tossing Frisbees on the water's edge. "Lonely. Humph."

"You have *Trenton's* friends," he said, but then quickly, almost nervously, back-pedaled. "I mean, don't get me wrong…we're your friends…but you know what I mean. We're Trenton's friends, and he's why you know us at all."

"You mean I don't have any straight friends."

"That's not what meant. I just...you aren't like those guys, and they're the only people you hang out with." Poor Mark was trying to find a way to make his point without sounding clumsy.

"I'm hanging out with you right now."

"I guess." He shrugged. "But you and I aren't really in that much alike either."

"I guess when I left St. Paul, I just...." Now it was clumsy for me too. "Trenton's always been there for me. He's a great friend. Right now, I guess I'm good."

"Trenton told me about Shannon." He tossed a handful of sand toward our feet. "Says you haven't been the same since she moved away."

I stopped scooping so I could stare at him. He was less than a foot from me, both of us facing the ocean. Why the hell did he have to bring up Shannon? I hadn't thought about her in almost an hour.

"Childhood sweethearts, I'm told."

"Trenton sure likes talking about me to his friends, eh?" My sarcasm began bubbling up.

"Don't blame him." He stared back at me. Then he ran his eyes down and back up my torso. "I pester him about you. He indulges me."

I chuckled again, like when he swore.

"Did I say something funny?"

"No, no, no. It's just that...you are lot more 'open' than I thought you were."

He shrugged. "I don't keep secrets from friends."

"Obviously." I politely smirked. "So, you're my fan?"

"Hell, I'm your fan club president."

"Gads. You are just not afraid to say that to a guy, are you?"

"I'm a poet. Saying sensitive things is what I do. Besides, I'm not afraid of you beating me up for it. And trust me, I'm not this open with everyone. You're just...super easy to talk to."

I broke eye contact to stare back at the ocean and begin scooping sand again. "What else has he told you?"

"Well, let's see." He relaxed and resumed his own fidgeting in the sand. "You've been friends since you were four. Shannon moved to your street when you were five. Everyone knew you guys were going to get married someday. You used to be 'Mister Popular' with friends everywhere you went. You're a hell of an athlete, and you're 'the greatest photographer' he's ever met."

"I'm the *only* photographer he knows…is that all he's said?"

"Pretty much. There's a big block of time that he's left to mystery."

"Mystery?" I laughed. "There might be more to me than that, but not much of it is worth writing a biography over."

"All his stories about you stop and then skip ahead. It's like you two were kids, you fished a lot, then you were here. He never talks about your high school years. He just says that when Shannon left, some beautiful part of you left with her."

"He really said that? A beautiful part of me?"

"Don't let his sarcasm fool you. Trenton thinks the world of you."

"Can we change the subject?" A wave of emotion exploded from my chest up through my face.

"Sure. Yeah… It's just… I mean…."

"What?"

"It's just strange, that's all. No one will talk about a whole section of your life. It's like you're in the witness protection program or something."

I laughed once. "Trust me, I'm not that interesting. I just…don't like talking about Shannon."

"Why not?"

"Stick to your business degree. Shannon's gone. Nothing's going to bring her back. I just want to forget about it is all."

"But Tuck…is forgetting her working?"

"I wish."

"If you're going to be a psychologist, don't you think it might work better to open up and…you know…explore?"

"Explore? The way you do? Mr. Poet?"

"Yeah. Explore your heart. Your soul. It works good for me. If you feel something for someone, you should admit it to yourself. Those missing years in high school—you should face them." He shrugged "I mean, isn't that the whole idea behind the science of psychology?"

I pushed my feet forward, dropping the backs of my knees into the warm sand.

"Someone will eventually replace her. You know that, right?"

I let my eyes follow a pair of girls walking past us. One of them smiled and I nodded politely.

"See? That just proved you can get girls. There's someone out there for you."

"I'm just…." I sighed. "Honestly, I meant it when I said girlfriends are hard work. I really don't *want* one right now."

"You're a little young to be celibate, don't you think?"

"Sex isn't everything, Mark."

"Oh. I might only be a freshman business major…but even us bismos know that's not true."

I laughed.

"Sex might not be everything to you, but it's up there on *my* personal list of the top one or two things to live for."

"Maybe…" I aggressively threw a handful of sand onto my legs, "you've been having better experiences than mine. Sex is hot and exciting, but sometimes I think it's easier done alone."

"Ha!" Mark's laughter sounded nervous.

"You're picturing me in the shower right now, aren't you?" I slapped his shoulder. "With my bar of soap?"

"All I can say is if I had your body, I'd have a hard time keeping my hands off myself." Through his nervous laughing, he blushed. "People *want* to touch you. You should let them."

"I never had a girlfriend *want* to touch me," I complained.

"Bullshit again," he said, but this time louder.

"It's true."

"I've seen plenty of girls ogling you. Like that one that just walked by."

"They ogle. But they don't *want* me."

"Bull-*shit*, Tuck. You're a catch and I'm telling you I see girls…and guys…licking their lips when you're not looking."

"Gross, Mark."

"It's true. They lick their lips." He smirked. As gentle as he was, he seemed to like talking openly about sex. "They *want* you, man."

"What girls *want*…is to be touched *by* men…but…" Anger swelled from my gut, "I get the sense that they touch me back because they know they need to keep me interested."

"Interested?"

"Ya, So I'll open pickle jars and buy them a house and stuff like that."

"I have to trust you on that. I'll never know what girls want. They *say* they like sex as much as men do."

I looked at him.

"Never been with one, though. And not really planning to start."

"Sure, they like sex, but I'll say it again; they seem to like *being touched* more than they like touching."

He stared at me, deep in thought.

"Sometimes I feel like I'm a necessary evil. Something they think is disgusting but needed," I mumbled. "They teach themselves how to touch me so I don't leave them."

"Shit, man. Shannon really did a number on you." He threw one last handful of sand toward the water and finished our talk. "Now I see why you look so lonely all the time."

18

The Devil Attacks

Posttraumatic Stress Disorder (PTSD) *is understood like this: a trauma happens, for example, a car accident, a plane crash, house fire, or battlefield explosion, and then the sufferer spends months, years or a lifetime suffering with seemingly uncontrolled physical, mental, and emotional reactions, or side effects, from its triggers. Example, hearing screeching tires triggers panic in a person who was once nearly killed in a life-threatening car accident.*

Complex-PTSD *is understood differently. A person might spend months, years, or a lifetime suffering with seemingly uncontrolled physical, mental, and emotional reactions, or side effects, but doesn't remember having been in a car accident, a plane crash, house fire, or battlefield explosion. That person may believe he or she was born broken, or is simply too emotionally weak to handle stress. Complex-PTSD happens, not after a crash, but after serious long-term, life-threatening abuse, such as being a prisoner of war, years of child or spousal abuse, or nearly dying from long-term* *disease. The cause wasn't recognized as "a trauma," and is too complicated to put a finger on, so the triggers are also complicated and not recognized, meaning the reactions are complicated and seemingly without a cause. The sufferer may never receive a proper diagnosis, and subsequently may never be given the correct treatment.*

Soldiers often receive treatment, as well as civilian accident victims, and even women who are aware of childhood sexual abuse. But for non-military men, the diagnosis is much more difficult to acquire. People don't readily recognize that a man who never went to war, but who suffers with emotional triggers, still may have Complex-PTSD. If a man doesn't know he has PTSD, his suffering can be difficult to explain to himself, and if he can't explain it to himself, how can he explain it to others?

It might actually be easier for a mother to explain the feelings of childbirth to a man than it would be for a non-military man to explain the feelings of Complex-PTSD to anyone at all.

But with this chapter, I'll try.

For me, a dissociative posttraumatic episode feels like a nightmare that "may or may not be happening for real." In my opinion, PTSD and Complex-PTSD are traumatic damage, not mental illness, but during an episode, I might as well be medically insane. Nothing is real, and everything is real at the same time. Past and present blur into a single moment as memories become lifelike. Am I awake or asleep? Are the memories recreations of actual events, or did I dream them out of imagination? Am I dreaming now? Back to that first violent PTSD episode on June 22, 1974, Dr. Krieg recreated the humiliating terror he'd started years earlier at Voyager Scouts and tipped the first summer domino that would ultimately knock over the rest.

Until this bike accident disrupted my crazy sense of daily stress, what Krieg used to do with me in his clinic was private. If he'd have left it that way, I'd have limped along for years, maybe for my entire life, comfortably uncomfortable, not remembering the shadow-like shame-filled dreams that I'd never have to deal with in the waking day. Or worse, maybe I'd have done like two of the other voyager scouts did. They slowly sank into drug addiction and died of overdoses before they were twenty.

But like a blessing in disguise, that day, Dr. Krieg sent me into a Complex-PTSD dream, which ultimately woke me out of a long, slow descent I didn't even realize I was in. He "shook my world" and changed its course for the better.

By Kyle Rickett

I woke up. Summer vacation smelled like disinfectant. I was still in Krieg's evil clinic. Still on my back staring at chrome lights. Still wondering whether this was an alien abduction or a nightmarish Christmas party. Still naked.

At least the trees had stopped growing inside me. My arms were now comfortably clasped together on my bare chest. I hoped it was all over with and everyone was going to leave me alone now. I looked around. The nausea was almost unbearable, and a familiar bitter taste—fear— seeped up from the back of my throat. In case of a vomit attack, I turned my head to the side, but I wasn't sure exactly which room of the clinic I was in: one or two. The slow process of reorienting myself placed me into 1974, but there were no women. Only Dr. Krieg hovered over me on that stool to my right.

"Good morning, champ."

"Where am I?" I mumbled almost incoherently.

"Your stitches are in…and you're welcome." Krieg reached behind himself to put what he was holding down on the countertop. "I saved you." He snapped off his gloves and tossed them onto the counter for Kathy to throw away later. "And that was quite a show you put on back there. You're a little more…*responsive*…when you're not on your pills."

Responsive? What did that mean? I remembered hearing, "*It's show time*" and seeing flashbulbs. Had I actually done it? Had I put on a show?

"Where's my mom?" I tasted more vomit in the back of my throat. My body felt like someone had pumped it full of cold water. Krieg stared into my eyes with a smirk. Intimidation transmitted from his eyes to mine, scaring the living shit out of me and sending me into a fearful trance. The room was warm, but shivers were rising from deep inside my chest, then quickly spreading to my arms and legs. I shook like I was soaking in ice.

"Well, you kept asking her to leave." He gently raked a hand through my hair, which made the nap of my neck stand up.

"Can she come back now? Please?"

"Oh, I don't think so. You don't want her to see the rest of this show, now do you?"

"I don't?" What the hell did *that* mean? Through the growing fear, I politely kept my hands on my chest, fingers interlaced to keep the arms from falling to my sides. Krieg's big hand stopped its gentle caressing of my hair and grabbed my two small hands tightly, forcing out another "Ow, ow!"

"You're a fine-looking lad, Kyle." Krieg closed his hand around my two like he was squeezing water out of a sponge on the hood of his Corvette. "Thaaaat's right." He craned them up together and moved them over my frightened cheeks. He then put all three of our hands, mine still interlocked, over my mouth and pressed down hard. "As I remember, you always liked this," he said in a quiet, but gravely strong voice. "But you're a bit of a screamer. That'll only be worse when you're not medicated."

I stopped breathing. *Oh, dear God—no.* My lungs held in as much oxygen as they could. I wanted to die before he did anything else.

"Don't forget to breathe now." Krieg's eyes pointed toward the closed door. "We all saw what happens to boys who don't breathe, and it sure would be easy to explain an accident while you're this hurt."

Jack's face flashed. Terror soured my heart and lungs and mouth.

Krieg looked back into my eyes, his face only a few inches away, and in that same strong, cracked voice, he admitted, "I've been hoping it would grow in white like this. A perfect little elf." A finger gently raked through my pubic hair. "We don't want your mother to hear any of this, now do we?"

I shook my head no as best I could beneath the pressure of his grip. I sensed the life drain from my eyes. I felt every facial and neck muscle relax as though I were preparing to be killed.

"That's good. She doesn't seem like the kind who'd understand."

I blankly shook "no" again. There was no question in my mind that he was correct. She was *not* the kind to understand, nor to help. If he covered my nose now, my final prayer for death could actually be granted and he would never be accused of killing me.

I was alone with this. Helpless. The world and all of eternal time then shrunk into a five-second window of existence. I remembered shaking my head no, but nothing before it. Only the current five seconds existed. How had I gotten onto this man's bed? I was now the same age as Jack was when he…*vanished*. The knife's edge of reality was now stranger than any fantasy I had ever had. How I was supposed to understand it? The answer was: *I wasn't going to understand it*. Somehow, I knew my mind was shutting off the past and future to protect me, and I welcomed the help. In fact, I also knew that as soon as this moment ended, it would never be remembered. My brain had gone off-line for this, and the memories were never going to be recorded with the rest of the day.

I was actually *inside* a blackout. Here, and only here, I could actually remember *some* of what happened during other similar blackouts, but the memories were flashes of photographs, and bodily sensations that didn't seem connected to words or explanation. The order of events was crazy. I was seven, nine, and thirteen all at the same time. Here I knew with total certainty that Jack was dead.

For now, I didn't ponder what might happen next—even though I somehow knew. I was only aware of what I was feeling at that, soon-to-be-forgotten, second.

I breathed again. My chest and stomach heaved from the chilling sense of entrapment. I wasn't able to lift my head or see past the doctor's, but I could feel. And what I felt was no surprise. A big sand-papery hand delicately touched my inner right thigh. My eyes burst back to life, then slammed shut tight. I tried to straighten that leg and curl the other one over it, but Krieg stopped me with only the power of his stern voice.

"Uh! Relax, champ. You started this by flashing those big, blue eyes at me. I'm only giving you what you want. So you owe me to keep it friendly now."

I'd started this? My eyes? I *owed* him? Like Dad always owed him? The words worked. I'd forever been obedient to my elders. My mind raced to how many times Mom had scolded me into being so. "He's our doctor," she used to say. "He knows what he's doing." I also somehow knew that Mom was right outside and that she would hear about any disobedience. Then I'd have to endure the long days of silence as she'd punish me for embarrassing her. Mom changed sides depending on who scared her the most. This was Dad's friend, and Dad was scarier to her than I was. For me, this was a checkmate with no choices left. I couldn't run with a crotch full of stitches. Of all the possible things I could do at this moment, surrender seemed the least dangerous. I relaxed both legs for the old man and searched my mind for another distraction. That's when I knew this wasn't the first time I'd relaxed and given in to him. In fact, I remembered at least a dozen other times I'd been in his hands. This wasn't the first set of memories that were being sliced out of my recall system. I'd definitely been here before. And I'd definitely been afraid for my life before too.

The rude hand moved upward. I sucked in another breath of surprise and my eyes opened wide to let me search the ceiling for God or a policeman or—oh, who was I kidding? No one was coming to save me. No one ever did. I slammed my eyes shut again. I was a rabbit in the mouth of a wolf. It was over for me.

"That's right; let's finish what you started here. It's going to feel a little different this time without your pill. Enjoy it. You always did have a special spark. These new changes of yours just might make you into a big star."

For the duration of five seconds, I knew what the words "make you into a big star" meant. I even tried looking over his shoulder for the usual cameras. But during the sixth second, I forgot the words had even been uttered. A hundred screaming voices took over inside my head. What were they screaming? Where were they coming from? I tried to think over the top of them—*This is only a dream; it's only a dream; wake up; wake up.* I didn't feel any more movement from the doctor's hands because at the moment the inner-screaming commenced, the spinning room overpowered all sensation. Like the rabbit, I'd prepared for my fate by shutting off all pain and pleasure sensors. I couldn't feel the weight of my own back against the table. Maybe this really was only a dream. I'd been pulled airborne into a spiraling tornado and couldn't touch ground or feel the difference between directions, up or down.

Then the pleasure sensors went back online. I didn't want him to stop. My body began to shake and convulse. Stomach and thigh muscles cramped. I'd never felt anything like it. My squeaky voice, from beneath the ugly hand, groaned. My eyes opened wide and then slammed shut again. My head wanted to explode from pressure. My back arched. Faces flew by behind my closed eyelids. First Jack's, then three of the other scouts.

To my surprise, Shawn Irwin, an older boy who had once lived in Connor's house across the street, appeared. He was about to kiss me on the lips. What the hell was that about? Why Shawn? Then Santa Claus and a skinny man with dark hair all over his body flashed in my face. The clinic lobby appeared with a Christmas tree towering almost to the ceiling. Why were these visions in my head? They came from out of nowhere. I hadn't taken my pill, but I spun and numbed like I had.

Krieg's hand kept moving. I moaned in a new way as every muscle in my legs and stomach flexed and shook. The visions intensified to the point where I felt the dark-haired man's fingers combing my bangs. I'd never felt such sensations before this, but they triggered another flash vision of Shawn's face. It seemed to be extraordinarily important to me at the moment.

Oh, my God; now I knew why Shawn had moaned like this. After all these years, I'd finally grown to an age where I knew what it felt like to *be* him—but wait a minute; where the hell did *that* thought come from?

Even with eyes closed, the lights blinded me. I must have been trying to scream for help because Krieg's hand tightened around my mouth.

I stopped breathing for about eight intense seconds. Everything calmed and darkened. My body relaxed, exactly like Shawn's used to. Wait another minute—why did I know that? I hadn't seen nor even thought about Shawn since…well, since Jack disappeared. Why were there so many people inside my crazy head?

Once relaxed, I continued breathing hard, but I was too confused to make sense of anything that had happened, or how these people I'd trusted could have done this to me.

As Krieg lightened the pressure from my face, I sensed my own disappointment that he hadn't killed me. Even though God didn't help, I had fully expected to be in his presence. But it didn't happen. I didn't die. Mom, who was probably only twenty feet away, never came through the door. She didn't catch him in the act. No one will ever believe that I didn't want this. Maybe I didn't believe it either. Krieg *said* it was my fault. Maybe it was. That's how the event will forever be tucked away in some secret vault in my brain. As my fault. My shame.

Right before going out cold, I found enough clarity in my head to beg God for one last favor.

Please...please make this stop. Please, God. I can't trust anyone! Please send someone to save me. Then, as I envisioned looking intently into God's compassionate face, the bright lights went out.

19

Losses

Throughout my writings, I will say in many ways that normal people struggle with abnormal, big problems every day. To look at a man, even a young one, it's easy to see the casual face of the simple moment. It's when we dig into their pasts, into the dreams and fears of people, that we learn of the bizarre events and unbearable losses from behind the curtains that have shaped the deeper complexities of who they are now. We really can't judge a book by its cover. We need to read every word that's inside if we're truly going to know the whole story.

By Tuck Taylor

Mark eventually joined the other guys in a volleyball game. Since I'm a daytime sleeper, the warm sand helped me doze off. But just before

I passed out, one more of Trenton's friends showed up with a four-year-old nephew who reminded me too eerily of someone I'd once known.

I faded to sleep and had a dream.

I was busy playing with my son, which I did a lot in my dreams. If Micah had lived longer than a few months, he'd have been three by now. In my recurring dreams, he *was* three. Blond. Always happy. And Shannon was still with us both.

Suddenly, that dove from years past returned with a message.

Take me with you.

"Take who where?" I thought.

A ball bounced near my head and jolted me out of the dream.

"Micah?"

20

The Devil's Cover-Up

In 1974, I didn't know about three key types of Anti-Social Personality Disorders (ASPDs): narcissists, sociopaths, and psychopaths. As it turns out, all three are cold-hearted vampires, disguised as friends who charm their way into your family, your government, or your upper management at work. Millions of people are fooled by them everywhere. Like vampires, once you've invited them in, you become spellbound by their interesting stories (manipulations) as they maneuver to get your blood (or money, or children) and satisfy their hunger to take possession of what is yours. Not everyone agrees on how to tell one from the other, but here's how I personally see the difference between the three;

Anti-Social Personality Disorders (ASPD): *The three ASPDs in my story share the ASPD signature lack of remorse or empathy for other humans. To me, the differences, subtle as they are, might circle around intelligence and self-control. In my own words, and my own understanding—not those of the* *medical community—this is how I personally see the differences between the three:*

Narcissists believe they are the only people equal to God. Each honestly believes he or she is the only human alive who matters.

Sociopaths are narcissists who use lies and tricks to abuse other people, mostly for enjoyment. Like puppeteers, they don't share the world with other people; they pull puppet strings. They also believe that only they matter. They blame someone else for all their problems and take no responsibility for anything done wrong, but they take full credit for everything done right. They can be hot-tempered, and if they feel foolish or outmatched, they come unglued. They are often unable to hold jobs because of these things. They may seldom make more than one friend in life. If they steal or murder, it's because of a moment-by-moment inability to control urges and temper. They believe they are entitled to free money, awards, and praise, and they are intrinsically jealous of everyone.

Psychopaths are sociopaths with agendas. A psychopath is just as cruel and cold-hearted as a sociopath, but intelligent enough to premeditate, plan, and execute his or her hateful agendas, while exhibiting enough self-control to remain cool and believable when it comes time to pass a lie detector test or defend himself/herself in court later.

As an adult, I've learned that these seemingly complex, all-powerful, intelligent ASPD strategizers are, in actuality, quite simple and easy to predict—as long as you take off the blinders and look at them without pretending they're better than they are. ASPDs are people who lack any ability to feel empathy. They see other human beings as sheep. All three types learn how to pretend they love and care because they notice we follow them and respond to it. They're not complicated. They are nothing more complex than selfish children in adult bodies who will lie and get away with it because reasonable people around them don't expect them to be as simple and uncaring as they really are.

Dealing with narcissists and sociopaths is so easy to do that it's difficult to grasp: Just don't listen to them. They want something that you have. Like water seeking the lowest point of gravity, they continue finding new angles until they get what they want. Then, the next day, they want something else and they start all over again. They get worse with age because each success makes them bolder. Their lives are much more likely than yours or mine to end up in prison one day. If you trust a sociopath once, you're a trusting person. If you trust one a second time, you're in his trap like a fool. For years and years and years and years, I was a total fool.

Dr. Krieg, more of a psychopath, could hold a job and could strategize better than Fran or Andreo, who were sociopaths. He could build armies around himself of people who would fight for him. He had tricked my dad into feeling indebted to him, which then tricked the family into not believing he was really as evil as he appeared. In truth, he was worse. Krieg, like any ASPD, simply goes after what he wants (in this case, me) without the annoying burden of a conscience telling him to feel compassion for the people he hurts. He wasn't complicated. He wasn't great—hell, he probably wasn't a real doctor. He was just another in a large population of lying, selfish, greedy, abusive psychopaths vying to satisfy his daily lust. The most frightening thing about Krieg was that he was progressing to doing his crimes practically in front of people who could jail him. He was becoming deadly dangerous.

He also wasn't the only ASPD in my life. Andreo was one. Even before he turned on me, the fact that I didn't remember meeting him, and that I had somehow found myself completely isolated from the rest of the class, and engulfed only in him, was a warning sign I didn't know to watch for. ASPDs often swarm and overwhelm their victims. They move so fast you often don't know what hit you until it's too late and you find yourself committed. You're married to one, or you're his best friend, or you suddenly realize you owe him (or he owes you) a substantial amount of money.

As you will soon see, my sister, Fran, not as smart as Krieg, was also a common sociopath. I could have avoided years of grief if only I'd have learned earlier to spot these variations of ASPD and to understand their simplistic evil. How I got three ASPDs in one childhood is a mystery no one can answer. I survived them all because I still had Scooter and Connor, and because I could escape within the dissociative properties of Complex-PTSD. While I may have had a target on my forehead, at least I can thank God for Complex-PTSD— that little gift of helpful crazy.

By Kyle Rickett

I woke up in peace. Still in the clinic. Hands clasped over my tummy. The women were there. I'd blacked out again, but this time, a few bizarre, surreal, and unbelievable memories had somehow followed me out. But it had to have been another stupid dream. Shame on me for thinking Dad's friend would really do those twisted things to me.

At least now, a warm blanket covered me from neck to toe. My right shoulder hurt from a bee sting or something. I was cold and shivering slightly. The nausea was now a stomachache, which I would drink chalky pink stuff for when I got home—a product I was building a relationship with.

"Well, Marie, I hope he didn't embarrass you earlier," sounded off the gruff old voice from somewhere behind me in the room.

"Oh, that's okay, Lee. He's thirteen. I guess that's just what they do." Concerned, she then asked, "That shaking, though. Are you sure he's all right? It looked like epilepsy. I thought he was going to vomit."

"That was shock," Krieg lied. "He lost a lot of blood. It was a rough day for him. It's not uncommon for a little ninety-pounder like that to get the shivers when a pint of blood spills out."

Mom bought it. "What should I do at home if he does that again?"

"He shouldn't. I gave him a shot while you were out of the room. He should be feeling it by now. If not, it'll kick in here pretty soon." As Dr. Krieg confessed to drugging me, I recognized the bee sting as being from a needle. He continued, "He'll calm down before it wears off. But if he starts to shake like that again, call me. Put him in a warm tub. I'll come over to make sure he's okay."

"All right," Mom agreed.

"Oh, and one other thing, Marie." Krieg shook a finger as if he'd remembered an important detail. "He was pretty confused there for a while. So if he tells you any strange stories about…oh I don't know…anything at all, just ignore him. He'll gain his faculties back soon enough, and he may remember this day all differently than it really happened. That little thing you saw happen to him…he might remember it happening, but he might forget that he did it on his own."

Intentionally ignoring me was something my mother was good at. If I'd had a dollar for every memory of her telling my siblings to "*just ignore him until he behaves*," I'd have been a millionaire by only thirteen. I knew Krieg's instructions would be followed. My telling her what I think he might have done, in my dream, would be "misbehaving," and it would fall on her deaf ears.

"Okay." Mom smiled. "He does have an active imagination."

"He could be in the movies someday," Krieg replied, and as if gloating that Mom was completely under his lying spell, Krieg shot me a private wink. God, how I hated his ugly, antagonistic winks.

I tasted vomit again while the adults spoke about how Mom was to care for me for the next three weeks and then bring me back for stitches removal. I wanted to cry but felt too defeated.

Instead, I escaped into my imagination. The answer to my prayer— a rescue, a beautiful gold GTO, roared out of nowhere and screeched into the parking lot outside the window. I leapt off the table and jumped out through the window of the clinic, then slid in through the open window of the GTO. In the imagined escape, a nameless but faithful superhero had finally rescued me from my out-of-control life.

I started to feel drowsy. *Oh God, now what?* The GTO vanished. I was still on the table. The room spun again, but gently this time. I hadn't escaped. I was trapped and needed to accept that.

"I give up," I slurred.

The drugs kicked in.

21

The Message Returns

Again, I speak of an inexplicable connection transcending time, space, and people. It had been three years since a dove had simultaneously connected a single intense moment for three strangers: me, Ronnie Taylor-Donovan, and Tuck Taylor. Somehow, that day was happening again. The bike crash seemed to have opened the door to that room in my mind where I felt victimized and vulnerable. It was the same room Andreo had locked me into with his jealous betrayal of friendship. In that room, all my past emotions were as present as ever. Psychologically, that connection makes sense. But what doesn't make sense is that at the moment I gave up and passed out on Krieg's table, Ronnie got another visit by that same dove.

By Ronnie Taylor-Donovan

At a little past 1:00 a.m. on Sunday, June twenty-third, and just two days after Tuck's twenty-first birthday, the dove came to see me once more. In this dream, Tuck was just seventeen again and was flying through a blue sky with it. *I need him,* said the dove without moving its beak. They soared away, but one more message came back toward me. *We're strong together.*

I awoke burdened. "Oh, no. I hope he's not sick again."

22

Reorientation

Obviously, since you are reading my memoirs, you know I lived through my childhood, and as you can see, I grew up to become an author and storyteller, which are two positive outcomes of being a person of lively imagination.

Among the pitfalls of being imaginative, however, is the fact that reality becomes difficult to trust when imagination so easily interprets my understanding of the world I'm in. Today, my sense of humor draws people close, but my sudden bouts of depression confuse those same people. I'm often likened to the proverbial comedian who is both funny and troubled at the same time. All in all, I'm having a great life, and I am so grateful that I've survived any suicide attempts. I just have to manage some down times once in a while.

These days, spiritual people who don't know my story call me a sensitive, friends call me a dreamer, and fans hail me as a visionary while critics accuse me of being delusional. Personally, I just call myself imaginative. I don't write for attention or glory; I write because I have to. I'll go crazy if my world stays locked in my head for too long.

Back then, at thirteen, I had some big realities to sort through, and since no one around me was ready to explain them, my gracious imagination and I had to find—or create—answers out of thin air.

The long day of the bike accident finally became a long night alone, where I and my pliable adolescent brain could work together to try to make an acceptable story out of all that had happened. I used some tricks to decide that the day wasn't as bad as it had seemed. As you read this chapter, here are the tricks you'll see me use:

Minimizing: I minimized Dr. Krieg's affections as something all doctors probably did to all boys.

Chanting: As a proven brainwashing technique, I repeated the chant "It was a dream; it was a dream" until I believed it to be so.

Denial: I allowed the chanting to work. I just chose not to believe the clinic visit had happened for real.

Diversion onto someone else: I intentionally distracted focus onto Connor, hoping he was okay after the crash.

Rage-Turned-Inward: I punished myself by wallowing in shame for not noticing what a good friend Connor had been for a long time.

Acceptance: I accepted the shame of being a bad friend and of overreacting to a routine doctor's visit. I normalized. I was Kyle again.

But then, just as I was comfortably settling into acceptance of the day's events, I overheard family in the next room talking. This night was only going to get worse. More alliances were shifting.

By Kyle Rickett

I woke up again, and again with a blank mind. I scanned the area to see that I was in my bedroom and in the dark, but still on my back. My muscles were stiff. I'd been asleep a long time. Stretching both arms and legs, I ignored a mysterious sharp pain in my crotch, and I wondered why I was not wearing my usual tight underpants and pajamas.

"Ow!" A headache covered the whole top of my head. "Shit!" I whispered. "Fuck. I haven't had one of these since…tuhhh…*I thought I was cured*." With hands on my forehead, I rolled toward the open window. Krieg's pills used to give me the same sort of headache.

The day unfolded fast. The second streak of pain in my groin proved the accident had really happened. It wasn't a dream. A bike crash had led to a fight with Mom, but things got hazy after that. I remembered hating Dr. Krieg. I then recalled being stripped, but I wasn't positive yet whether the rest was real or imagined. So I decided not to think about it.

"Fuck, I hate that guy," I whispered.

I returned to my back to let the scar rest in a position that hurt less. At least I'd gotten one of my wishes—I wasn't at the clinic anymore.

"That was then. This is now," I chanted. "I'm alone and safe *now*. Guess I should be grateful for that."

Up in my room

I loved my room, the only place on earth that was mine. Even though Mom cleaned and routinely searched it, it was my private space. I was allowed to arrange it how I wanted, so I rearranged it a lot, always trying to keep it interesting and new. During this time in my history, I had the head of the bed pushed against the north wall, perfectly equidistant between the east wall, where the door was, and the west wall that had the window and my desk. My closet was to the south at my feet. The symmetry was practical and balanced—which made me feel a *little* more balanced also.

On the shelf above my headboard was displayed my only allowable creative expression: three dozen perfectly crafted models—twenty-eight cars, two pickups and six semitrucks were parked in an angle facing the window. I'd built them over the years while wearing headphones and listening to classical music records or to my granddad's accordion tapes. With a Bic lighter and some clever use of paints, I was able to bend or color them to look realistic and detailed. My customizations gave me joy and a sense of personal control. The finished models were uniquely mine.

Listening to accordion and classical music in the privacy of that room brought peace, but it was an important secret I had to guard with my life. Other kids would tear me to shreds and burn the pieces if they found out I didn't listen to rock 'n' roll like they did. Looking back now, I can see that I had a lot of secrets I shouldn't have had to keep.

Ultimately, it seemed that it was just never okay to be me.

Foreboding messages in random patterns

Comfortably interlaced fingers rode my stomach up and down with my breathing. I stared into the ceiling cracks that had appeared after the 1964 earthquake. Where another person might only see cracks, or bunnies or butterflies, I always saw drawings of God and the old bearded men of the Catholic Bible staring scornfully down at me. An angry God comforted my subconscious. How sad is that?

"I'm a worthless piece of shit," I mumbled groggily to the stern faces.

Shame: The gift that keeps on giving

Obviously, I'd slept through family dinner and evening TV. I glanced at the clock. A little past ten. I'd been in bed for a long time and had to use the bathroom. I pushed back the covers and tried to slide a leg toward the floor.

"Ouch!" A streak of pain triggered the sound of two crunching bicycles. Two fingers of my left hand gently massaged the right wrist.

"Connor!" I whispered, and then I immediately defaulted to worry. Worrying about someone else was a good diversion from thinking about myself. It's honorable to worry about a friend, but selfish to focus on oneself, right?

"Dear Lord, please let Connor be okay. He's my best friend. I never realized how nice a guy he is." I wondered how long Connor had felt so close to me, and I immediately thought of myself as a jerk for not noticing before.

"Maybe tomorrow I can see him." I slowly got out of bed. My crotch burned and itched at the same time, but only on the right side. I cradled my aching testicles like baby birds, holding them up and away from the painful burn. My fingers touched loose threads while I allowed myself to recall Krieg's rough hand tugging on me, but nothing else. At the moment that I nearly remembered his comment about being in the movies, I stopped myself.

"No, no, no, *no*! It didn't happen; it didn't happen, it didn't happen." I pressed my hands tightly against my ears. After a deep, cleansing breath, I was again able to turn off the memories by calling him an asshole and refocusing on the pain itself. Chanting worked well for me at that age. I could repeat something until it overpowered other thoughts and literally became my truth. Who knows? Maybe this process is one way clinical levels of denial begin in a person.

Changing alliance to the winning side

I shuffled carefully toward the closet door to grab a bathrobe I knew would be on the left-most hanger. Unlike my family, I obsessively controlled my closet by organizing garments on the same hangers each week. It gave me a sense of predictability over some part of my life. My robe was always on the left.

I quietly slid open the closet door. My parents' muffled shouting resonated through the sheetrock at the back of the closet. I heard my name.

"Oh, God. *It's about me.*" My heart sank an inch. A shot of adrenaline thumped it extra hard. The bitter taste of numbing fear coated my throat. Even though my father had never hit me, his disapproving fits of rage felt just as painful. I worried that if he didn't continue to love me, he'd somehow just leave me. Terrified, I stood like a statue trying to make out the words that followed my name. Generally speaking, my parents loved me and I loved them, but they could be scary. Whenever I made one of them unhappy, they both came down on me—then things were usually followed up days later with snide remarks from my sister and even some of my aunts. Somehow, without actually throwing me out of the house, they'd all gang together and abandon me emotionally.

Even my niece, Fran's oldest daughter, Jayne, who was eight, had recently begun eye-rolling me at family functions before I could open my mouth. My sister had recently informed me that since girls mature faster than boys, she wanted me to be aware that her precious eight-year-old Jayne was already more adult than I was. Those eye rolls looked just like her mother's and were all the evidence I needed to be certain she was definitely getting in on their malicious women's gossip that a dork like me wasn't privy to.

I was normally a comedian at family functions, but only until the first hint of eye-rolling, when a blank mind would clam me up. No one ever seemed to notice me change. Or maybe they insulted me on purpose to get me to stop talking. Either way, the derision worked to annihilate completely any hope of a positive self-image, so I'd close down and try to slink out of the room when they weren't looking.

Once the Rickett family criticisms began in those days, the teams typically sided against the victim. Whenever that victim was me, which it often was, clamming up proved to be the only way to shorten the abuse. If I fought back, or sought an ally, the disappointment only worsened because everyone in earshot would side with whoever was winning. They were sharks. Humiliation and vulnerability were blood in the water. I'd learned well to retreat from battle quietly to avoid becoming the meal for a certain and violent feeding frenzy.

Another shifting alliance

Still standing motionless, I could tell Mom and Dad were trying to be quiet, so I had to work extra hard to make out full sentences. Single words rose for emphasis, like "Connor" and "school." I hated hearing "school" because I had life-altering secrets to keep there. Hearing it spoken in anger pumped several more shots of adrenaline through my body. What did they know about Andreo and my humiliating school nickname? My stomach always had a knot in it, but this wrenched at it. My pulse and breathing detonated into near hysterics. My thumping heart started to hurt. Then I heard "Krieg!" My mind flashed to the memory of an erection in front of Mom. The shame I'd been wallowing in suddenly made sense.

"Oh, no!" I whispered. My face cooled as blood drained and all the memories I'd been ignoring flooded in to laugh at me from inside my head. She was telling Dad. *But he didn't need to know that part.* Why would she volunteer that? My knees weakened. I looked down again and gently inspected my raw, red penis.

"Oh, shit. It's happening again," I whispered.

I can't describe the confusion that overcame me at that moment because when I tell you now that I didn't know why I expected to see the rawness, I am telling the truth. I didn't know *why* it was familiar. An emotion welled up, but I couldn't place it. Did I want to cry or kill? Did I want protection with my family or escape *from* them? I glared into the closet wall, not knowing what to do with the swelling rage.

"I can't let them see this." I covered my bare crotch with both hands. Then I heard "Kathy." I remembered her breasts, and then again, my erection, and Dr. Krieg winking at me. More of the day came back.

"Oh, no." My mouth went dry. I finally heard a full sentence in my father's rising voice.

"Lee is our friend. We can't *ever* talk about this!"

My nervous hot breath cooled. Lee was their friend. Lee. The gorilla. I—their son—was the outsider. It shouldn't have surprised me, but it did. The shouting stopped. I was like an innocent bystander who had just walked into a crime scene and seen something I wasn't supposed to see. My spine chilled and my legs roared into action, shuffling me fast back to bed. How terrifying it would be to confront them if they knew I'd heard that. Hoping not to tear open the aching new scar, I skillfully and swiftly slid under the covers.

Thump in the hall

Something thumped in the hall. *I had to play dead.* I pretended my heavy breathing was from being in deep sleep, almost snoring. The hall light glared right through my closed eyelids when someone—not sure who—opened that door and walked across the creaking floor, between my motionless feet and closet. My breathing skillfully sustained its rhythm. No changes. The sickening screech of the aluminum-framed window was fingernails on a chalkboard as it slid shut and ended with a crash, then a click. Still no changes in breathing. The floor creaked again, and the door closed quietly, followed by the rattle of the doorknob being let go slowly, like the mysterious visitor was a character in a movie. I sighed deeply and sat up. I still had to pee, but holding it long beyond comfort was a skill I'd grown proud of.

Bathroom skills

I hated not being able to pee when I wanted to, but ever since Andreo had turned the school into a war zone, I'd learned to be selective of when and where doing so was safe.

When I was eleven, three of my classmates, all larger than me, surrounded me in the boys' room, held me back, slid my pants down to my ankles, and tried dragging me out to the crowded halls. But I screamed loud enough to raise the attention of the nuns. Fear of the nuns was universal across all classes of students—even the tough boys. They let me go. I never again set foot in the bathroom at school. Or at a mall. Or at a fair. I just learned never to drink fluids if I weren't at home.

The bathroom was only the beginning of my public stress. By this time, Connor and Scooter had become the only minors I'd ever purposely let myself be alone with. I tried never to be anywhere with other children if adults couldn't see me. I also learned never to let anyone, anywhere, get between me and an exit. (I still tend to be a little bit that way today.)

That night, alone in my bed, I had a different kind of bathroom problem. I'd played dead and had enemies stationed between me and the facility. I figured I'd have to wait until the whole house was quiet. I would hold it for at least an hour past the final sound.

23

Supportive Coaching

It's said that every cloud has a silver lining. My experience in life is that it's true. If we want to learn, there really is a positive lesson in every bad day. Whether we choose to embrace that lesson or not is our personal choice. I've also learned that a little bit of humor can make almost any problem seem more manageable.

When I was learning how to withdraw and hide from people whom I thought wanted to ignore me, Tuck was acting out a whole different strategy. He had learned, instead, to get squarely into the faces of the people who were trying to ignore him.

Same lesson; different learning.

By Tuck Taylor

At just about midnight, I finally went to bed, but I could only get halfway between awake and asleep. For some reason, I was feeling connected to the darker times of my past. Believe it or not, the illness wasn't my worst memory. It was what the illness turned me into that had churned in my brain ever since.

I had stayed in school for about a month once I'd been diagnosed with cancer. The medicine thinned my hair quickly, and I'll never forget how it hurt when classmates reacted. Mark was right when he said I'd once been 'Mister Popular.' During the cancer, a small number of good people stuck by me. But for the rest of the school, they reacted in different ways. Some made fun of me, like bullies would do, but they didn't bother me; they were idiots. Others became ridiculously nice to me, like sugary sweet. They bothered me more than the bullies. But the ones who hurt the most were the majority of them who pretended not to notice me anymore. They pushed it further by avoiding me altogether. For the most part, I'd become invisible to a large percentage of the population. It was angering to be bullied, embarrassing to be pitied, but *horrible* to be ignored. More than ignored; *Erased.*

My sister, Ronnie, constantly asked me how things were going at school back then. When I told her what I just told you, she coached me to get in their stupid faces and be as obnoxious as I needed to be until they saw me again. So I did. I'd intentionally make hooping sounds when I'd enter a classroom, and I'd wave at everyone who tried to sneak a peek at me, pretending not to. I'd have rather had my classmates and teachers irritated with me than ignoring me completely.

The funniest example of that was when one of the girls in my German class was ignoring me. I got up next to her and asked a question she couldn't ignore.

"Want to know what cancer feels like?"

"I'm sorry." She acted like she had no idea who I was or why I was talking. "Are you talking to me?"

"It's like I got kicked in my *balls* and now they're on fire and ready to explode."

She kept up the façade, and except for turning red as a beet and swallowing hard, didn't react at all, but Tony, the boy next to her, burst into laughter. While she made sure never to get close to me again, that guy, Tony, quickly became one of my best friends and stayed tight with me right up through graduation.

Ronnie's advice definitely helped, but mostly because it proved my sister was 100 percent on my side. Her advice, whether it was right or wrong, was evidence for my heart to know that she wanted me to stay strong and relevant, rather than to vanish from my own life and suffer alone.

Thinking about Ronnie's support and wondering where Tony ended up after high school helped me relax enough to fall asleep finally.

I've come to believe that there's nothing a person can't handle if his family or friends stand up and support him.

24

The Devil's Fingerprints

This is what it feels like to be trapped in another person's delusion, and it happens to a lot of abused teens. All the evidence was right in front of her, but Mom couldn't see it. What my mother feared the most was being publicly shamed for failing to raise a strong family, so since she couldn't stop embarrassing things from penetrating the family unit, she instead controlled the evidence. "Don't talk about it" was her most commonly used strategic instruction.

My dad, I now know, was suffering with undiagnosed PTSD (shell-shock) from a particularly long and bloody island battle in World War II, and Mom only knew that, for whatever reason, keeping peace at home meant keeping him calm at all cost. In essence, when a parent or other guardian suffers emotional damage, his or her family suffers it too by walking on eggshells and becoming neurotic and hypersensitive to an unstable authority figure. At thirteen, I didn't understand any of this dynamic. I only knew that my protectors lived by a fragile sense of peace that I had to find ways to support, and they were allowed to say whatever they needed to say in order to quiet any situation as it was unfolding. I was trapped in their denial—their version of reality—with absolutely no way out.

Rather than standing with honor and being willing to protect at any cost, they sought peace by giving in to the greatest threat of the moment. In order to live safely in their world, I learned from them how to shut-up and stuff down problems.

If trust is little more than the ability to predict how someone will behave, then how was I supposed to trust my protectors if I knew I couldn't predict whose side they'd be on at any given moment?

By Kyle Rickett

The wait tortured both mind and bladder while I studied the old men of my ceiling. At 12:34 a.m., my heart went hollow. Something I didn't want to recall had happened exactly twelve hours before. Sadness overcame me. Then sharp pain gripped the top of my stomach. I groaned and got up. The lonesome stillness of the house meant it was time to risk the hallway to the bathroom and relieve at least one of the pains.

Being naked was unsettling. This was my longest stretch of being nude since the womb. To feel normal, I put on a pajama top and shook my head at how different it was going to feel not wearing binding briefs, but I had no choice. They would hurt. I retrieved my bathrobe and began my adventure into the darkness.

The hallway was lit. How strange. It was *never* lit. The venture now felt like a trap. Why else would Mom have broken her own rule and left the light on?

I made it safely into the bathroom and sat on the stool to pee quietly, which took a while but felt so good. So no one would hear me, I didn't flush. I washed my hands by barely turning the water on to a trickle so the faucet wouldn't hiss. I dried them, folded the towel, and set it next to the sink, where a small sheet of paper lay beneath two white pills. *For Kyle* was scratched across it in Mom's handwriting. I thought about throwing them down the toilet, but I didn't have the nerve to be that defiant. So I simply didn't touch them. That way, the bathroom would appear unvisited.

I pulled the two end sections of the big three-piece mirror outward to view the sides of my face, which still hurt. My large front teeth had cut the upper lip inside my mouth. Some predictable gravel burns decorated my forehead and faint markings of red colored my cheeks and chin.

Krieg's fingerprints

"Oh, no. That wasn't a dream either," I whispered. Some nausea returned. The blackout couldn't disappear this time—I had physical evidence proving that what had happened was real. The house was dead-silent except for some whisper-quiet gurgling in the trap below the sink I'd just used. I clasped my hands and placed them over the pattern of the marks. Beneath the hot lights of the bathroom mirror, I could see a perfect match. I watched my skin flush. "Oh, dear God, please, please, please don't let Mom see this. She's not the kind who'd understand." Anxiety built up quickly. I wished the blackout could have remained intact. Krieg's words had apparently become mine. "She'll never love me again."

I wanted to see the wound. I rounded my shoulders. The bathrobe dropped to the floor. Then I grabbed Mom's hand-held mirror, spread my legs through the pain, and held it beneath my crotch to count the stitches. "Thirty-*six*! They're real. They're *fucking* real."

A picture of Santa Claus shot through my mind, then vanished.

"Oh, God!" I whispered loudly, and then I closed my lips tightly and shot a panicked glance toward the door. Out of nowhere, I remembered that I used to perform this self-evaluation years earlier in the same secrecy and with the same mirror. Were *all* the blackouts going to open up to me at once? "Oh, God," I said again. I saw another Christmas tree, then shook my head briskly once in each direction. *Why does that keep happening?* I delicately—ever so silently—set the mirror back exactly where I'd found it so no one would know I'd looked at myself. My face in the big mirror showed a panic I couldn't control.

"Oh, God," I whispered a third time. "I'm going totally crazy. This is *not* real! I want to wake up."

A new dizzy spell made me nauseous, and bending down hurt more than I had figured on, but without letting the floor creak too loudly, I eventually retrieved the robe and covered myself again. "I have to get out of here." I gathered my wits and slowly switched off the light with all fingers so it wouldn't snap. I pulled open the door gingerly to avoid the usual squeak.

"Yikes!" My arms reeled back and my eyes sprung wide open.

Late night confrontation in the hall

I gasped and jerked backward, slapping the door loudly with an open hand. There was Mom, three feet away, beneath the glaring hallway light like a vampire, leaning against the wall with folded arms, chuckling lightly at my nervous jump. Next to her, the pair of wooden crutches from Daniel's motorcycle accident rested against the family-photo-wall. She had obviously been waiting to speak to me. I laid an open hand across my chest to indicate she'd scared the hell out of me and conveniently angled my face downward to shadow the bruises.

"Are you okay, honey?" She pushed off from the wall to stand on her own. "Sorry if I spooked you." She giggled again. It was strange to have a meeting in the hallway with Mom at midnight. I was surprised by how many of her own routines she'd broken. Accident or not, this was so unlike her that it was confusing.

"It hurts pretty bad," I reported. There had to be a reason why she needed to stay up to talk to me. I figured it was about how I would get ready for church tomorrow. "But at least I can get around okay. I promise I'll get ready in time to go to Mass in the morning."

"No, no, no, no. We'll skip this one Sunday." *Oh, my God, another rule broken.* She jokingly excused, "God'll understand us skipping one single Mass." She ran the fingers of one hand through my hair. I barely felt it.

She noticed my lip and grabbed at it without asking. I flinched away. A hot blush of terror streaked across my face.

"Does that hurt?"

"A little," I blurted out without thinking.

"Did you hit your face on the handlebars?"

"No," I answered nervously, but then I immediately wished I'd said yes to take advantage of a perfect excuse. "Maybe.... Um...I can't remember." I hoped she couldn't hear my pounding heart.

"Oh, my gosh." She looked a little closer.

"What?" I responded like I had no idea what she was seeing.

"Are those bruises? They look like *finger marks*."

"They're *not!*"

"Then what are they?"

"I don't know." I was an innocent angel as I feigned complete ignorance. As far as she could know, I saw no bruises of any kind.

"Okay, well then...uh...your face looks like you've been sleeping wrong on your pillow. Or did that happen during the accident?" She tried hard to figure out the bruises.

"I don't know." Nervous dread was turning to panic. "I...I slept face down. My hands were on my pillow—that's probably it."

"No, those are bruises, and you weren't sleeping face down when I closed your window."

I went blank. Pure innocence meant keeping my mouth shut. I couldn't play dead now, but I could play *brain-dead.*

"That is just *so* strange." She let go. "You poor little guy. It had to have been from hitting the ground.... It's just so strange how they look like finger marks." Then she looked toward my crotch and asked, "How do the stitches look? Are they holding okay?"

I glanced down. What did she mean, *Are they holding okay?*

"Kyle? Are your stitches holding okay?"

"Uh. Well. Uh...they're pretty red, but I don't see...blood or...anything." I relaxed at her not questioning whether Krieg had given me the bruises. The stitches were okay as far as I could tell, assuming that's what *holding okay* meant. They weren't leaking blood, and organs weren't squishing out through them...so I *guess* they were holding.

"Here." She grabbed and wiggled both crutches with one hand. "Good thing we kept these around. I'll leave them here." She let them gently fall back against the wall. "Did you take the pills I left?"

"I don't need them." I suddenly felt like fighting for at least *one* right.

"They're pain pills. You should take them."

"Who gave them to you?"

"Dr. Krieg. He said you'd need them."

"Even if I don't want them?"

"Take your pills. It's going to hurt worse in the morning."

"Then that's when I'll take them." I couldn't believe I was standing up to my mother. But I was.

"*Kyle,* they're just *pills.*"

"Mom, please don't make me take any more of his pills!"

"Oh, for Gosh sakes, Kyle…! Well, starting tomorrow morning, I've got antibiotics for you. Those, you *have* to take."

"Why?"

"So you don't end up with an infection. There was a lot of grease and grime around that wound."

"Okay, but…" I deflated at the shameful image of my body's reaction to Kathy wiping the grease out of my wound. Slowly and almost sadly, I reiterated my position, "no pain pills...*please.*"

"Oh, you're being silly now. He's been giving you all kinds of pills for years." Mom shook her head with a roll of the eyes. "Fine, but you'll be begging me for them tomorrow."

"Okay, leave them here. I'll take them then." I didn't know if I was winning an argument or being a bad son—but I was absolutely not going to put those two pills in my mouth.

"Such a tough little man." She shook her head slowly and faked a smile. "So much like your dad." She stepped forward. I turned my head to the side and she squeezed it into her breasts for a moment.

I loved Mom's touch. When the side of my head pulled into her soft bosom and both of her hands covered my shoulder blades, I closed my eyes and tried to soak in the warmth. My heart grew to twice its size, and warmth filled all my veins. Heaven. I didn't want it to end—me and my mom sharing a moment.

But it did end. She let go too soon. As usual.

"You've had quite a day, haven't you?" she commented. I hoped she was building toward an apology for the humiliation she'd allowed at the clinic.

I puffed in acknowledgment and gave a single nod. I wanted to say more. The pressure in my chest built again as I got ready to come clean with her. I needed to know that everything she saw happen was somehow okay. I *think* I knew she knew I was a thirteen-year-old boy and that what had happened today was nothing to be ashamed of. Oh, who was I kidding? I was terribly ashamed of it. And I hated not being able to share my thoughts. I looked at Mom's nose, which was near her eyes, but not quite as intimidating.

"Mom—"

"I know, Kyle," she interrupted. "It was a rough day for all of us." She continued, still not with an apology, "And don't worry about your dad."

My warmed heart froze like ice. Why would I possibly need to worry about my dad? And why was she telling me not to?

"I'm not going to tell him about anything, except that you got stitches."

I remained silent as she pushed the knife in deeper.

"I hope you don't think you need to talk to him about it either. It's best to let it all go now."

"Let it all go?"

"Like it never happened…. Let's all just forget about it."

"You're not going to tell him about any—"

"*No!*" Mom's intensity rose, but her volume dropped to a stern whisper.

"I can't talk to Dad about—"

"*No!*" she interrupted again in that whisper, which was building in anxiety. "Your dad doesn't need to be bothered with *any of this!*"

I knew she was right. Dad couldn't handle emotion or sexuality on any level. But I wanted a man to talk to. If I couldn't talk with my father about what it meant to be a sexual male, then who? Dr. Krieg? Thirteen-year-old Connor? The nuns? Santa? I sighed and closed my eyes in defeat. Mom probably interpreted it as thankfulness. The energy between us became dry like we were strangers now. Two hours before, I had overheard her *tell* my father enough to make him demand we protect that doctor with silence.

The adults were allowed to discuss my life, (and then lie about it), but I wasn't. As far as I could see, they were definitely ganging up on me, and leaving me with nobody to talk to—*again.*

Retreat! Retreat!

My mother's rising anxiety meant it was time to run. I was a master at reading signs of danger. I had never been taught any self-protection skills. Forbidden from fighting, I instead kept my eyes peeled and legs ready for escape twenty-four hours a day. I was small and almost always outnumbered. People hurt me easily, and they usually did it in groups. Any arguments I ever won were lost later through cold revenge. There was no winning in this clan. I routinely tried to map an escape-route for every situation, physical and emotional, even when it was with my own family and in my own home.

This was one of those moments. My anger at Mom scared me. Retreat was my only option. I couldn't take her on, so I had to flee before I said something confrontational and got myself into *real* trouble. I smiled so that my high cheeks wrinkled the way she liked.

"Thanks, Mom." I turned and escaped toward my room. She couldn't see that my eyes were wide open in combined anger and fear, and without looking back, I added, "Good night, Mom. I love you." I shuffled through my door and closed it.

The hallway light leaking beneath the door went dark. The automatic nightlight in the outlet right outside flickered on. Mom's laws of normal life ruled once again with *lights-out*. She was in charge of the house and ran it like a tight ship, but today, I'd seen weaknesses in her I hadn't noticed before. The way she cowered at Dr. Krieg, and then protected Dad from having to deal with his son's mess, made me wonder who *really* had ultimate control over this family.

It sure as hell wasn't me. With no one in my corner, my long night of processing the complexities of life—by myself—had only begun.

25

Connor's Worry

I wasn't the only accident victim that day. I wasn't the only one having a long night. I also wasn't the only one whose night was made so by past memories being awakened by present events. Connor had his stress to deal with too. But because he lived within an atmosphere of openness, he was able to feel his stress with much more simplicity and clarity. He only had to deal with one emotion. With no alliances shifting he could trust his family. His sadness would appropriately pass.

By Connor Mason

I woke up at about 12:45 a.m. because my head hurt. Mom had left a few aspirins out for me in the hall bathroom. She checked me over about a dozen times after the bike accident because she was worried about me maybe having a concussion. My head hurt, that was for sure, but I didn't need a doctor. As I headed back to my room, her voice softly rang out from her open bedroom door.

"You okay, honey?"

"Yeah. It's just time for another aspirin."

"Okay. You'll let me know if it gets worse, alright?"

"I will, Mom."

"I love you, little man."

"I love you too, Mom."

"We'll check on Kyle in the morning. Okay?"

I stopped. My plans changed. Mom and I had been closer ever since Merrick died. Sometimes we would just cry together over photos without saying anything. She knew Kyle was my best friend and she liked him too for her own reasons. She used to tell me that "the little shit" sure did a good job cracking me out of my shell.

There was no doubt in my mind then, or even now, that, because we were so used to mourning Merrick together, Kyle's accident was drawing us closer together again on this night. She's had practice now and knew how to handle my emotions.

"Mom?" I asked.

"Just a minute, honey." She got up quietly and tiptoed out of the bedroom. She closed the door enough so Dad could keep sleeping. She ran her fingers through my hair and asked, "What's on your mind?"

"I...don't know." I started to cry. "I'm so worried about Kyle."

"Oh, oh, oh...." She wrapped her arms around my shoulders. "We'd have heard something by now if things were bad."

"He was bleeding so much, Mom." I huffed and choked. "I wanted to go with him, but his mom wouldn't let me." Tears streamed and she squeezed me harder.

"I know, honey. Mrs. Rickett..." She tried to be as polite as she could "has her hands full over there. I wish she'd have let you go too, but...like I said, we'd have heard by now if things were bad."

What more than that could she have said? Perhaps if we hadn't been through Merrick's death together, she wouldn't have been quite so empathetic to my exaggerated emotions. But Mom knew I still had a gaping hole in my life from losing my big brother. She knew that Kyle was my mentor now that Merrick was gone. She had seen me cry a lot, and she had learned to let it happen.

I went back to my room and sat on the edge of my bed where I could reach the nightstand and grab my old picture of Merrick and me fishing with Kyle off his dad's boat.

I quietly fidgeted with Merrick's dog tags hanging around my neck as I stared at the photo and Kyle's face.

"I can't lose you too, man. God damn it, I hope you're okay."

26

Redesigned Memories

Regarding the age-old question of nature versus nurture: It seems to me that a person is born to be something, and then raised to be something, but only for a lucky few, the two somethings are the same. For the rest of us who were born to be one thing, then raised to be another, life can be a chronic inner battle. I wasn't one of the lucky few. I'm social and expressive by nature, but raised to be quiet and ashamed. The hallway conversation with Mom proved I was required to remain alone with my questions no matter how badly I needed to talk them through. To keep stress off poor Dad, no one could talk about what might be bugging his son.

I was also well-trained never to fight for myself whether at home or at school. If a humiliating call were ever to come in from the school over me fighting for myself, Mom would look like a bad mother and all her love would be withdrawn from me for several days as a punishment. That hurt too much to deal with, so instead, I learned to control my emotions by finding ways to accept every shame, and just try, try, try to avoid conflict.

I had the rest of the night to accept all that had happened that day by developing a new fantasy—one that would make real life bearable again. The first step in rewriting the day's history in my head was to process what had happened—so I could change it.

By Kyle Rickett

I had slept soundly for the whole afternoon, so I knew I'd be up through the night. I lay still, staring into the darkness while the branch's shadows partied on my walls without music. The only sound was a limb squeaking against the glass.

"I'm in hell." I was an accident victim, impulsively reliving the crash and the humiliation over and over again. With eyes closed, I'd watch my hand reach for Connor's bike. Then Krieg's face would stare down at me. Kathy's lacey bra would appear. I'd see Mom staring at my naked body. I'd see the clock: 12:34. Krieg's wink would force my eyes open again. It was horrible.

Like after any bad accident, the flashbacks menacingly caused me to relive the story every time I closed my eyes. But the nice thing was that each time I restarted the story, I trimmed out a few more details.

Like most kids, I was a fan of science fiction. Its characters used mind melds and ESP to control thoughts. I believed it could be done, and I practiced it a lot. I once cured a headache by imagining soaking it into my hand. When I lifted that hand off my forehead, it actually removed the pain that one time. So now I held that healing hand over my chest in hopes of soaking my shame into it. Each time I closed my eyes, I'd crash into Connor again and then think of ways to change what happened next. I'd pull my hand away and imagine it had worked. Each time, another ounce of the shame left.

Of course, I couldn't really change what had happened, but I could come out of it feeling better than the time before by telling myself it was a dream. Two things had happened to me on Krieg's table: a physical attack, and a series of unexplained flashbacks. It surprised me how quickly my memory-erasing techniques worked to expunge the flashbacks. The first to vanish were of the hairy man. Then Jack and Shawn Irwin's faces. Santa and the flashbulbs ceased on the third time through the scenario. I guess it makes sense that those memories would fade fastest since they weren't real anyway—only bizarre flashes of a crazy mind. *Easy come, easy go.* Right?

Think about the good stuff!

I had strong arms and a strong will. Changing out memories was a skill I excelled at. As nice as Connor's emotions were, I now wanted the rules of ordinary life back, so I focused on happy times. I was Kyle Rickett, running and jumping in the neighborhood. Being called *Half-pint* and *the cute little shit that never slows down* were reputations that brought pride. I received brief moments of positive attention when I'd mow a lawn quicker than an adult could, or when I could carry more wood to the truck than Dad. These were real things that I could do, that consistently bought short moments of glory and gave temporary evidence that I had value. So I diverted my thoughts onto them.

It worked!

After about an hour of doing this, I'd relived the whole day a dozen times, leaving only a memory of embarrassing myself to Kathy, and then relaxing my legs to let her boss jerk me off in private. No big deal, right? Maybe he really did need to see if there was nerve damage. He *was* a doctor. I ignored the sinister things he'd said about being his favorite, and of remembering me as a screamer.

Or did it backfire?

So now, with all the *bad* stuff swept back into the blackouts where they belonged, I still had one huge problem. Now I was ashamed of how I'd overreacted to such a little thing. My sister Fran would often say, "We all know you're a drama queen who *always* makes mountains out of molehills," and so here I was, proving her right again. A doctor had cut my clothes off to save my life, and I'd freaked out like it was the end of the world. That was so like me.

If I thought about it logically, what little I remembered was nothing more than a free hand-job. In fact, it felt good at the time, and would have for hours if I hadn't been so ashamed of it. No one got pregnant or hurt. I needed to be grateful it was me he'd held down and diddled, and not Mom or Connor. I guess I could feel proud that I'd taken one for the people I loved. Again, it felt right to protect others, but selfish to protect myself. Somehow, I was again the only person in my life I didn't feel the need to show any respect to.

Go with him

Ashamed of myself for being upset, I asked God to help me make sense of it all. I laid back to rest my head and fell into a short dream.

A white bird hovered in the wind, like when our seagulls would hover over moving ferries waiting for French fries. Then a slender young man appeared in a yellow tank top and walked up a wooded hill. With him, a shimmering golden cougar growled rhythmically. The man's smile warmed my whole body. He motioned for me to follow.

I hesitated.

"*Go with him*!" ordered a familiar elderly man's voice from above.

"Huh!" Both arms and legs jolted. My bed shook. I woke up.

27

Bed Jolts That Make No Sense

The dreams. How do I explain the dreams? I have come to believe there are at least two kinds: 1) Those the mind uses to process events and concerns, and 2) Messages that come to us from...well, from I don't know where.

By Tuck Taylor

"Huh!" My bed shook.

I woke up.

I had been dreaming of peacefully walking up a steep hill into the woods, but with a sudden jolt, both legs and both arms shot straight out as I unexpectedly fell off a cliff.

I thought maybe it was time to get up and go to work, but the clock said it was only 3:55 a.m. I sighed and stared at the ceiling to ponder the impending sense of dread I couldn't place, but which had been bothering me all weekend.

28

Three Sides to a Page

I believe we are three parts: spirit, mind, and body, and that in order to make something real, one must engage all three parts. In a perfect world, I'd have used spirit to know what I'd been through was wrong. I'd have used mind to know I was not at fault, and I'd have used body to yell at my parents until they saw the truth. That's a healthy response to an attack: know it, understand it, yell at it.

But I could do no such thing. My family and their church had been blessed with full access to my body, mind, and spirit since birth and used that access to shame the fight right out of me. This is where too many anti-bullying campaigns fall short. People who, from birth, have been convinced at the cellular level that they are not worthy to stand up for themselves can't "just stand up" to bullies.

So without properly storming my parents' bedroom, my body, instead, needed to find another way to enter into the activities of what was torturing my spirit and brain. Expressive people like me feel more stable once our thoughts are made real on paper, canvas, film, or sheet music. Perhaps this is why so many talented artists are also tortured souls. They've learned the same trick.

By Kyle Rickett

"I'm so stupid. I hate this." I got up, shuffled quietly to my writing desk, and carefully draped a handkerchief over my small brown metal desk lamp. Having been born with over-active sinuses that kept me stuffy all winter and hay-feverish all summer, I always had an abundant supply of handkerchiefs on hand, and always at least one in a pocket. Once the white cotton shroud was in place over the lamp, *then* I turned it on. The handkerchief shroud was another secret I had to keep after a time when my brother Daniel had tattled on me by asking my parents why I was still up on a school night. From then on, it was me against the darkness and the handkerchief-of-secrecy was my standard operating procedure.

I silently tore a page from my school notebook and delicately fished a pencil from the drawer. I was bursting with the need to express myself somehow. Maybe I could write a poem or a diary entry. I stared at the page for a few minutes, whisper-humming one of Mom's favorite songs from *The Sound of Music*. She had a smooth, pleasant, melodic voice. I used to practice alone, hoping that one day I could sing them at least as well as her. Tonight's tune was "My Favorite Things."

"Yesss!" I got an idea. My back arched and my tongue pushed through the corner of my mouth. "I'm a genius." What were a few of *my* favorite things? I drew a line down the center of the page, dividing it in two. Atop the left column, I wrote: *Why I love my home*, and on the right side: *Why I love my school*. I was going to force myself to think positive thoughts because I was *miserable* being *miserable*. I wiggled my head side to side, and as I quietly sang the words, the pencil became a maestro's wand. This would definitely make the bad thoughts stop dripping poison out of my brain into my bloodstream. It *had* to. Writing about the joy in life would make me feel comical again. I was so sure of it that I giggled.

"This is going to work," I whispered.

The first entry on the list of reasons I loved home was *It's not school*. I commented out loud, "That's for sure." After that I wrote, *I have my own room*. Then, *My parents don't know what I am at school*. Then, *I am safe from bad kids*. Then, *My bed is comfortable*. And finally, *I have a bike*. The word *bike* reminded me of the one favorite thing I most loved about home. I smiled and wrote in enormous letters *CONNOR!!!!!!*

"Connor's so cool," I said. And then I underlined my buddy's name so many times it left no room for more words.

I set the pencil down and leaned back. Two fingers gently rubbed my wrist as I enjoyed knowing that Connor cared about me as more than a simple bicycle-buddy. His heart was so much bigger than I had ever before considered. And he was *my* friend. I looked at my scar and then back at the paper. Staring at the blank half, I asked, "What can I write about school?" I tried to find something good, but it burned my stomach. It repulsed me even to think about liking *anything* at school.

I looked at Connor's name. My best friend in the home column. I'd once had a best friend at school too. The truth is that I had felt closer to Andreo than I ever had to Connor, who'd inherited the number one position as lifetime best friend after Andreo pulled out through the unexplained slap during the fifth grade.

I still didn't understand what had happened on that normal school morning. I remembered excitedly greeting him and then getting slapped across the face with no explanation. He had then launched a shit pot full of rumors that spread across the school like wildfire. The mysterious slap had happened three-and-a-half years before this night, and Andreo was *still* attacking. The whole school had now hated me for nearly all of my adolescent life. Andreo had never explained what I had done to deserve it. Because of him, I had no friends at school. Not even one. But *why*? It was the *not knowing* that constantly drove me crazy.

Blind hatred

My body wasn't getting the relief it wanted. I leaned forward with anger in my gut, grabbed the pencil, and crossed out the word *love* and wrote over it *Why I hate school!!!!!* Then I wrote *ANDREO*. The muscles in my fingers tightened and shivered. I wrote it again, and again, and again. Once I'd used up the right column, I then used the space between the lines and wrote *Homo* beneath each spelling of my former friend.

I still didn't know what the word meant. (*I know this sounds strange: How could a teen not know what that word meant? But remember; my brain had been split into fragments. Total denial around sex and sexuality gripped me. The word was connected to parts of my brain that I'd purposely put to sleep. The word was now a sound that had no meaning*). I hated it, though, because from the moment I was pinned with it, I became an outcast from the girls and boys both, and no matter how hard I tried, I was never again able to feel safe there. Near as I could figure, the name had something to do with the fact that I was small, emotional, and couldn't catch a ball—another unfair attribute of being me. Because of my woodcutting, I had probably become the strongest boy in the entire class, but not having a competitive spirit and being unable to catch a ball, made me appear weak on the playground. My girlish sparkling blue eyes and that damned white hair played a part in it too. They also called me "Alby," short for "albino." Those were the things used as proof for three years running that I was a "homo." Therefore, I must have earned the name. Right? I may not have known what it meant, but I sure took a lot of punishment for it—and I *hated* it.

Bold, black borders

I found a black felt-tip marker in the drawer, uncapped it, and bolded the line between home and school. I made sure the line went all the way off the paper top and bottom so there could be no way the two worlds could sneak past it and see into each other's territory. I was drawing the wall between the home and the school columns that I knew was needed for survival.

My home and school lives were just as divided, and thank God for that. Today, kids who suffer the same kind of mob-style treatment can't always escape, due to modern social media. But in 1974, with the exception of the family phone, I had the luxury of being out of touch when out of school. My bold line represented the wall between the two worlds—and I needed the two worlds not to know about each other. Whatever it was that Andreo knew about me had destroyed my social life completely—*but only at school.*

Even so, I lived in constant fear that one day, whatever it was that Andreo knew, might sneak past the wall into my home life and I would become "Homo" here too. It was my life's mission to protect the secret identity I had at St. Tiberius Catholic Academy so that my parents, friends, brother, and sister wouldn't jump on that bandwagon also. Even on a normal day, it took a bit of effort to keep them proud of me. My good standing with them seemed delicate.

I once forgot to mow the lawn on the day they'd expected me to, and instead of reminding me, Dad got mad and mowed it for me—then didn't talk to me for the rest of the night. Whenever I'd fallen from grace, my punishment was to be ignored by family. As I've mentioned before, I was born to be a social butterfly and raised to be isolated. During each punishment, my stomach burst into flames and my heart smoldered painfully until they'd start talking to me again. I often wished they'd yell and hit me and get it over with. Ignoring me was a hell I couldn't bear. Imagine the shame of finding out their son was a homo. Whatever the word meant, it seemed to be something I was born with, meaning they'd never stop ignoring me. I'd never not be whatever it was. They'd ignore me to death. I'd never recover. This secret had a messy, sloppy, thick core, but a thin shell that must never crack. The pressure to keep it protected gnawed at me twenty-four hours a day.

Oh my gosh! There's a third side to this page!

Thinking I was finished, I folded the page along the bold line. Now it had *Home* on one side, and *School* was face-down.

"Genius," I muttered with another self-assured smile. The two couldn't be seen at the same time. I wrote *Kyle* at the top of the home side. This was a cool trick.

"Heh-heh-hehhhh!" I chortled like a mad mastermind-scientist-inventor. But as I studied the page, I discovered yet another angle.

"Oooh," I squinted, "look at this." Neither side could now see what was hiding inside the fold. "Hmm." I carefully peeked into it like a book, but when I opened it, my bruised face and raw penis both hurt.

"That was weird." Anger swelled. "Oh *shhhhit*...I know what's hiding in there." I picked up the pencil, and with a numbing, quaking hand, I wrote inside the blank fold *Santa's favorite boy*. Then I added *Jack*, and then for some unknown reason, I wrote *death*. I closed it fast. A short, painful burst of acid climbed up my throat. My shoulders shivered from a chill. I belched.

Leaving it folded, I flipped it back and forth so I could only see the home *or* school sides. I did this for a few moments, trying to forget the Santa side hiding within this single sheet of paper.

Not *one* of these worlds could see the other two. All three were real. All three were happening at the same time and occupying the same space, but they *couldn't see each other*. Such a relief.

I belched again as my stomach calmed as quickly as it had erupted. I used tape to seal the edges. It worked. I smiled with relief. Then, silliness came along, and like a bored child, I fidgeted with the tape dispenser, tearing off a little piece for each fingertip, and one for a strip across my lips. Muffled through the tape, I sang the final verse again "...and then I don't feeeeeeel...so bad."

I stared at the repeated name *Andreo*. My thoughts moved to survival. The tape across my lips broke loose when I prayed quietly, "Oh, God, please don't let Andreo find out what happened at the clinic." My gut hurt again from terror. My world had fallen apart before. It could do it again. The shell really *could* break and my private embarrassment could be spread across the schoolyard like mustard on a sandwich. It was a fact that Andreo could, and would, twist any truth into an insult and then bully the rest of the class into helping slap me with it. I flipped the page back over and saw the home side, realizing, in an instant, that Andreo wasn't my only problem.

"Shit," I whispered. "Fran's exactly like him. Dear God, pu-leeese don't ever let Andreo *or* Fran *ever* find out!"

I wished this paper I was holding was a fiction novel, but it wasn't. It was my real life that looked like fiction. "It even has villains!" I said.

Of Fran

"Why do both of my worlds have to have a villain?" I asked aloud. For the first time, I realized that Fran was the Andreo on the *Home* side of the paper. I flipped the page a few more times.

"I love my sister, but she can be so much like Andreo. I have a Fran *and* an Andreo. I have a *Frandreo*." I giggled at my clever name-blending. If my life really were a series of fiction stories, then all three of mine—*Kyle*, *Homo*, and *Santa's Favorite Boy*—had the same evil character in them, but played by different actors. Krieg was a little different. He did more icky stuff to me, but if Fran and Andreo were to find out what he'd done, they'd tell everyone. They were the voices—no, the *megaphones*—of evil, as far as I was concerned.

Fran and Andreo both laughed often and loud, but their laughter seemed to be more of a weapon than joy. They both seemed good at gaining support from the people around them—who were the people around me. Because of the amount of damage they could do, how were these two better than the pedophile Krieg? Right? My misery would be unbearable no matter which of those three attacked next. But since Krieg usually kept his abuse secret, Fran and Andreo were way more dangerous.

Fran was twenty-eight. Even though she was on her second husband, Bob, and fourth job, she hadn't gone far from home. She remained a constant entangled force in my home life. In fact, some of her gossipy customers were my friends' moms, so her tentacles reached wide and deep into my social life.

She would sometimes invite me to stay overnight on her couch when Bob was out of town on business, which I thought was fun—eating pizza with my nieces and drinking all the pop I could down. The next morning, I'd show my appreciation by cooking chocolate chip pancakes for her girls, earning the honor of being named their "favorite uncle." But then, feeling like I should pay for my fun night, I'd scrub the kitchen and bathroom for her while she slept in. What I hadn't noticed during childhood was that the sleepovers were almost always timed only to a day or two before Bob was scheduled to come back to a clean house.

As a general rule, I knew to behave myself so she'd give good reports to Mom, or I'd hear about it from both of them. She'd talk on the phone with all my aunts too, but she was almost never honest with her gossip about anyone. It seemed like she would report something that really happened, but change the details ever so slightly so she could assign her own meaning to the event. A neighbor lady once asked me why I rode such a big bicycle, and before I could tell her it was because I felt connected to my brother, she accused me of doing it only to be a rebel with the other kids who rode spyder bikes. Coincidentally, Fran had accused me of that very same thing only three days prior, once again leaving me to feel like I'd naïvely ridden into a meaningless snare. Those insignificant communication traps happened a lot. Even though the neighbor's opinion of my bicycle didn't matter, the mere ambush itself taught me not to trust what the people of Torano Island thought of me because of what they'd been hearing behind my back. The whole island was a team. An "alliance of bullies." I was alone.

Fran could turn on the charm, and laugh and make friends quickly, so people listened to her. They had no reason not to. After all, why would she lie about something so insignificant as my choice of bicycles—*right*? Well she *did* lie about it, and they *did* believe her. So I'd best *never* trust *anyone* with my *real* secrets. I knew I was alone with the truth.

With a heavy sigh, I flipped the paper back and forth again. The phenomenon of these three separated worlds was true for now. Fran didn't know Andreo so I was safe for as long as I kept those three worlds from seeing each other.

"I love Fran. I love Fran. I love Fran," I chanted.

I kept a roll of antacids in the top desk drawer. I popped one in my mouth and crunched it quietly. I flipped the page back and forth a few more times, knowing that as long as *Santa's Favorite Boy*, *Home Kyle* and *School Kyle* couldn't see each other, I could keep ignoring problems within my evenings, weekends, and summers.

"Everyone always believes Dr. Krieg," I mumbled. "Everyone always believes Fran. The whole school believes Andreo." I sighed. "No one ever believes *me*."

If word of what had happened at the clinic got out, my three worlds would crash together. Krieg would lie and be believed, and Frandreo would make sure everyone on the whole island knew I had seduced him with my stupid sparkling eyes. I'd have no choice but to kill myself then.

Of God

A villain was built into each of my lives, but so was God—*or was he*? Why would an all-powerful being be in one life but not in the other two? Maybe he wasn't an all-powerful being. Maybe he didn't even exist in any of the three lives. I prayed often, as taught to by school, church, and parents, but it didn't change anything. Had God left me? Or had I simply stopped pretending he was ever with me? Either way, I didn't feel him in the room with me anymore. Each prayer that night sounded similar to those I'd prayed my whole life, but on this night, they had become hauntingly empty. In fact, hearing my voice beg him for miracles for the thousandth futile time irritated me now. My sense of normalcy around faith was leaving me for the first time ever. Krieg had almost literally blown my mind that day. He wouldn't stop. While I begged God to block him, or turn it all into a dream, Krieg's real hands kept going until I exploded. Nothing, not even the God of the Universe, was able to stop him. Was this monster more powerful than God? An even more important question: Was there a God at all?

I saw the uselessness of prayer. I finally began to understand that begging God to keep my secret from Fran and Andreo might actually *not* work. Prayer hadn't kept me safe from Krieg. How stupid of me to have kept praying all these years. I was on a prayer-treadmill, running after the carrot of hope, believing that the *next* prayer would be the one finally to reach God.

Kids I knew who didn't pray at all seemed to have a better grasp on self-confidence than I did. Maybe this failure to feel safe wasn't about a God. Maybe this was about me. I was no better off than a gambling addict, repeatedly believing in the next roll of the same dice.

The Catholics taught that God answered prayers, but why then did he never answer *mine*? From above the desk, I carefully lifted a handcrafted wooden crucifix off the wall. A plastic dead Jesus, painted gold, was nailed to it in traditional fashion. I rubbed the face and hair with a finger as I pondered its meaning. For the first time, the scales fell from my eyes and I saw it as a powerless trinket. At school, Andreo had uncovered some truth about me to prove I was unlovable to anyone in his reach. I feared that somehow this doctor's visit was going to leak across the home/school boundary and Andreo was going to turn this part-time humiliation into absolute despair—*whether I prayed for protection or not.*

I quietly placed the lifeless crucifix into the trash next to my desk.

Of the dangers of love

Andreo had once been my best friend. How could someone I loved so much do this to me? I looked toward the old men in the ceiling cracks.

"I thought you wanted us to love people. But no! I can't trust anyone. Can I, God…Huh? *Can* I?" The angry sarcasm of my ranting at God only agitated the frustration. "I guess I'm too fucking *stupid* to know who I can trust! Isn't that right?" The theatrical anger didn't help. My questions kept building, but no answers came from *anywhere*. Nothing I did to try and stop the cruelty worked, and between Andreo and Fran—whom I also loved—every goddamned day only brought more unprovoked abuse and more traps to walk into. What had caused this? How could loving people have returned this much hatred?

And now abide faith, hope, and—futility

Somehow or other, I was beginning to see the truth: I had to find the strength from within myself to fix my own problems. I just didn't know how to do that yet.

It became clear that if God wouldn't solve my problems, then I had to. I didn't have much power, but I had a pen.

"Mightier than the sword," I said. I used that felt-tip marker to cross out Andreo's name in big, bold, zig-zagging lines, each drawn with a burst of emotion. Soon the whole room smelled of marker ink.

I knew this solution wasn't real. Writing a name on paper, then crossing it out wasn't solving *anything*. And neither was praying to the supreme God of all the universe. Hmm, how were these two pointless acts of desperation similar? Neither was a *real* solution to a *real* problem.

I placed the cap back onto the marker, twisted around in my chair, and threw the pen onto my bed so I could have a final angry explosion, but, because I was still Kyle, I made sure to "explode" without marking anything, or making noise against something solid.

"This is so stupid!" I whispered hard. "Nothing ever works!"

Rage from the depths of hell

There on my desk sat the paper with the *School* side facing me. Then, from swelling rage, my hands clenched tightly. One fingernail punctured my palm, drawing blood. My teeth gritted down as they had done hundreds of times during the three years, but this time something inside me wanted to take action. I just didn't know how. The frustration nearly tore me in half. I shook as the fires stoked in my stomach and waves of hatred came up through the floor, possibly from hell itself. They roared through my body, building with heat as they scorched my heart, and then ripped through me, up my throat and out my tightly clenched mouth.

"*I hate you, Andreo Castro!*" resounded from a deep-throated whisper like Satan haunting a dark basement. My eyes then focused up and through the ceiling as I tried to aim the whispery curse all the way to God's ignorant ears. I pictured looking straight into God's scornful eyes and instructing him to send my enemy to hell.

"I *hate* him! I fucking *hate* him! *Why* won't you make him *leave me alone?*"

I sat and shook. Blood trickled along the wrist that Connor's concerned fingers had stroked earlier. I put my mouth over it. What would he think if he saw *this*? Funny little blond—half-pint-Kyle—that cute little shit who never slows down, was now licking blood from a self-inflicted wound, on that same, now shaking wrist. I glanced at the folded paper. This was real, but which Kyle was I now?

"Oh, my God," I whispered dramatically toward my bloody wrist. "I've never done that before." I wiped it off with a tissue and shuffled to the mirror by the door to glare at my white hair and pool blue eyes. "Why can't I look like everyone else?" I lifted my red, raw dick and curled my upper lip in disgust. "What the hell is happening to me? Who are these people? Who am *I?*" I licked again at the blood. It tasted of copper. I sat back down and put my forehead on the paper.

Tap-tap-tap—someone was at my door.

29

Revisiting Heaven

Tap Tap Tap. From 2,000 miles away, tapping woke Tuck...into a dream. But again, I can't prove any of our parallel lines were more than coincidence. If we were somehow connected, then he was the lucky one because I needed help while he was enjoying beautiful, peaceful walks in a place that had no stress.

By Tuck Taylor

I awoke into that dream I'd once had when I'd died for three minutes. Ever since, I've always called that peaceful location The Place Without Shadows. I didn't know how I got there, but for the first time in a while, all my problems were gone. The usual green grass became a cobblestone street and the trees became people. As I slowly moved through the crowded city, I first sensed that I knew my way around it. Then, I noticed my feet were not moving but hovering about six inches above the pavement. Nobody in the crowd was acknowledging me. It was as if I were a visitor they simply didn't notice. The place was alive but silent.

I stayed for a long time. Probably close to half an hour. All the while, I assumed I was being prepared to come back soon and stay. This time I was not blessed with any visitations from the dove or from any voices overhead, until the very end when a *tap-tap-tap* woke me up out of the dream. It took a few minutes for me to come to. It was 4:33 a.m. Texas time.

30

Not so Brotherly Alliance

Having been born looking different (small and white-haired) while having my defenses taken away by family meant that I was basically born and raised to be bully-bait. With the exception of Connor and Scooter, I never knew who was going to be on my side on any given day. When I originally decided it was time to write my story, a successful novelist warned me that a good novel has a simple plot and a single villain. But my life wasn't a novel. Nor was it simple. My villain(s) kept changing names and weren't easy for me to spot. My life was a turbulent tornado of multiple confusions. So that's what my novel is about. The complexity itself was my problem. This is what the Complex in Complex-PTSD is referring to.

Complex Posttraumatic Stress Disorder, in my own words, is the mess that is driven from a series of layered issues, none of which alone are so terrible, but together, and over time, weigh heavily, interact, and entangle into a complicated mess of realities that don't mix well.

Writing the three-sided page shocked me into realizing I'd been living a dual life, which is something that, on some level, everyone does. The art of living dual lives has always intrigued me. I'm not talking about the extreme stories of international spies living in normal neighborhoods. I'm more struck by the fact that most of us normal people aren't wholly known by anyone. At home, I was highly capable, comical, stronger than average, and made friends quickly, while in school, I cowered inside my head, mumbling only when spoken to while striving for invisibility. I never talked about school at home, or about home at school.

On any given day, I was funny and depressed both, and neither was an act. To make it worse, I wasn't living a double life, but I had suddenly become aware that I lived a triple. Who was I really? The cute little shit who never slows down and feels bad when he swears? The depressed "homo" who never stands up for himself? Or Krieg's favorite slutty blond, living in fear of being murdered by "forgetting to breath"? The freakiness of all this is that I'd lost complete touch with the middle ground where good and bad can coexist and negotiate. I was not balanced. Depending on location, I was exclusively only one of the three. An even scarier thought crossed my mind, that if I had been blind to the fact that I was living three lives, were there more? Could there be a fourth, or fifth one still hiding in my confused brain? I was losing my ability to trust what I knew to be true at the deepest level—my own mind.

Taking turns with each identity could only happen if each one didn't know about the other two. But holding that page in my bare hand, where I could see all three identities in one place, changed me. I couldn't hide two of them from my thoughts any longer. I was integrating them now, but without the help of a qualified mentor. Maybe this was the moment in my life that often claims the innocence of confused teens. The allure of defiantly going bad and feeling personal control by becoming untamable by others is difficult to resist when being good seems to have yielded no positive results.

The arching overview that I'd lost touch with didn't know how to handle this much diverse exposure. Fantasy was crashing and reality seemed too horrible to bear. I was terrified the secrets would explode in my face and kill me—or at least would kill one of me. Thanks to that paper, I could never again be as sure of what I thought was real as I had been up to that moment. Could I?

By Kyle Rickett

Three gentle taps came out of nowhere. I didn't know if they were real. Maybe it was the tree outside bumping the siding. I glanced at my clock: 2:33 a.m. I switched off the handkerchief-covered lamp and turned quietly in the chair to watch the space beneath the door. A shadow moved. Someone *was* there.

Oh, shit! I have to put things back how they were.

I purposely bumped my desk and noisily turned my light back on, but first, I removed the hanky so I could trick whoever it was into thinking he or she had gotten me out of bed. I kept the hanky wadded in my hand to hide the bloody puncture wound.

"God!" I whispered. "One more stupid secret!" I knew I could pretend allergies were making me keep the cloth in my palm.

I took a few more seconds to slide my important notebook and ink-soaked list into the drawer and to pull the crucifix from the trash and put it back on the wall. Was I a changed person or not? Obviously not. This was cute little *Home Kyle* attempting to normalize again. Dumping the crucifix was a bold new move by a different part of me altogether. All of a sudden, it was much too bold.

"I didn't do nuthin'," I quietly joked as I opened the door. I had no pants on, so, like my old self, I screened my lower half behind the door and cranked my head around it.

"Daniel."

"Did I get you up?"

"Yeah…" I lied. "But I wasn't really sleeping. Just laying here." I scanned downward. He was fully dressed, all the way down to his cowboy boots. "When did you get home?"

"I rolled in about dinner time. I'm going to do some local runs for a few weeks before I leave again. You were out cold when I got in. Now I can't sleep."

"Like me I guess." I looked down at my own bare legs. The new Kyle washed over me. I smirked and invited him in, and in a surprisingly new change of values, I dropped my guard to let my fully dressed brother gaze all he wanted to at my naked ass as I shuffled back to my desk. It was exciting to me, but in a non-sexual way. I felt liberated. "It hurts to stand," I said, sitting down.

"Can I see your stitches?" He closed the door quietly and followed me to my chair, limping slightly from his childhood injury. Daniel was now twenty-five years old and a truck driver who'd recently moved back home, but he only occupied his room on the days when he was in town, which, when added together, totaled to probably a week out of every month. Except for facial hair and twelve years of age difference, we looked alike, both with protruding cheek bones and dimples, but he was tall and gauntly thin. His once yellowy-blond hair was now medium brown, and like most truckers in those days, a large cap covered most of it while tinted eyeglasses and a scruffy reddish-brown mustache hid his lonely, now skeletally thin face from the world.

"Shit, kid. How many are there?" He took off his glasses and cap while leaning forward. I was surprisingly okay with him looking into my spread legs. Something had definitely changed me that day. My "dirty parts" were public property now. I casually held my scrotum out of the way for him, feeling no more embarrassment than if I were showing him the inside of a sandwich.

"Thirty-six."

"Man, I can't get over how white your hair is. Even down there."

I gasped. My eyes widened for a brief second. Daniel was from the wrong world—the wrong side of the paper—to be referencing Krieg's favorite part of me. I closed my legs quickly and then put my hands over my pubic hair, half-pretending to rest them casually in my lap.

"What?" he asked. "C'mon, Kyle; I used to give you baths, for God's sake. What the hell'd you show it to me for if you think I'm a perv?"

"I'm sorry," I mumbled. "It's just...." My right foot started quaking nervously, an involuntary action that often got me yelled at.

He pulled away to sit on the foot of the bed about three feet from me. The sweet aroma of a freshly finished joint wafted from his thick mop of uncombed hat-hair.

"It's just—"

"Don't stress over it, man." Daniel liked to present himself as a laid back dude who never let anything offend him. Like a hippy, he wanted to believe he was always the neutral party, there to live and let live. Pacifistically to accept people for who they were.

"Okay." I smiled shyly at being let off the hook.

"Mom said you had a pretty rough day." He squirmed, reached beneath himself, and presented the black marker I'd thrown earlier.

Evidence of a core change

"A really fucked-up day," I said as my eyes bulged again. A missed detail. I'd hung the crucifix and hidden the paperwork, but I'd missed the thrown marker. I was getting sloppy. I pictured myself in a witness stand, being accused by the prosecutor of illegally documenting my secret lives, and breaking the laws set by my authorities who'd clearly told me to keep *their* secret sins to *myself.* Faking innocence, I casually reached to receive the evidence. I shrugged as if I didn't know why it was on the bed.

The whole marker handoff incident took up only five seconds of clock-time and meant absolutely nothing to Daniel, but it served to teach me a powerful lesson about a decision I needed to make. Do I stand boldly and embody my three-sided life? Or do I focus harder on not leaving any shreds of evidence that I'm secretly falling apart at the seams? I obviously couldn't go on playing like I was standing up for myself *unless I was ready to do it for real.*

"She said Connor knocked you down."

"Oh, fuck!" I rolled my eyes and raised my voice slightly. That was a word I wouldn't normally say, but hearing Daniel tell me that Mom went after my best friend, the anger hit me hard enough to shock that word right out of my mouth. "That's *not* how it happened!"

"Whoa, little brother. I'm on your side here." He jokingly put up two blocking hands.

"I keep telling her we crashed *together*!"

"Shh-shh-shh." He put a finger to his mouth.

"We crashed together," I whispered.

"Not how she tells it." He shot me an inquisitively raised brow, "and when did you start using the 'f' word?"

"She wasn't there." I ignored his question, but with a boastful smirk.

"I know. But that's her story…and she's sticking to it." He smirked back like he was proud of me.

"What's so funny?" I laughed quietly under my breath.

"Them's pretty grown-up words there, kiddo." He jokingly tapped my shoulder, then ran his eyes down and back up my frame. "But you're still a cute little fucker." He playfully pinched my cheek and I chuckled.

Brotherly advice

"Daniel?" I was being drawn in. I was letting out swear words and sitting half-nude, but as vulnerable as I was, he was acting proud of me. The twelve years between us started to shrink as I began feeling warmth toward him, like when he'd tickle me as a kid. "Why does she hate my friends? I'm nice to hers. Why can't she like mine?"

"Oh, I don't know. She wasn't friendly to mine either." He looked around the room as if he'd never seen it before. "It's like she thinks neighbor kids are her responsibility when they're in her house."

"She hated your friends too?"

"She didn't 'hate' them. But, yeah, it was no different for me. I never could bring my buddies over."

"Me neither." Oh, my God—*more bonding*! My brother and I shared a common enemy.

"And girlfriends?" He waved. "No way. I never brought any of my girlfriends by." He tapped my knee and then pointed into my face. "You shouldn't either."

"But…" I challenged, "you've never *had* a girlfriend."

"I never *brought one by*." He raised a brow.

"You had a girlfriend? And we *never knew*?"

He held up four fingers.

"*Four*?" I slacked my jaw in surprise.

"Almost married one. Mom couldn't know, or she'd make sure and ruin it for me."

"How?"

"I don't know for sure. But I promise you, she'd have done *something* to make them go away and never come back."

"Where are they now?"

He chuckled.

"What?" I asked with another smirk.

"They went away…and never came back." He laughed.

I laughed with him.

"Here's the sick part…. Most of them left because they thought I was too controlled by my mom." He poked at me once. "So look at that—she ruined it anyway."

"God, I never knew any of that."

"Yeah." He glared inquisitively at my first ever use of God as a swear word. "Fran knew."

More sudden shifts in alliances

"She did?" Bam! Again I was the outsider. Fran knowing his secret restored the twelve years between us. I was the dumb little kid while he and Fran were soulmates. Excluding me from his secret meant he didn't trust me—like I was part of Mom's play to ruin his life. Another unfair shifted alliance. I'd have never taken Mom's side.

Or would I have? The family theme—which seemed common in other Catholic families we knew—was to band against anyone who threatened to upset the status quo, and sometimes, I got caught up in it too. Sometimes I didn't even know I was caught up in it. Or I wasn't on her side, but I didn't know that he *thought* I was.

"In this fucked-up house, she was my only supporter." He quieted to a serious tone. "Why do you think I was invisible my whole life?"

"You sure didn't hang around here much." I broke eye contact and looked down at our knees a few inches apart. "Still don't."

A wave of sadness reminded me of how often I'd tried finding ways to connect with him, by doing things like wearing his shirts, riding his bicycle, and wishing I'd have been part of his childhood.

"If I wanted friends, I had to go to them," he said, interrupting my thought.

"Then why did you move back home if you can't bring your friends here?"

"Dad talked me into it."

"He *did*?" In shock, I looked back up into his face. Dad was always bitching about having to take care of too many people. Why would he talk Daniel into coming home?

"Yeah. He said it was stupid to pay rent on an apartment when I basically live on the road."

"*Dad* said that?"

"Yeah." Daniel appeared surprised at my shock. "It makes sense...don't you think?"

Not to me it didn't. "Are you glad you moved back?" I was still taken aback at Dad's two-faced message, but there was no point in telling Daniel that Dad talked shit about him behind his back. What exactly did our dad expect of us? Did he want us *out* or *in* after we grew up?

"What's the difference?" Daniel, who obviously didn't know Dad talked like this behind his back, naïvely went on with his story. "I might as well live here. I don't have a ton of friends to bring to my own place anyway."

Anger started to creep in. One of them was lying to me, but I wasn't sure which. Dad was always making snide remarks that Mom had to defend, about having his grown son mooching off him in the back bedroom. Was Daniel lying? Was Dad two-faced? Was this whole family just fucking crazy? I needed to let this go. As shocking as Dad's comments were, the fact that my family members talked out of both sides of their mouths was something I had to stop pretending I didn't see. There was no point in pursuing an answer at that moment, so I returned to the original conversation about my friends.

"What about Fran?" I asked.

Whose side is Fran on?

"What about her?" he defended.

"Why doesn't she like any of my friends either?"

"Don't worry about Fran, Kyle. Just give her some space."

"Why?" Unexpected anger surfaced again. "She never gives *me* any! She hates my friends. She's been calling Connor stupid ever since he moved here, and she's never even talked to him. It's probably why Mom says the accident was his fault. Fran's convinced her he's an idiot. She says crap like that about me too. She says I'm awkward and I need extra care. And even Jayne looks at me like I'm a freak now."

"Oh, be the man." He flicked my shoulder with a finger. Apparently, he thought I was joking some more. "Grow some hair on your balls for God's sake. She's your *sister*."

"I grew that already." I couldn't believe I'd blurted that out, but I was pissed. Growing ball-hair was one of his favorite tough-trucker insults, and after having heard him use it about a thousand times on other people, it was out of character for me even to address it. Normally, I'd ignore him and pray to God to forgive him for talking dirty. But this time, I had answered it—and with an off-color comment of my own. It was liberating not to hold back. But the sensations of liberation brought with them a taller wave of anger. Why the hell did he think a smaller-than-average, thirteen-year-old boy was supposed to be the one defending an adult woman just because she was *technically* my sister?

Daniel's eyes flickered toward my crotch.

"See? Ball hair. And it's white!" I became overwhelmed with a bizarre new need to shock him. "I'm a cute little fucker, aren't I?" The vulgarity exploded. "It's going to make me a big star someday!" Rage was shutting down my filters as I skirted dangerous boundaries between my home life and being Dr. Krieg's favorite boy.

His brow furled like he was confused by the bizarre comment.

"Wanna take a *picture*?" Even angrier, I opened my palms and sarcastically framed my pubic hair. Then I jostled my hips so all the flesh would wiggle left to right. As frightening as this moment was to Home-Kyle, the defiance empowered Santa's favorite boy. After what Krieg had done *to* me, I felt an intoxicating sense of control at *choosing* to expose my dirty parts on *my* terms. If you can't beat 'em, join 'em, right?

"Gross, Kyle." He rolled his reddened, glossy eyes and leaned back with a blocking hand gesture between his line of sight and my crotch. "It's an expression. She's trying to help."

"Bullshit." My lips loosened even more. "She's a bitch." I was on a roll. Empowered anger was loosening Santa's favorite elf to say things cute little Kyle had previously only thought.

"Kyle, I mean it—you're too young to understand. She's our sister. Brothers take care of their sisters. Don't call her names. She's had a hard life."

"Oh, she has *not*."

"Yes, she has." I could hear a rage building in his voice. As I've mentioned before, Daniel *liked to present himself* as an amiable pacifist, but I'm here to tell you, right now, that when Daniel Rickett's personal opinions were challenged, he could lose control pretty goddamned fast.

"What makes her life harder than yours or mine?" I asked more timidly in order to try to keep him calm. I wanted to learn what I could about his and Fran's relationship, but not at the expense of a shouting match. What he'd said so far didn't make sense—that brothers stand up for sisters—when it seemed to me that *adults* should stand up for *kids*. The two of them were nearly equal siblings in age, and then more than a decade had passed before I was born. I knew they were bonded. I was the family's child who'd almost killed Mom simply by being born— another fact Fran occasionally enjoyed reminding me of. I'd never changed their diapers, but they'd changed mine. This was an unequal match. They were not siblings to me; they were elders. Because of that, there were never any *fair* Rickett fights. I was tiny comparably, but if I so much as disagreed with one of them, even in my childhood, they'd gang up and aggressively retaliate as if I were a formidable enemy who'd *attacked* both. They were not safe people to be related to.

Poor, poor Fran

"She's told me some things." He simmered down to sound sympathetic to his abused sibling. "Mom and Dad have been pretty rough on her. She didn't want to be a hairdresser. But because she's a girl, Dad wouldn't pay for any other kind of school."

His words hit me hard. Fran always had a reason why her problems were someone else's fault. What I knew about all three of us kids was that Dad and Mom gave far more attention to Fran than to both of us boys put together, *and* that they disrespected all three of our career choices.

"She wanted to be a lawyer, right?" I thought I'd try to trick some sense into him.

"That's what she's always said."

"And you wanted to be a trucker?" Zing! I knew he hated the fact that Dad had pushed him into trucking, but I was hoping he'd see the foolishness of buying into Fran's accusation that she was the only victim of family control.

"Hell, no. I wanted to start a business. Be my own boss. But Dad told me to stop dreaming and get a job like a man. He'd only pay for trade school so I could learn a job. College was for sissies trying to milk their old man for four more years of childhood."

"He says that to me too."

One would think that I had now won this argument. But Daniel wasn't emotionally evolved enough to hear his own words. Within only two sentences, I'd gotten him to tell me that Fran was worse off than us because Dad had unfairly stopped her from being who she wanted to be, and then with his next breath, I got him to state that Dad had also stopped *him* from being who *he* wanted to be. Maybe he'd smoked too much pot, but Daniel could not bridge his own two sentences.

I'd learned the hard way that if reasoning with him didn't work on the first try, pushing the argument would only piss him off. He'd increase his defenses and drive further into blindness. Fran had him by his own ball-hair and he couldn't see it. He never seemed able to see through Fran's chronically twisted logic. He was either too protective of her, or too afraid. Either way, if she were playing the role of the wicked witch, he'd have been her obedient flying monkey boy.

It was time to stand down. I knew from experience that this conversation was about to go into circular rounds. It would get crazier by the sentence until he'd fall back on his advantages of age and authority to make me shut the hell up. So I forewent the pain and conceded early, kept quiet, and avoided being told to. Essentially, I sensed danger and used my skills of escape: *I changed the subject.*

Another new thing

"Can I get stoned with you some night?" I blurted out without thinking. Little demons had taken over my mouth. I was swearing, exposing my dirty parts, asking for pot. I was going to be in jail by morning if I didn't gain control of myself.

His eyes lit in shock.

"Well?" I boldly demanded.

"I...I guess. Sure. Uhmmm…wanna do it now?"

"No!" I retorted. I hadn't expected him to call my bluff.

"Okay, well…tell me when."

"Daniel?" His invitation to tell him *when* felt like bonding. It shouldn't have. I knew him well enough that I shouldn't have trusted him even then. But I wanted an ally so badly that I blinded myself into believing he was my friend. I became myself again, "Why didn't you have to go to Catholic school?"

"I don't know." The distractions had worked and he'd calmed down. "We were in Minnesota when I started kindergarten. We moved a lot. Maybe it wasn't convenient. And I don't believe in God anyway."

"What about Fran? She believes." I rolled my eyes at my own words.

Whatever Fran believed in, it was at her own convenience. Fran was a devout Catholic but not much of a Christian. During that summer of 1974, she volunteered in the church second-hand store every Saturday, but she seldom went to Sunday Mass. None of her charity was out of kindness. No one will ever know her true reason for volunteering, but I assume she was trying to prove she was "good" to someone somewhere. Also, she had authority at the church store and loved every second of it. Her public dedication that short summer bolstered her power over others. Righteousness must have given her influence over the other volunteers, whom she often referred to as her sheep. But then again, maybe she was just there to steal office supplies, for crying out loud.

Her daughters were both in catechism, and if she hadn't been so bad with money, she'd have put them in Catholic school, too. Mom had refused on several occasions to pay for it, which Fran had then labeled as more unfair abuse of her and her precious daughters. Thank God Mom held to her guns on that demand. I was closer in age to Jayne than I was to Fran, which was dangerous. If my own niece had attended the same school where I fought for my life each day, my secret shame would have been leaked to Fran to do with as she pleased for sure.

I'm not who you see

"Fran can believe whatever she wants to believe."

"I hate it, Daniel. I *hate* Catholic school."

He shrugged.

I shrugged back sarcastically.

"Kyle, I didn't think you hated anything. You're such a happy kid. A freaking comedian."

"Not when I'm at school."

"Why don't you ask Mom to let you out?"

"Oh, fuck you!" Another angry outburst I hadn't meant to launch.

"What?" He appeared genuinely shocked. "Who the hell are you, and what have you done with my cute little brother?"

"I've asked her a million times. I've begged."

"What'd she say?"

"She said that whatever's happening to me there, it will be worse anywhere else. She thinks the Church is safe."

"Isn't it? What happens to you there that's so bad?"

The hairy man in the dark clothes flashed in my head. Who was he, and why did he appear when the Church was brought up?

"Kyle, you okay?"

"They hate me; that's all." I shook the vision out of my head. The statement felt too close for comfort. I cinched my lips and didn't say any more. I'd accidentally asked him for pot and then dropped the f-bomb. I needed to zip up before I gave up to him and his teammates my life-or-death secret nickname, Homo.

"Huh." Daniel was stoned enough that after a pause, it appeared he'd forgotten what we had been talking about. So I ended the Catholic school conversation before divulging too much.

Do you know Jack?

"Daniel?"

"Yeah?"

"Do you remember Jack? Do you remember when he disappeared?"

"Vaguely." He pinched his nose and rubbed his eyes. "What made you think of *him* all of a sudden?"

"I think about him a lot. I always want to know where he went. And if he's okay."

"I'm sure he's fine," he said.

"Why? Why are you sure he's fine?"

"Why wouldn't he be? Kids run away. He had no dad."

"But no one ever found out where he went." I gathered my strength. "What if someone killed him?"

He laughed quietly.

"What? People get killed."

"On TV maybe."

"Oh." I quieted down. It did sound kind of theatrical to suggest that an actual murder could happen in real life.

"The only thing we know for sure is that he left. Kids do that sometimes."

I noticed he was still looking in the general direction of my stitches. My face warmed and I asked the question I needed the most help with.

"Daniel? Has Dr. Krieg ever touched your…" I took a long breath and jumped into the deep end "your dick?"

"No-ho-ho," he laughingly responded. "What do you think I am? A homo?"

I felt sick at his comment.

"Oh." He looked at my scar. "I didn't mean…that you…" His head jerked upward about a quarter of an inch. Then, after a short pause, he reasoned, "But then I've never had to have stitches in my balls either. I supposed he had to touch you, right?" Then he laughed like a supportive big brother and tapped my arm twice. "That thing of yours is getting kind of big. He probably had to hold it back. You stud, you."

I guess I deserved that. I'm the one who'd wiggled it in front of him. And if this were a different day, I would have laughed. But my face was still warm, and now my heart was pounding harder.

"He did more than hold it back."

"What do you mean?"

It was great that Daniel was letting me confess, but I could tell he was fighting to stay with me. I kind of knew I should clam up, but I wanted his help so badly that I couldn't stop myself. His face showed that the pot was obviously settling nicely, and my own mind briefly wandered to sneaking into his room and stealing some of it. I snapped back on track. This could be a once-in-a-lifetime opportunity for help, so I needed to talk it out before he collapsed.

"He made me get a boner."

"Oh, wow. Oh, shit."

"I think he did it twice."

"You think?"

"Things got hazy."

"I wonder if that's why Mom said you had a *hard day*."

"Not funny, Daniel!" I felt stabbed at. A cold sweat coated my forehead. Fear returned. I was vulnerable now that he knew.

"Did she see him do it?"

"She saw the first one—the fucker did it right in front of her and she didn't do *anything* to stop him." Unwelcome anger came from nowhere. I stuffed it back down and calmly continued. "She was gone when he did it again."

Daniel's eyes focused, then broke away, then focused again.

My breath went sour. My heart throbbed. The next words weighed a pound each as I forced them up and out.

"He told me to keep my legs spread apart...so I did. He told me to be good. So I was."

"Did he threaten you?"

"He made me feel like I owed it to him to be good." I swallowed hard. "Then his hand made me go...all the way...all over myself."

Daniel stared. Was he going to make me say it?

"You know..." I paused in case he would indicate he knew what I was saying, "he made me...ejaculate." I used the word as Dr. Krieg himself had taught us in school.

"And you just...*let him*?" He looked at my legs like he was expecting to see it was still on me.

"I didn't just *let* him!" Oh, God. He was putting me on the defensive. "He *told* me to be good. He's Dad's friend."

"So what? He's not *your* friend."

"But...Dad...I have to be nice...." Confusion completely overwhelmed me. My brain started unraveling. Almost in tears, I pointed to my mouth with a quivering finger. "I have bruises from his other hand."

"Kyle, those bruises look a little small to be from his big hand."

"Well...." Confusion was tearing me in half "Well...I mean from my own hand. But because he...made me...."

"You bruised yourself with your *own* hand?"

"Well...yeah...but...no...not because I wanted to...."

The room hushed with a terrible, frightening pause. My shoulders tensed. I'd gone too far. He was accusing me of letting it happen. I was starting to accuse myself now...I think. I could never take any of it back. Was he about to explode on me for my accusation?

"That sounds wrong," he mumbled, squeezing his nose.

Voices screamed through my stressed mind. *That sounds wrong?* What the hell did *that* mean? My confession had already taken me too far out of my comfort zone to be able to handle any challenges. Were those words saying that my accusation was wrong? Or was Daniel agreeing with me that Dr. Krieg's *actions* were wrong? With this family, it could go either way—but usually it defaulted to treating me like I was too stupid to know what I was saying. Suddenly, the whole story felt like a lie even to me. Maybe I *was* guilty. People in 1974 didn't comprehend that boys could be sexual targets. The story I'd told Daniel was too strange for anyone to believe back then. I was too terrified now to find out what Daniel's words meant. I felt like a hot knife had been shoved into the top of my stomach. I groaned and wrinkled the cloth of my pajama top with both hands.

Oh, my God. What had I done? I suddenly wanted everything to go quiet and for everyone to forget anything said. Meanwhile, Daniel had started to fade off. After a minute or two of dead silence, he got up, wobbled slightly, and squeezed my shoulder.

"I think I'd better hit the hay." He stumbled to the door, and as he slid through, glanced over and said, "Good talk, kid." He closed the door and vanished into the night.

I sat, frozen in disbelief of all that had happened. I retraced the conversation, regretfully asking myself what I'd said and what I should have kept quiet. Daniel was Fran's brother, not mine, and all the miles I put on his bike wanting to be his sidekick didn't change that alliance. Thankfully, only the marker was found. The three-sided page was still mine to protect.

Alone again with my memories

"Fucking truck drivers," I whispered. "I should'a kept my *fucking* mouth shut. Hopefully, he'll forget everything...*stupid stoner!*" I pulled my precious paperwork from the drawer and slowly, quietly tore the list in half, then in half again, and then again, eventually transforming it into confetti. "I swear to God, I'll never talk about this *again!*"

I had a routine of protecting sacred privacy by shredding my writings, letters to God, diary pages, poems, and stories. When I'd shredded this night's evidence of my home life plus my two secret identities, I then shuffled across the room to stuff it into my socks. My routine was then to wear the socks out of the house the next day, find myself a private hiding spot, usually deep in the blackberry thicket, dump the contents, and dispose of them in some way that wouldn't be traced back to me.

I put the loaded sock back in the "tomorrow" slot, closed the drawer, and found myself face to face with the year-old family picture of all of us, including Daniel, Fran, her daughters, and second husband Bob, in a San Juan Island campground. Then three-year-old BJ was sitting on my hip, arms wrapped around my neck. A gentle smirk graced my face. Jayne, who was seven at the time, hung off Bob's hip in the same way. I studied the image of my father holding a fish while the family posed with him. As in the hallway pictures, everyone was smiling.

"I wish that was my family. They look happy." I put the picture back, but face down, then waved an insulting middle finger at it and went back to my desk. "Bunch of fucking liars."

I kept another photo, a special one—a very, very special one—in a small five-inch tall frame next to my pen caddy. I picked it up to gaze at an eleven-year-old version of myself sitting beside my granddad, Papa Louie, behind two accordions—a large one strapped to his shoulders and a smaller one to mine. Scooter, then fourteen, stood tall behind us with a hand on each of our shoulders. All three of us wore German lederhosen. Papa was half-German, half-Norwegian, and he embraced both cultures in turn. He performed once a month on a local TV show in Duluth, Minnesota, that had less than a hundred viewers total. He also entertained every year at a cultural folk festival. When Scooter and I visited, he'd dress us up so we could feel like we were a part of the festivities. (Before she died, Grandma had sewn up costumes for us boys. She was full-blooded Swedish. I always figured it was her genes that somehow detoured into me and bestowed the blonder than blond hair.) Papa Louie had taught us how to play some simple, but festive accordion songs, and how to dance a small number of extremely easy folk-dance moves that, if we repeated them just right, let us participate in the entertainment, hoping no one would notice how we really weren't that good.

VCRs hadn't yet been invented, so all I had were a dozen or so audio cassette tapes of Papa's TV appearances to listen to. But that was more than enough for me. I cherished them. These were the parts of my life that balanced out the difficulties. Thank God for those scattered moments of celebration. One weekend with Papa and Scooter could lift my spirits enough to carry me through a full year of Andreo and Catholic school. Of all the photos I'd ever been in, this one showed the most genuine of smiles. The photo was my prized possession.

"I wish that was my family," I whispered again, but this time minus the insulting gesture. "I love you so much." I was looking at both Papa and Scooter when I said that.

My team

Many things had changed in the past half-day, but sleepiness was coming and I could now move forward. I was about to embark on a maturing friendship with Connor, which gave the dark cloud of the day a brilliant silver lining. Again, two fingers scratched at my wrist as I contemplated the three-sided paper. Three fantastic years had passed since Connor had come into my life at almost exactly the same time Andreo had turned against me. It's like it was meant to happen that way. And like with the folded paper, the two best friends, one from school, the other from home, had never met. Thank God.

Connor, Papa, and Scooter were the only people I could think of whom I'd never expect to hear mean things from. These three weren't a dream. I got up and looked through the window into the night. At this moment, Connor and Scooter were both out there, sound asleep in their beds, probably dreaming about girls or Camaros. I knew that my true allies, however distant, were real, alive, and on my team. If it weren't for their mere existence, I might have gone completely insane that night. I stood the photo back up on my dresser so no one would notice I'd moved it, and slipped into bed.

When I climbed under the covers, I pictured myself with them.

"I wonder what they see in me that no one else sees?" I whispered. "Thank God they don't know the truth about me." I eventually dozed off.

31

Missed Opportunity

*So many people live with so much pain. We never really
know what has happened to someone unless that person tells
us. And many never will tell because they can't face their own
life stories even within themselves.*

By Tuck Taylor

It was about 10:30 a.m. on Sunday and I'd been cooking for nearly
three hours. The first wave of church people, the Catholics, were just
starting to light up their after-breakfast cigarettes, which meant more
table clearing work for the waitresses and less cooking work for us guys
in the kitchen. The Methodist church was going to let out in about a half
hour, bringing the lunch rush of people wearing Walmart suits and
dresses, but my shift was ending so I was off the hook.

I made no bones about my personal bias against church people, but I didn't mind receiving a paycheck for cooking for them. It wasn't the crowd that got to me. It was the heat. For a guy who hated heat, I had sure picked the wrong job to get myself through college with. The kitchen was hot even before the Texas temps ruined every summer day. From the kitchen to my hot apartment, at shift's end, I always had to go from one hot place to another.

Marla was the cutest waitress there that morning. Her dark hair, as well as some well-applied dark eyeliner, exaggerated her huge brown eyes like she was a character in an enhanced painting. She stood about four inches shorter than me and couldn't have weighed eighty-five pounds. There's no doubt she was cute. Real cute. And she tended to get into my physical space a lot. She touched my arm a lot. She came home with me in my imagination a lot. She was definitely on my list of girls I thought about when I was horny. Beyond that, there really wasn't a soulful or intellectual connection. Both of which were important to me.

"You're sexy when you sweat," she joked.

"Then I'm sexy a lot," I teased back.

"I think it's the hair net that gets me all hot and bothered."

"Let me remove the temptation." I reached up and slid it off.

"Going to bed now?"

"Nah. I had the night off. Slept already. I'm…." I didn't finish.

She stayed nearby until she was sure I wasn't going to invite myself over to her apartment or ask her out to lunch…or whatever she was waiting for. Eventually, she shook her head, said "Hopeless" and wandered away.

Getting past Shannon

At that time in my life, Marla had no chance of getting through my thick shell. Ever since the cancer, casual sex wasn't a good fit for me. I needed emotional and intellectual attachment to be there also. Otherwise, casual sex felt empty. It had been two years since Shannon had left, and I still hadn't found a reason to put myself through another attachment.

How could I start another relationship when I was still involved in the ghosts of my last one?

If I'd been an adult when Shannon and I'd met, losing her may have been easier on me. But our life together had roots that went all the way back to early childhood. Our story in a nutshell went like this; We'd been friends since I was five and she was seven. I fell in love with her when I was still just little, and I honestly grew up believing we were going to live out our lives with each other. We'd survived a horrific car accident together, and then, years later at seventeen, I got cancer. I used the sympathy card to get her to sleep with me. She got pregnant. I died for three minutes—but came back to life. She had Micah. Then a few months later, he died—but stayed that way. I changed. So did she. The trail of tragedy was something she couldn't deal with. Still a nice guy and all, I just didn't have the perky energy I'd had before dying, coming back, and losing *my son*.

Shannon left in a fog. Depression had completely overtaken both of us, making it easier for one of her girlfriends to talk her into going with her to California and starting over. I tried to let go, but some part of me just hollowed out when she left. For me, there had been no closure to our life together, and so these days, I still suffered. I couldn't blame her for trying to find her own spark again. Blaming myself for ruining her life is likely the reason I couldn't let it go. Too much shame and guilt tied to it all. Too much fear I might ruin another life if I get involved again.

Letters I'd received over the years told of her making a little headway, but by reading between the lines as she spoke of who her friends were and what they did with their time, I was starting to wonder if she had begun drinking too much. Alcoholism ran in her family. She admitted to struggling with depression, and that through partying, she'd found some release. She'd made friends and a new boyfriend, and she said it helped her slowly regain some sense of release. I knew I'd lost her forever, probably now to alcohol, but I just couldn't stop mourning who she had once been, and what we'd once had together. In my guilt-ridden mind, I just figured it was *me* she was releasing from.

I wasn't interested in drinking my depression away, but I still had to find a friend who could help bring my joy back. Marla wasn't that friend. I wasn't really connecting with Trenton anymore, and I didn't want to connect with Mark, even though I found myself oddly appreciative of our conversation on the beach, which was the closest anyone had come to reaching into my lonely mind in years. I'd forgotten how good it felt to be listened to by someone who truly wanted to get to know me.

How out of synch; With Marla I had a sexual attraction and with Mark I had emotional and intellectual attraction. Damn.

PART 4

New Day:

SURVIVING A NEW NORMAL

32

The First Next Day

My stoner brother's late night visit was wonderfully disastrous. Because of him, in his normal off-balance state, visiting me in my newly disillusioned bad mood, I was able to see him more for what he really was, and less for what I'd always fantasized him to be. I learned then why you should never meet your heroes. They're usually not as great as you imagine them to be. For only being one strange day, I'd learned a lot more than I yet realized about how things really were in the world. With Daniel's tumultuous visit over, my long night alone had finally ended.

By Kyle Rickett

Relief! The long night was *over*! It was about eight-thirty. The walls that hosted the late night shadow-party hours before were bright and still, proving that reality can shift with lighting.

I had shifted too. I was my bright "cute little shit" self again—exactly how I wanted to be. And it was summer break still! As far as I knew, the whole ugly mess was behind me and now I could go get some good buddy-time with my best friend. Being with Connor always felt comfortable, but now that I knew he cared about me as more than just a playmate, I champed at the bit to return the sentiment. I wanted to show him that I too could revisit a mature, sensitive side, like I'd shown at Merrick's funeral.

Something about surviving a life-altering bike accident with a guy my own age felt connected. I also needed to know that he was okay. We were both about to turn fourteen, and maybe these new emotions were the kinds we couldn't really feel as little kids. I wondered if the words I'd heard in my head during the night, *go with him*, were about Connor—maybe about us growing up and going off to college together, or sailing around the world or something.

I slid out of bed in a good mood, keeping legs together like I was dismounting a horse side-saddle, then grabbed for the dresser drawer. I dug through the neatly folded briefs to see if there were any old loose-fitting pairs, but Mom would never have let anything worn go un-disposed of. I didn't own boxers, so if I were going to have to go without underwear that day—I guess there's a first time for everything.

I shuffled to the closet, looking for shorts that might be loose enough to wear over my trouble spot. Again, all tight. And too short. In fact, in 1974, shorts for boys could be so short that not having briefs on beneath to hold things in place could set me up for an embarrassing display of *dirty parts*. So no shorts for me that day. And unfortunately I only owned one pair of loose fitting pants—my school uniform.

"Damn," I whispered. Then I repeated what I'd written on the confetti, now in my sock drawer, "Why I hate my school." I yanked them off the hanger and carefully slipped them on. "Fucking school pants."

The burning pain was almost unbearable, but the thought of taking Krieg's pills was too unnerving. I'd never worn pants without briefs, so even while dressed, I felt naked. The freedom of movement was a new thing, too. My brother's joke from last night was right. Things "down there" were getting bigger, and without briefs, the equipment swung around a bit. In some cultures, this transformation from boy to man brings pride. But not on Torano. Not in my world. Nothing about my anatomy was giving me joy that day. If anything, my body was becoming a target. Everything about my body, from the girly-white hair to Krieg's favorite part was a humiliating vulnerability.

Forbidden apparel

I slid a sunshine-yellow V-neck shirt over my head from the play-clothes shelf, but the pants still looked like school, which sucked. After eight years, I honestly had never once worn my school clothes anywhere but to school. Now I had to wear half of the uniform-of-shame into summer vacation—another unhappy merging of worlds.

Connor, who'd known me for over three years, came home each day a half hour after I did and had never once seen me in uniform. I was the reverse of a superhero. I was a super-homo, so I needed to protect my identity for the opposite reason any comic book hero did. Changing out of the uniform was my important transformation each day. I could almost feel the heavy weight of Catholic school leave my body with the removal of its baggy pants, red-and-black-striped tie, and white button shirt each day.

But on this morning, I had to carry the disgrace with me by wearing half of the shameful uniform into the sanctity of summer vacation. I refused to glance at the reflection of myself in my hideous pants as I passed the mirror; then I headed down the hall to live life as normally as possible.

"Damn," I whispered. Before this, I would have said, "Dang," but I'd crossed a line during the night. I'd seen things that aged me ten years in twenty-four hours. Two things had changed: Connor had worked his way into my heart as a real human being with deep feelings, and real swear words felt more powerful than the fakes. Now I knew why Scooter swore so often. It *felt good*. Almost like I was taking a first step at fighting back. It felt mature.

Of strength and determination

I froze, hovering my sore leg over the top stair. But where another boy would have called for help, I *wanted* to descend under my own firewood-stacking power. Mom was right. I *was* like my dad—tough and self-sufficient.

"Ow! Shit!" The scar stretched as I lowered my eighty-seven pounds of body weight, slowly using the combined strength of my good leg and strong arms, taking care not to hit the step too hard.

"Whew, that wasn't so bad." I shifted weight and repeated the action exactly. I smiled with pain and pride after each descent. I hit the living room floor a pro, then slipped a hand into my pants to make sure nothing was bleeding. "Ow."

I shuffled into the kitchen. It didn't take long before Mom came in with a small box of magazines to go through and get rid of. She sat next to me and checked again.

"Good morning, sweetheart. How is it feeling now? Were you able to sleep all right?" Her silky, compassionate Mom-voice soothed the room—and my heart—like milk and honey. I was her sweetheart again. Life was normal once more. While Daniel slept off his late night high, it was only me and her at the breakfast table.

"Morning, Mom. It hurts, but I can handle it. I slept fine; did you?"

"Oh, sure."

"Where's Dad? Did he go to church?"

"Still working on the McNaughton tractor. I guess it's giving him a real run for his money."

"On Sunday?" I laughed to be polite.

"He knows how bad Frank needs it." Then she repeated one of her favorite sayings: "He's a good man, yer Dad."

"The best." I smiled with pride for my great father. "Mom, can I go over to Connor's and play Monopoly or something?"

"I saw Connor this morning…. He came by about eight."

"Oh, good. Can I call him so he can come back?" I asked excitedly.

"I don't think so, honey," she said, lifting magazines from the box.

"Why, Mom?" A look of begging was emerging across my face, which she didn't see because she wasn't looking.

"I'm still mad at him for what he did." She was still not looking up.

The magic moment of mother and son was over. I had just spent a grueling long night staring alone at my ceiling. I didn't want to spend the day that way too.

"Mom! Connor didn't do anything. It was an accident. It was both of our faults." That made sense—until I heard the trap slam shut.

"There you go then, son." She stopped her magazine shuffling and looked at my agonized face. "You both caused this, so it's not a good idea to be together right now." She looked back at the magazines. "I don't need any more accidents."

With my jaw slung open and my neck pushed forward, I tried to look as offended as I could, but without actually saying, "I'm offended."

"I had things I needed to do today, and now I have to stay here and take care of you, thanks to Connor."

I rolled my eyes, dropped my hands, slumped back in the chair, and sighed. I had been listening to her complain about my burden on her life for as long as I could remember, but that day—and I'm not sure why—it *really* hurt.

I wanted to reason with her, but my survival instinct told me to give up while it was safe. Nobody ever really won with her. If it seemed like they had, she'd make them pay for it later by proving they'd unfairly hurt her somehow by winning.

I took my antibiotics, ate some cereal, and shuffled back up the obstacle course to my bedroom, where I closed the door, pulled out my Legos, Hot Wheels and Matchbox cars, which Connor and I called "Matchies," and set up a city on the floor. I established myself as the king. In this little city, everyone loved me and drove over to my house in their small cars to party with me.

I focused all thought onto the miniature world of my bedroom floor because if I looked up at the sun-soaked walls, they seemed to close in on me.

33

The Hard Way

In five decades of observation, I've yet to see a man drastically change personality types because he, or anyone else, wanted him to.

To really, truly "change one's ways" is extremely difficult. Old habits die hard, and so do old paradigms and old biases. When we see a person who has drastically changed, it could be because of a traumatic event that changed his brain's wiring and his biases for him. A bad car accident can change a person's driving habits for life. A near-death experience from eating bad shellfish can change a person's love for seafood for life. My papa, Louie, for example, became a better, much more forgiving, attentive, and patient grandfather after the shock of Gramma's sudden death proved to him that relationships can end before apologies are made.

Tuck's near-death at seventeen, followed by the losses of his childhood sweetheart and his son, gave him the trauma that changed him for life. Like Papa, he became a better man, but *at what cost? He made a commitment to help others make sense of their lives, but in the process of helping others, he hid from the magnitude of his own chronic loneliness. By this time in 1974, his depression had gone untreated for so long that he didn't notice it anymore. Depressed was his new normal.*

Being forever depressed about something we can't go back and fix can wear us down over time, especially if our original DNA was to be cheerful and energetic. At times, through the unremitting ache of persistent memories, we can reach for short bursts of relief in whatever wanders into arm's reach. Drugs, alcohol, sex. Anything that provides a dopamine rush that lifts us up and out of the constant, daily torture of unwanted depression. In the heat of especially dark moments, our decision-making process can become somewhat compromised.

By Tuck Taylor

Sunday evening, 9:00 p.m. Trenton was gone. When we were kids, in St. Paul, he'd kept his sexuality private and discrete. But in Texas, he unleashed, which is a personality change that had caught me completely by surprise. He had found some friends who could help him let loose and become the person he had apparently always wanted to be—a partier. Texas had its own problems with sexual freedom, but as long as he knew when and where to let loose, he was finally free to express himself in a small, but active sub-culture with the like-minded. He deserved a happy social life as much as anyone does, I guess. But I was finally realizing that I was losing him to the release of partying just like I'd lost Shannon. I was taking it personal too. Like in both cases it was *me* they were releasing themselves from. Did I have the power to turn people into drunks?

Like being married to a cop, I now had a constant awareness of the dangers he faced every day outside the apartment and that one night he might just *not come home*. He might let loose a little too much and could end up dead in a ditch behind some macho, homophobe tavern or something. I worried more than I wanted to, but I also knew not to expect the partier home again until two or three in the morning, *and* to complicate things further, I was getting to the point where I didn't know whether I missed having him home or not.

His friends were not like me, but I wasn't out making new friends who *were* like me, so by default, his friends *were* my friends, and I sort of liked being with them, but only for short bursts, and only when they were doing "normal" things, like going to the movies or the beach to play Frisbee or something. I didn't go to their bars with them. It was easier to be alone most nights.

The problem is that the apartment was becoming more like a prison I didn't have the energy to leave. Before losing Shannon and Micah, boredom would have pushed me out to make friends and put together a ball game, but by now, my confidence in the staying power of friendship had been shaken at the cellular level. On some days, the years of pain I'd endured after losing them were greater than the joyous time I'd had with them. That old saying, "It's better to have loved and lost" wasn't resonating with me. Planning an exciting future with someone I could believe would always be with me wasn't something I could trust doing anymore.

I figured becoming a psychologist was more responsible. Helping others in exchange for a fee could somehow help me live productively within life's certain letdowns without expecting a lasting friendship out of the exchange. It made sense logically. So I did what was right instead of what was fun. Those days, I followed my head because I had to. My badly bruised heart didn't want to lead anymore.

A sorely needed visit

A knock at the door could have been anyone. It also couldn't have come at a better time since I was lonely and had started developing a second wind. I don't know how to say this without sounding like it's a joke, but anxiety does this to me; *I was becoming horny.*

"Please be Marla," I whispered as I pulled open the door, hoping to see a tube-top and skimpy shorts.

"Hey, Tuck."

"Mark!" I squeamishly—*and abruptly*—stopped being horny.

"What's up?" He chuckled as if he could tell I thought he was someone else. "Surprised?" His thick, light-brown hair was freshly brushed. His blue t-shirt was skin tight.

"Uh…" I cleared my throat, "you have no idea."

He chuckled again. "You're cute when you're befuddled."

"Then I must be very cute right now."

He smiled and shook his head.

"Trenton's out—like usual," I said. Stepping aside, I welcomed him. "Come on in if you're still interested."

"I'm interested." He poked at my shoulder as he stepped past me.

I knew his comment had double meaning. A joke with a sense of wishing behind it. I ignored it.

"Not here to see him anyway."

"You came to see little old me?"

"I'm not up for his bar scene tonight. I thought maybe you and I could just chill a little for once." He held up one hand. "You okay with that?"

"Of course I am." I searched my social intelligence for a meaningless conversational reply. "Chillin' is what I do best these days."

"So, it's okay that I dropped by?"

"Absolutely." As he passed by me, the lonely apartment came to life. "You know what? It's not just okay. I'm actually glad you're here."

"Good. Because I combed my hair for you. Wouldn't want to have done that for no reason." He pulled a small bag out of his pocket. "I bear a gift. I have a little weed…if you're…ya know…into that."

"Really?" Rapidly, the emptiness filled with social energy, so I joked, "So…what is it if I'm not into *that*?"

"Huh?"

"You said, 'I have weed *if you're into that*.' So I'm asking, what do you have if I'm not into it? Is it still weed?"

"I guess it's still weed…" He laughed again, "whether you're into it or not." Then he added, "You're nuts."

"Oh, good. *And I'm into it.*" I waved him toward the brown couch. "In fact, you couldn't have picked a better day to bring it over." I didn't drink or smoke pot often, but I needed a break from the shrill screech of reality. "A little weed sounds soooo good right now."

He sat to build a joint. I brought two beers from the kitchen. It felt good to have a friend in the apartment with me. I snapped and fizzed the tabs on both cans and put his on the floor.

Mark was a nice kid. Quiet but not shy. He wasn't aggressive, so his crush on me didn't offend. His siblings were both in college on their parents' dime, but he was putting himself through business school because after they'd discovered he was gay, the family withdrew all their support—and *all* their love. His writing poetry made perfect sense to me. It's pretty normal for people who'd been through so much trauma-drama to be late-night writers looking for some expressive release. Partying and drinking weren't his chosen methods of coping. Writing was. I guess that, to his family, the fact that he was awesome, and compassionate, and kind didn't mean enough. As often as he joked, I saw his pain at the mention of my family, so I tried not to bring them up much.

"You're scantily clad," I said of his gym shorts and blue t-shirt.

He shrugged and guiltily smiled like he'd done something mischievous. "I *was* kind of hoping you'd be in your undies again."

I laughed politely.

The seriousness of friendship

"Tuck…" he paused, "I'm not really here for me. At the beach yesterday, I could tell you were pretty stressed out." He stared for a brief moment. "I'm worried about you."

"*You* are worried about *me*?"

"I joke a lot, and we haven't known each other that long, but believe it or not, I care."

When some people say *I care*, they aren't to be believed. But I knew Mark was genuine. He could easily see the loss behind my eyes because he'd felt so much similar loss in his own past. Empathy. He'd been in my shoes and tonight he wanted to reach out a hand and offer a rescue.

"Trenton says you were a fireball before Shannon left you."

"A fireball?" I cocked my head back.

"He called you 'a force to be reckoned with on any sport court.' He said you never lost a battle—and you *liked* rubbing that in. But I gotta tell ya…" He paused and looked directly into my eyes, "I'm sure he's not lying, but I don't see *any* of that in you at all."

"Not any at all?"

"I've seen you let people cut in line at the store…and you don't even *drive* your fast car fast."

"Well…I'm still a force to be reckoned with," I joked quietly.

"No, you're not. I've seen you swim and run with perfect athletic form, and I can see how you *could* be a force. You've got an athlete's body, but you're a pacifist's pacifist. I've never witnessed a boastful bone in your whole body."

"Is there something wrong with being an amiable person?"

"Not at all—unless it's not who you are supposed to be. His stories of you before Shannon don't jive with what I know."

"Hmm." I sighed.

"I think something changed you. Something really big."

He wasn't going to let me joke this conversation away. "Okay, okay…there was more to the story than just Shannon."

"I hope so. Because if one girl could make this big a change in a guy…well…that'd be crazy. Every guy loses his first love. We're kind of wired for it."

I tipped an interested head.

"Don't they teach you that in shrink school?"

"Maybe they just haven't gotten to that chapter yet. That's pretty profound."

"Just seems to me that you changed waaaaay too much for having lost a high school girlfriend. Normally, some rebound sex with a crazy bitch would have fixed all that. So I'm worried. Your life change isn't computing."

"Again, you're right. It's not normal. And I promise I'm not crazy. It *was* more than that."

"It always is." He put a hand on my shoulder. "People see the last thing that happened and blame your big reaction on that. But from what I've seen in all my years, there's always a longer, more complicated backstory."

"In all your years?" I laughed, but not from politeness "You're *nineteen*. You're not a psyche major, so how, exactly, do you know these things?"

"I've lived a long, *long* life in just nineteen years." His deeply introspective poetic depth was exposing itself. "I may not be a shrink, but I've been on the couch plenty. Enough to learn these things." He removed his hand and resumed rolling his joint. "I know from experience that your big change was because of a bunch of stuff. I just never heard the whole story. That's all."

"I've just...well, I've just had to grow up a little more than most twenty-one-year-olds. Trenton knows more than he's telling you. He needs to respect that. He's remembering me as a kid. Time passes. I'm an old man now...in a young body."

"That's for sure, Gramps," he teased. "Only big shit makes us change as drastically as you did. And to top it off, you said something yesterday about running off. So again...I'm worried."

"You think I'm going to run off? Is that why you came over tonight?"

The cushion sank beneath me as he shifted to look me square in the face. His right eye twitched nervously.

"What?"

"Running off is only where it starts, my friend. Next thing you know, you're alone. Isolated. Hopeless. Wondering what there is to live for...." He paused for me to fill in the rest of the sentence.

"Oh, my God," I slowly muttered. "You think I'm going to kill myself?"

"It happens."

"Not to me. Why do you think it could happen to me?"

"I'm gay; it happens all the time in my world. People go quiet. They start making little dark jokes about giving up. Then 'BAM!' Funeral. I'm used to seeing it happen."

"You are?"

He slowly looked down. "Have you ever noticed that I never turn my wrists up?"

My eyes followed to what he wanted to show me. His wrists. For the first time, they were turned palm up. Both scarred.

"Jesus, Mark." I gently rubbed a finger on one scar. Then I looked into his eyes with my jaw slack and brows compassionately raised.

"I didn't do this because I'm gay. I did it because I was alone. I didn't fit in anymore. People told me I couldn't be loved anymore. So…if it could happen to me…right?"

"Loneliness made you do that?"

"I love my family, Tuck. I just…can't believe they turned out to be such…FUCKS!" A brief and unusual redness shot from his normally calm face. He looked down to hide the anger and quietly continued, "I didn't change who I was. I was trying to be honest with them. All I said were two short words and all their love for me just…stopped."

A half-rolled joint lay in one upward facing palm. I put both my hands over his.

"Someone found me bleeding and called 911." He looked up at me. "That's where I met my shrink. State hospital. I was committed for a month. I was saved. But I fall apart again every time someone doesn't save one of my friends."

"So you're here to save *me* now." I stared into his eyes for a second. More and more I understood why he was the old soul that he was. "I promise. I'm not there." I spoke gently. "I'll never do that to you or to Trenton, or to my own family. I'll never kill myself."

248

"I hope not. Because on the beach you said you didn't think girls wanted you. That sounds like you think you're unlovable. And all your friends are really Trenton's friends. You hang out with us even though you don't fit in. It all sounds too familiar for me."

"Well…" I didn't know exactly how to respond. "I…I guess all I can tell you is suicide hasn't even crossed my mind once."

"They're the worst funerals in the world." The words quivered. Another, more sorrowful glow of redness lit his face.

"I know…. I mean I don't *really* know…but ..yeah, I know." I compassionately kept a low voice. "I guess I can see how you'd worry."

"Okay. Good. Thank you." He quietly mumbled, "Now that we've cleared that up, let's celebrate with the only woman I'll ever kiss…*Mary Jane*."

I chuckled. Then suddenly sensed his body heat radiating across the cushions. I looked into his face as he resumed licking the joint paper to close it. He was more real to me than ever before. "You're a good friend, Mark."

"Oh, yeah, some friend." He laughed politely. "I'm polluting you with drugs." He teasingly wiggled a scolding finger "Your awesome mother would be veeeeery unhappy with me right now."

I held a deep breath and readied to say something, but I wasn't sure what. Finally, before suffocating, I simply exhaled a casual conversation-ender. "Mom would be grateful I'm not alone tonight."

"You're not just a pretty face, Taylor." He jokingly knocked his knee against mine. "You treat Trenton and me like we're human people. I've learned the hard way to appreciate when someone does that. You're one of my closest friends."

A moment of abandon

I was gladder than ever that Mark had come by, and I trusted his motives. He had never proven to be a manipulator. Tricking me into getting closer to him would have been out of character for someone who'd always been open and honest with me. But, then again, we don't always manipulate intentionally. Our billions of miniature micro-thoughts work like bees in a hive sending tiny fragments of bigger ideas into our perceptions and…well…long story short, sometimes we don't realize what we're doing until someone catches us in the act and makes us ask ourselves where we got the idea to use a trick.

It's also possible that this was no trick at all. Maybe Mark was being himself while I was being myself and the moment simply happened when it happened. Sometimes a cigar is just a cigar, right?

"You need a backrub."

I stared, somewhat stunned.

"I only have two talents, Tuck. I write poems and I give great backrubs." He laughed. "No shirt, but you can keep your pants on."

"Um. Well…." My stunned expression became a gentle smile. He wanted to help me feel less alone and this was the only way he knew how to do that. "Okay, what the hell? Why not? I guess a nice friendly backrub would feel good right now."

"Let's smoke this joint first." He proudly displayed the end product as he wedged it between his lips. It wiggled when he continued speaking. "Getting a backrub is the second most amazing thing you can experience when you're buzzed."

As he flicked the Bic lighter, I asked what the first most amazing experience was and fully expected him to say it was sex.

"Pop-Tarts." He coughed out a puff of bitter smoke, then smiled a full-faced grin.

I laughed a lot harder than I normally would have. His answer provided comic relief that broke through my tense shell like a rock through glass.

Setting the mood

We put *The Dark Side of the Moon* on the record player and let it repeat itself over and over while we lost track of time. We shared the joint and each sipped only the top half of our beers while Mark told me about his family. After a long while, I went to use the bathroom, removed my shirt, socks, and jeans, and asked my mirror if I knew what I was doing. Then, clad only in what he called my "tighty-whities," I slowly reentered the now darkened room.

"Hey…where'd you go?" I glanced at the green glow of the dials on my record player. "Slow jazz?" All the lights were off in the living room. I walked toward the bedroom door, and to where his voice was now coming from.

"Don't get your whities in a bunch." He chuckled. "Massages deserve ambiance. Slow jazz is peaceful. And you're a photographer, so you already know lighting sets the mood." Now shirtless himself, he was busily laying towels on my bed. "You need to relax. So…" He pointed to the dozen or so of Trenton's candles that he'd brought from the living room and lit atop my dresser, "the flickering fantasy of firelight."

I stopped in the bedroom door to stand quietly in the dark hall.

"Tuck, I swear, it's just a massage."

"I know," I quickly fibbed. "I'm just letting my eyes acclimate."

"Just, come lay down. You don't have a massage table. If you fall asleep, you'll already be in bed."

"Where's your shirt? And why the towels?"

He huffed a laugh. "Again…it's a *massage*. I found baby oil next to your beach stuff." He pointed to my towel and swimsuit which I'd sloppily thrown on the floor next to the bed. "The towels are easier to wash than my shirt and your sheets."

I smiled. He had a legitimate answer for each concern. I knew he was a touchy-feely guy. Might as well jump in and enjoy the gift.

"Come on, Tuck. Trust me. I'm your friend first. Admirer second."

"Okay." I shook my head. "I'm sorry, Mark. I'm being a jerk."

The missed calling

Within minutes, I knew Mark had missed his calling. In the same way I'd given up photography to be a shrink, Mark was in business school, *not* learning to turn his amazing touch into that of a world-class masseuse. His hands were otherworldly. Perhaps the fact that he was a deeply compassionate and empathetic friend put a little extra nurture to the touch of his hands. With no professional training, he knew exactly how to guide them through my tangled back muscles while coaxing moans of ecstasy from my throat. As usual, my mind drifted to Shannon. *If we could have stayed together, it would be her rubbing my back right now. Or vice-versa.*

I knew Mark wanted me. I didn't want him back, and it's humbling to admit this now, but dang, it felt satisfying to know I was the object of someone's desire. Someone who *wanted* to touch me was touching me. Talk about a much-needed boost to my ego. He knelt on the bed beside me and worked magic. The music was perfect. The room warm. The candlelight soothing. This was a legitimately top-rated experience.

He deserved something in return for this, so while he worked, I paid him with something I knew he wanted: the truth. I turned my head so my face wasn't buried in the pillow, and in a quiet, relaxed voice, I came clean. I told him my story. My whole story. *Everything* Trenton had glossed over. I started with the car accident I'd survived when I was seven, and the fact that Shannon's dad was a drinker and I watched him die at the wheel. He listened while working my back and neck. But at the reports of my cancer, his hands stopped. Then as I recounted every step in The Place Without Shadows, he lay still and stared into my face with a look of awe on his. I reported on how quickly I had recovered once the medications were changed. His rhythmic movements restarted, but were now even more nurturing and warm. I heard a few gasps at the mention of how Shannon had given birth to my son, whom I had also watched die, and that his funeral was the worst day of my life.

"My God, Tuck. Oh my God. I knew there was more to you, but…God. I had…no idea…."

Coming clean

What happened next was innocent enough, but it didn't look that way. We had both lost all track of time when I rolled onto my back to let him finish my shoulders, pecks, and legs. We both sported reddened eyes from the combination of a joint and my story. My trust for him had improved since he had been keeping his hands respectful for this long. He poured a bit of oil on my chest and massaged it in from belly to neck. I'll never know whether it was intentional or not, but some of it soaked into my underwear, revealing skin through the now transparent cotton. I didn't care. Let him look. He was a friend first, admirer second. Right?

"Tuck, I'm almost speechless right now. In fact, I'm almost in tears. Like I said, I knew there was a longer story about you, but…wow."

"I'm glad I finally told it." I sighed with relief. "It's amazing how good it feels to come clean. Secrets suck."

He massaged for a quiet moment and then asked, "By the way, who did you think I was when I came to the door?"

I laughed slightly. "A girl I work with."

"I bet you wish I was her right now."

"Kind of." I chuckled. "No offense intended."

A key jingled in the front door. It clumsily opened with a thud. Trenton was home. I jolted a look toward the clock.

"Jesus Christ! It's two o'clock!" I blurted out.

Mark moved away and rested back onto his arm, precariously near the edge of the bed.

Less than a second later, a hand swung open my bedroom door and Trenton appeared, stunned and slightly drunk.

In a move of mindless knee-jerk panic, I pushed Mark the rest of the way off the bed. Down he went with a thud.

"Ouch!" he shouted. "What the *fuck*?"

"Hi, Trenton." I sheepishly covered my oil-soaked briefs and pretended nothing was different.

He didn't respond. He didn't move a muscle.

Mark collected himself off the floor and slapped me across the shoulder. "What the hell was that?"

"Sorry," I muttered. "I panicked."

"Hi, yourself!" Trenton barked and looked at my hand covering my briefs.

"Did you have fun?" I smiled. "Buddy?"

"Just exactly what the *FUCK* is going on here?" he shouted.

34

In the City of Safety, I Shall Not Lash Out

It wouldn't have been unreasonable for a kid like me to lash out at someone, but my compliant nature kept me on the high road and clinging to my long-standing values of obedience. I was taught never to fight back. So I didn't. My active imagination let me hide in my private world where I would not physically hurt myself or anyone else. Whether by natural wiring or through daily training from birth, different children who feel isolated by their parents react and behave in different ways. I let them do it to me.

Rage turned outward: *Some sufferers of Complex-PTSD might be inclined to turn their rage outward. Perhaps it's what made Daniel into such a hot-tempered "pacifist." They "go bad." They might act out by abandoning their values, stealing the family car and wrapping it around a tree, or turning away* *from their parents to link up with other teens who accept them, even if those other teens aren't exactly law-abiding citizens.*

Rage turned inward: *I am one of the lucky ones who turned my rage inward. No chance of a police record that way, just a lot of stomach problems, depression, withdrawal issues, and nervous twitches. Drugs, however, were available to me in my brother's bedroom, and despite my decision to stay the course, I confess I was beginning to toy with the idea of "borrowing" some of them—not for defiance, but escape. For the moment, I chose instead to stick to my long-standing ethics and give my imagination another whirl because it seemed to be the safest and most responsible option. However, anyone who was standing outside my head, looking only at my behaviors, would likely have misinterpreted my depressed sorrow as a rude, inexcusable, pissy teenage withdrawal. They'd have been wrong. But they'd have judged me anyway.*

By Kyle Rickett

Dad started working longer hours after Mom told him about my accident and its aftermath. At first, I tried to hang out with him, but because of my injury, I couldn't help with chores. I know I'm not perfect, but I'd dedicated my life to trying not to hurt anyone's feelings, and to always being obedient and "good."

What had I done wrong this time?

Why was he avoiding me?

I wished I could ask him why Dr. Krieg had done what he did to me, and if all doctors do this to all boys. If all doctors did this to all boys, then I didn't need to feel so damned ashamed of it, like I was a freak of some kind. Daniel said Krieg had never touched him, so maybe I was a freak. I knew my dad wasn't the man to answer questions like that, but I *wanted* him to be. He was my *dad*. Mom was right. He was a great man, strong and stoic. But he was also aloof and distant. And for now, he barely spoke.

I don't know whether my dad was born with a quiet nature, or if his life of PTSD had forced it upon him. I guess you could say that by the time I met him, Dad had only three moods. He was either: Normal Mechanic-Minded Dad, Angry Yelling Dad, or Quiet Disconnected Dad. He didn't transition between them slowly either; the switches were instantaneous.

We didn't always know what we had done to switch him from Normal Mechanic-Minded Dad to Quiet Disconnected Dad because he did it for a lot of reasons. For example, when he worried, or didn't like someone, or had money problems, or felt taken advantage of. It seemed to me that he couldn't handle anything but normal boring life. Anything out of the ordinary made him either mad or quiet—both were scary to me. I also knew that if I brought my problems to him, he'd eventually call them *his* problems, and become irritated at me for having laid them on him.

My sense of humor came down through Mom's side of the family. Dad wasn't funny at all. In fact, he was usually stone-faced, but really, really scary during his rare times when he was mad. So as horrible as it was to have him disappear into his mind, Quiet Disconnected Dad was a hell of a lot better than Angry Yelling Dad, and during this time of my own stress, I wasn't about to crack into that volcanic shell.

Closing in: Stage one withdrawal

After the first four days, I stopped trying to figure out why Dad had gone quiet. My chest felt hot but empty at same time. Maybe he wasn't afraid of me. Maybe he knew more than I thought he did, and was *ashamed* that I was the kind of boy whose "big eyes" could invite his buddy Krieg to do what he'd done—and now my problem had become his because he had to protect a friend.

I'd lived with secrets my whole life. Without knowing for sure, shame had me terrified that my secrets had caused this and he was going to call them out. By Thursday the twenty-seventh, I didn't talk anymore when he was around. Terrified of what he thought I was, I pretty much stayed alone most days. I steered clear of Mom too. The ache that traveled down my leg was almost unbearable. Knowing she could see pain in my face, I avoided her. That way she wouldn't make me take "Doctor Creep's" pills.

Out of boredom, I'd discovered the family library on the rec room shelves, as if I'd never seen it before. I started reading actual books to pass time. I'd spent most of the first week in my room, worrying about how to get that sock-full of evidence emptied before *that* secret was used to cut *me* into shreds. I was starting to dread, like panic, that someone was going to find it, piece it together, and read it.

Why did I have to fucking write it in the first place? That sock drawer haunted my conscience like the floorboards did in Poe's The Tell-Tale Heart, which I read voluntarily because I was *that* bored. Each day, as the scar pain hurt less, I built a little more confidence that I'd be able to sneak out to the thicket soon to dispose of the evidence of my secret triple lives.

My city of safety

On Wednesday, I was in the middle of a complex town meeting, where all my friends had joined together at City Hall, which was built of red Legos. My home, an eight-inch-long mansion, was built of white Legos, and was the only home on the top of Kylesbed Hill, built appropriately on my bed. The address of the meeting was the wooden plank floor at the foot of Kylesbed Hill, next to Homeworkdesk Bluff. The cars of my friends were parked in front of the red Lego building while we voted to have the blue Lego Catholic Academy torn down and to have the nuns and priests board the big Matchy bus, so I could drive them across the bridge and off the island. I unexpectedly pulled back into reality when an unfamiliar knock rattled my bedroom door. It was not Mom, Dad, nor Daniel's knock. I stopped breathing. Terror overcame me. I locked eyes on the door.

"Who's there?" I mumbled.

Nobody answered.

"I said…'Who's there?'" I mumbled louder. My heart went up into my throat.

The knob twisted slowly; the door bumped.

"Come in!" I found enough strength to holler instead of mumble, even though whoever was there was coming in anyway.

As the door swung slowly into the room, it gave off a mystery-movie creak.

Connor!

Terror turned to joy. The smiling, bright, blessed face of Connor Mason pushed through. Then the rest of his body, again in cutoffs, leather watchband, and puka-shell necklace. He closed the scary door and turned back to see my face light up for the first time in a week. His eyes were flashlights behind the dark-framed glasses.

"*Connor!*" I squealed in a raspy voice that hadn't been used in a while.

He had no words at first—I giggled as his knees hit the floor so fast they screeched against the wooden planks.

"Matchies! Can I play?"

"No, this is stupid. I'm done with this game." With a single swoop, I wiped the town and all its cars and nuns under my bed. He grabbed my white mansion off "the hill" before I could.

"What happened to you?" he sat back onto his legs, curled beneath himself. He dropped the mansion into his lap, grabbed my shoulders, and shook me. "You've had me so worried!"

"You mean you don't know?"

"Your mom won't tell me anything. I came by Sunday, Monday, *and* yesterday, but she would only tell me that you needed your rest. How bad did you get hurt?"

I almost couldn't believe my ears. He'd come by and pushed on my mom *every single* day. I felt like hugging him.

"Real bad, but at least I still have my wiener!" I laughed.

"Oh, good." Connor rested back on his legs and sighed in relief, which proved he honestly didn't know if it had been that bad.

"Did you really think—?"

"I didn't know, Kyle." His cheerful face suddenly flushed.

"It wasn't your fault, Connor. You know that, right? That it was an accident?"

His eyes darkened like with guilt or something.

I paused for a moment to absorb how guilt-ridden and worried he'd been. Should I show him the scar? A few nights before, I'd carelessly shaken my dirty parts in my brother's face. I wasn't that person today. But I at least wanted to joke a bit.

"What if I'da been turned into a girl?" I converted stress into humor. An inviting smile was meant to get him laughing. "Would you carry my books to school for me then?"

"Ha! No way!" he charged back. The guilt on his face turned to a smile of relief. "You'd be the ugliest girl in school." He slapped my shoulder. "Would you have a ten-foot pole I could touch you with?" He paused briefly. "Nah—even then I wouldn't."

We both had to work to stop the anxious laughter. It felt good to be together.

"Why was there so much blood?" He popped the roof off my mansion, then stopped, held it out, and checked. "Okay if I take it apart?"

I nodded.

He began removing windows.

"Because it took thirty-six stitches to make it stop. It was only my leg." Then, in a silly gesture, I wiped pretend sweat off my forehead. "It was really close, though. Whew!"

"Gross. But I'm glad you're okay." He stopped to smile.

I smiled back, amazed. He meant it. He was really *glad.*

Then he grinned with his signature over-exaggerated smile.

"How bad does it hurt?" he asked.

"Not that bad today. It hurt really bad the first couple days. I can't play outside yet. Probably not for another week."

"Oh." He sounded disappointed. "When can we ride bikes again?"

"Do I still *have* a bike?" This was the first time I had thought about it. I'd been cooped up all week, and no one had said anything about the bike.

"You do. I brought it back to your house and left it next to the garage after your mom took you to the doctor's. I know how good you are with tools, and you can fix it easy. The front wheel might be bent and the seat.... Well, you know...it fell off."

"Boy, do I know it!" I gently grabbed at my crotch, and we both chuckled. I laughed harder than him from the joy of his knowing that I was good with tools. "Connor, you're a super-good friend."

"I know." He giggled and elbowed me. "But why did you look so scared when I came in?" He paused to stare into my eyes. "I've never seen you do that before. You looked *really* scared."

"I don't know why." As I thought about it, I realized the fear was a new thing for me. Who the hell *did* I think was coming into my room? "I guess I didn't know it was you."

"Who'd you think it was, the boogieman?" He slapped at me teasingly. "C'mon, Kyle. You know I like you better than anybody."

"You *do*?"

"Duh—" he taunted. "That's what 'best friend' means, dummy."

Had I never heard him say things like this before? I blushed with a quick smile.

"What?" He stared at my hesitation.

"When did I become your best friend? When I sat next to you at Merrick's funeral?"

"Jeez, no!" He grunted. "The day you let me ride Fran's bike."

"That..." I dropped my jaw, "that was the first minute I met you!"

He shrugged like I was supposed to have always known that.

"Wow." I had an urge to apologize for how these past few days had gone. I threw a Lego at his face. "I'm really sorry about my mom."

"What do you mean?" He flinched and threw one back.

"I could have played here in the house with you all week, but she wouldn't let you come in."

"Don't worry about it. We all know about your mom, Kyle." He slowly spun a crazy finger around his ear.

"Hey! That's my mom! She's not crazy." I slapped his shoulder.

"Ow!" he laughed. "Well then, let's just say she's not very…warm…to any of us neighbor kids." He stopped fidgeting with the toys and stared into my eyes. "My mom wanted to call her to find out how you were, but she wasn't sure how stressed out she'd be…."

"I know." My shoulders drooped. "Mom can get pretty uptight. She's been good this week, though. Kind of quiet around my dad. And then she always says, 'I'm *your* mother, not theirs.' I think it makes her nervous when non-Ricketts are in her house." I snatched the discarded mansion roof from the floor by him and began disassembling blocks. "I don't care about my other friends, but I wish she liked you better." Then I punched him a little too hard in the arm and laughed again. "You're *my* best friend, too." I wanted so badly to thank him for crying for me, but that would have gone too far. The crisis' window of opportunity was gone. We were almost completely back in the realm of normal where teenage boys were not mushy with each other. I needed to say something a boy should say to a boy. "Scooter's coming for the Fourth. I'd like it if the three of us hung out together."

"You'd 'like it if the three of us hung out together'?" He mimicked me, still staring into my eyes. "Are you on pain pills or something?"

"No pain pills! Why?"

"'Cause you're being extra nice. I mean, you're always nice, but you're like…being mushy."

"Ha!" I'd thought I was doing a good job of *not* being mushy. "Well, get used to it." I fluttered my eyelids and dreamily joked, "I'm going to be like this now." Joking always smoothed the edges.

"Whatever." He leaned forward and pushed me aside gently to reach under the bed, "C'mon; I wanna play Matchies with you. It's been so long."

"'Kay." I laughed at being pushed. The two of us then set up a whole new city and put all our imaginative powers into building a scenario we'd never used before. As we worked, I sang quietly under my breath.

"What song is that?"

"I don't know what it's called. My mom sings it." I stopped snapping Legos, and turned serious. "Who's your doctor?"

"Martinson." Connor kept building and started humming the tune I had just sung.

A bully is a bully is a bully.

"Do you know Dr. Krieg?"

"Yuck. He's a bully." His nose wrinkled in disgust.

"Why do you call him a bully?" I laughed, realizing I'd never thought of him with that label. I thought of bullies as big children who punched smaller ones and took their lunch money.

"My mom says bullies are people who have power over someone else, so they use it because they can."

"You mean *adults* can be bullies too?" Maybe I needed to think this through. People taught the stereotype that bullies were mean kids on playgrounds, with big muscles and not much brainpower. But a *doctor*?

"I hate bullies," I droned.

"Me too."

"But at least you've never had to go see Dr. Krieg, right?"

"Only for a few visits when we first moved here. But I told my mom I didn't like him, so she switched me. She didn't like him either. She said he wasn't nice to women and children. We even looked into the Island Voyager Scouts, but when I saw he was the scoutmaster, I told Mom I didn't want to join. Chad says he likes him for some reason. He even goes to his house and does yard work for him." He looked curiously up into the room with a tilted head and added, "He goes there a *lot*."

"So that's how Krieg knows Chad." I recalled the conversation about Chad with Mom and Dr. Krieg when I was still bleeding.

"Huh?"

"Nothing." I tossed another block at his face to make him laugh. "Do you play with Chad a lot?"

"Only when your mom won't let me play with you, so yeah, a lot lately."

"Do you like Chad?" I threw another block.

"Stop it!" He chuckled and batted. "He's okay. He talks about sex a lot. But he's someone to play with. He likes to wrestle on the grass. It's kind of fun…but just a little hard to get him to stop." He put his attention back onto the Legos in hand, "Do you like Krieg too?"

"No. He's a bully." I smiled. That was fun to say. "But my parents make me see him because he's my dad's friend. And he's always, always, always at my school." I rolled my eyes. "Sometimes he's in the nurse's office. And he teaches Sex Ed once every year."

"That sucks, Kyle."

"I know."

"I mean…no one's ever made me *stay* around bullies. Have you ever asked your parents if you can change?"

"They'll say no."

"You should at least *ask*. Doctor Martinson is super-friendly."

"I guess I could try."

"I would."

"I know you *would*, dummy; you just told me you *did*." I threw another Lego at his leg this time.

"See? There's your proof." He giggled at himself while swishing a hand through the Lego pile, collecting white pieces.

"I'm glad you don't see Krieg."

"Why?"

"I don't know." I shrugged and kept locking blocks together. "I just am." In my mind, I chanted *Thank you, God*. I pictured Krieg telling me to keep it friendly, and I couldn't *stand* the thought that Krieg might be doing those things to such a nice guy as Connor.

Connor looked up and saw something in me. Maybe it was my softened glance. "Are you okay?"

"Yeah." I smiled and huffed gently. "I am now."

"You need to get outside." He shook his head. "You're too emotional these days. Like a girl. You sure you didn't cut off your wiener?" Then he chuckled, held his Lego project out to me, and grinned. "Let's swap!"

I was genuinely glad to know he was safe from Krieg. I grabbed a wrist to get him to look me in the eye.

"I couldn't have a better friend than you, Connor. Thanks."

"You're...welcome?" He swallowed hard. "Well, duh— And...well...thanks, too...I guess." He shook his head and teased, "Weirdo."

"This is fun." I smiled at our brief emotional link and looked down at my project. "I'm glad you came over." We then swapped Lego projects. Something we did a lot. It was fun to see what the other one would do with what was started. The rules were that neither of us could ask what it was supposed to be, and neither could undo anything. We had to keep going forward with our own ideas.

Connor's visit lasted until dinnertime. The Lego projects ended up as two space stations linked by an "astro-bridge." Over the next few days, Connor was granted one daily afternoon visit despite my pleading for more. My life normalized in some ways, but turned lonely in others. I was happy when Connor was with me, and quiet when he wasn't. Dad was like a ghost that made nightly visits to the dinner table, the TV room, and bed. By Saturday, one week since the accident, I'd caught my sister using the new term "moody teenager" when she'd talk about me to Mom, whether she knew I was listening or not.

35

Two-Way Support

I've come to believe that the greatest strength known to man is found in the comfort of a simple friendship. Sometimes, I'm the recipient of a friend's compassion, and other times, I'm the giver. In a true friendship, I don't think it's always clear which person is giving to the other. But through mutual support, strength happens for both.

By Connor Mason

I'd never seen Kyle look so scared as he did when I walked into his room. Who the heck did he think I was? And why did he feel like he'd changed somehow? I couldn't put my finger on it. He'd always been kind of nervous, but I guess the best way to describe it was that his eyes had gone dark, somehow. I know that sounds strange, but it was true. They didn't light up like usual. I joked about the boogieman when I asked him about it, but I don't think he could tell that I really, truly was worried about him after I said that. I figured that maybe his dad beat on him, and he'd never told me. I've heard of that happening to guys my age. My family didn't have secrets, but I knew other families did. I wouldn't have been too surprised to hear that Mr. Rickett had a temper. I wasn't afraid of him or anything, but I just couldn't figure out who else Kyle would be so nervous around in his own home.

I hated that he was stuck in his house. Summer was supposed to be *our* time, so I missed him during the day. I brought his bike back to his driveway, knowing that as soon as he could get away from his mom, he'd repair it lickety-split. The guy was amazing with tools. I honestly don't think there was an invention in existence in 1974 that he couldn't have taken apart and put back together.

Our first visit was great. We played Legos and laughed a ton, but when I left, I wondered what he was going to do with the rest of his day. I was no stranger to alone time. Merrick was my only sibling, and he'd been gone for a couple of years. Kyle needed to learn how to get lost in books the way I had learned to. They can be good friends when the days are long—or *painful*. And God knows there's a never-ending supply of books in the world. We'll never run out.

I had just finished one I really liked, so I decided to give it to him. So on the second day that I got to play, I brought him *Dove*, a true story I'd read about a teenager who sailed around the world by himself in a tiny sailboat he'd named the *Dove*. Kyle loved boats, and the book was really interesting. So I gave it to him and watched him make a very strange expression like he'd already read it. When I asked him about that, he answered in an even stranger way.

"No," he said. "It's just a very interesting title. That's all."

36

Sibling Adventure

Things were eerily quiet at home. My parents were probably more afraid of me than I was of them. If they did know what Krieg and I had done, then they were the ones who had to live on needles and pins in hopes I'd stick to my silence. But no matter what was happening in the world, Mom and Dad were in charge. My job was to comply.

Life went on in a lot of normal and not-so-normal ways. I hope this story isn't bringing you down because I still had laughs and normal activities in each day. But this story is focusing on the isolation I was feeling, so those are the specific details I've written about. One day, for example, Connor brought me a book called Dove. It was such a great story that I read it in two days. The author was only seventeen when he sailed alone around the whole world. His parents trusted him enough to let him do it—that was different from my experience with parents. I wondered whether, if my parents were like his, I would have been man enough to do something that big too. I guess I'd never find out what my capabilities were because I'd never get the chance to test them. Meanwhile, like a slowly forming icicle, a sense of isolation was growing in my chest, making itself comfortable as if it had always been there. I was slowly resetting to a new normal. A quieter, lonelier normal.

For most of us, each day is a mix of good and bad moments that average out to an overall measure. Fran, whom I loved only because she was my sister, had a lot of moods that she seemed able to present whenever needed. Mom had, many times, coached me that as Fran's brother, I was a good person for forgiving her mischievous moments and making peace with her so she'd eventually be nice again. Years later, I figured out that Fran was a severely ill sociopath, so Mom's advice was the worst possible. Fran's technique for driving me crazy was called "gaslighting" and one of its methods, I'll call "alternating between raging and attracting."

Raging is the act of flying off the handle unprovoked, which pushes people away or makes them feel they've done something worse than they really did. Usually it comes out of nowhere and shocks the victim. The bully blames his or her misery on the victim with wild accusations, screaming anger, and self-pity. The confused victim takes the high road and the blame.

Attracting is the act of sucking that same victim back in by suddenly being extra nice, as if the raging had never happened. If the victim loves the bully, this makes him/her say, "He/She is a nice person, most of the time."

I forgave each of Fran's rage episodes because it's what Ricketts did, and I was caught up in the family cycle with them. When Fran attracted, she bought me stuff and said nice things about me to Mom. My brain was so fragmented, I couldn't see the big picture. Each instance, by itself, wasn't so bad. Like the gambler who keeps thinking the next lottery ticket is going to be the winner, my grand ability to forgive and forget just kept repeating itself. If I'd have stepped back and looked at the whole picture, I'd have clearly seen the endless treadmill I was churning on.

The reason sociopaths can do so much damage is because the people around them keep taking the high road by repeatedly falling for the attracting, and forgiving them over and over and over and over and over and—you get my drift. When she was good, she was very, very good. I enjoyed my time with Fran's good side.

By Kyle Rickett

On Saturday, Fran came by in a good mood and offered to take me that afternoon to see a new movie, *Herbie Rides Again*, at the Everett Theater. Bob and the girls were off to the zoo and then to his parents.

Daniel was still in town, making local runs that week. His final 4:30 trailer drop at the Port of Everett would put him at the Big T Steak House on the waterfront at about five. The plan was that he'd meet us for dinner after the movie, then take me home in the Kenworth—which I *loved* riding in.

I didn't know why Fran and Daniel had made the offer to take me to a movie, but that uncertainty, in and of itself, wasn't unusual. With my unpredictable family, the reasons for taking me out could have come from anywhere. It wasn't at all out of character for any of them to do things for, with, or *to* me without an explanation. Being unpredictable seemed to help them keep all the power in our relationship. Maybe Mom talked Fran and Daniel into taking me out. Maybe Fran wanted something from me, like babysitting, and was priming me to owe her a favor. Maybe she was mad at Bob and wanted to prove she could have fun without him. Or maybe, just maybe, Fran and Daniel really did just want a sibling adventure with me. I never really did figure out why they took me out that night. I guess I was simply grateful that for a single night, we all could act like siblings on a city adventure. Lord knows, I needed a break from the island anyway.

Happiness sometimes feels like a drug. On this unexpected free day, that drug spun dizzily through my veins as if I'd eaten spoonfuls of raw sugar on an empty stomach. Fran was playfully manic, in a bright pink pullover sweatshirt and pony tail. Riding in the green Duster with her was a sibling's joyride away from the gnawing parental stresses at home.

Her big square, white-framed sunglasses danced on her nose while she sang loudly to the radio. Her voice was as beautiful as Mom's. We competed to see who knew the most words to each song. After taking the Hewitt exit off I-5, we crossed Broadway and I burst with giddy excitement.

"Hot Wheels!" I shouted with a laugh. I pointed, intentionally nudging her face with my forearm, toward Carter's Hobbycraft, which usually carried a reasonable and fresh selection of cars.

"Get your hand out of my face, you nut!" Her slap made me laugh all the more.

"Please, can we stop?"

"You're the one who picked this car movie. It starts in twenty minutes, Kyle. You'll make us late."

"We're almost at the theater. I'll be fast. I promise. I know right where they keep their cars. If they have the one I want, I have my money ready."

I should have heeded the warning when she checked her mirrors and gripped the wheel. But I didn't brace. She hit the brakes hard, all four wheels stopped. The car heaved and spun leftward in a horrific scream of rubber on pavement, parking us sideways across both lanes.

"Ouch!" I'd hit the dash, laughing. "Are you crazy?"

"Did I stop quick enough for you?" Her devious smile proved the move was a humoristic revenge for startling her.

"Just get me to the door, crazy-driver." I lightheartedly rubbed my head. "Ouch—I'm on a mission. I've got two dollars and a car to find."

The blue GTO blues

Excitement overcame me. Carter's had gotten a few new cars in. I eagerly pulled every one of them off the display rods, but by the last uninteresting car, all that was left to sort through was my frustration. The only GTO there was blue.

This stop was my idea, but Fran had a shopping addiction that could be fed anyplace that had a cash register. As I stood staring at the display, hoping the cars would change colors by my wanting them to, she stepped into my field of vision with a handful of colored stationary she couldn't live without.

"Blue!" I griped.

"Huh?"

I held up the packaged car so she could see its color.

"A bird in the hand, Kyle. You need to take what you get."

"They *always* have the blue ones." I was pissed now. "Why the...?" I remembered not to swear. No doubt I'd be indignantly scolded if I swore. We Catholics could be deeply sarcastic, but technically, we weren't supposed to use swear words while hatefully scorning the unfairness of life and blaming other people. "Why can't someone just get it right?" I started turning red. "I had one in my hand on spring break."

"Well, that was stupid. You should have bought it, don't you think?"

"I didn't have two dollars, and no one would loan it to me." I angrily pushed the car packages back onto the rod. "Am I being punished for something? Is God mad? Why won't he give me a fu—a *darned*—gold one?"

"You called *me* crazy?" She rolled her eyes. "Who cares, Kyle? It's a toy." She unsympathetically shuffled through the packages I'd handed her in my flurry and gave me back a gold one.

"That's a Gran Torino," I mumbled.

"Then you have a choice: buy a gold Gran Torino or a blue GTO."

"Sure. Then I'll find the *gold* GTO five seconds later in the next store and I *won't have two dollars*!"

"There won't be a next store today, Buddy Boy." She snatched the car, still on its cardboard display from my hand. "It was nice of me to stop here, but I'm not taking you shopping all over God's green earth."

"Hey! You could'a given me a paper cut!"

"I'll buy it for you so you'll shut up."

"I don't want it."

"Too bad. You're getting it."

"Fine! As long as it's free. I can always crush it when I get my *gold* one. You don't have to do this for me, you know."

"This isn't for you. I'm buying myself two dollars' worth of peace. We all know how you are. You'll get in the car and start ranting over this again. You'll pout all night like you always do. When are you going to learn to stop buying them? Kyle, you must have a hundred of those dumb little cars."

"Fifty-six." I took the GTO from her hand. "Fifty-seven."

"And you play with all of them?"

"I *collect* them."

Connor and I loved sharing Hot Wheels and Legos, but I had the sense I was the only almost-fourteen-year-old left on earth who obsessively played alone on the floor with them. "Collecting" sounded more mature. The secrecy around driving small cars behind the closed door of my room was a humiliation in its infancy. I would become much more embarrassed by it as the next couple of years progressed.

Grownup fun

Herbie Rides Again turned out to be a lot of fun. The movie wasn't hysterical, but Fran jovially grabbed at my knee about a dozen times anyway while we shared laughs.

Dinner was fun too. We got to sit outside overlooking the bay. Even though I was nearly a generation behind my siblings, we were still "the kids." And with Mom and Dad not there, we could jokingly criticize them openly. As Fran and Daniel drank with dinner, I noticed their laughter got louder and their comments meaner. They ranted for a while about feeling trapped on the island by family, which quietly piqued my curiosity. What were they so mad about? They were adults who could leave at any time. Couldn't they? Daniel had even voluntarily moved *back* home. *How were they trapped?* Their boisterous energy unnerved me, so I laughed and shook my head along with them as if I understood, but truthfully, I didn't get it at all. I'd known them my whole life, but as a child. Somehow I was being treated a little more like an adult on this night and this was a side of them both that I hadn't really seen before.

At one point, Fran asked, "What about you? Don't tell me *you're* having a great time in that house."

"Mom and Dad can be hard to live with sometimes," was my careful, yet agreeing response. I wasn't lying; I also wasn't divulging much of my own confusing life.

The Big T Steak House was known for its seven-layer double chocolate cake. While my adult siblings finished their night with an after-dinner beer and a new set of sarcastic comments about their jobs, I slowly dissected a slice of the cake and laughed along with everything they ranted about. Angry as they were, they were funny, sort of like hot-headed comedians blowing off steam. I guessed this was what adults did when they got together. The best part was that they weren't taking any of their meanness out on me for once. I was a party to them tongue-lashing someone else.

The way they'd connected and enjoyed being with each other that night made an impression on me. I wasn't an adult yet, but I wasn't a child anymore either. I was in that awkward place in between. I wished I hadn't been so much younger. I wondered if Scooter and I could have a friendship like that in ten years when we turned twenty-four and twenty-seven. That would be cool.

37

Empathy Balance

At our cores, Tuck and I were alike. We were both empaths.

Empathy, in my own words, is the ability to feel what another person is feeling. Some believe that we can only feel true empathy when we have first walked in the shoes of another. With a healthy level of empathy, we share in each other's sorrow and joy. We feel pain when others get hurt, which drives us to want to help. We cheer when others win. We take responsibility for our actions and strive to do better. We are kind to people even when we don't want anything from them. We cry at sad movies, donate to charities, and obey rules even when no one is watching. Through empathy, we are the "good" in humanity.

The Hare Scale is a psychological test that places a person on the spectrum between a total empath at 0 and a total psychopath at 40. If you rate 28 or higher on the Hare Scale, you are a clinically diagnosed sociopath. (For me, sociopath is the umbrella term that includes psychopath and narcissist.)

As an adult in 2015, I used online free versions of the Hare Scale test and self-rated at an abnormally low 6. A score of 12 to 16 is a perfect balance between being empathetic to others' needs while successfully defending one's own personal boundaries.

Tuck never saw what happened between Mark and him that Sunday night as being Mark's fault. He did exactly what I would have done. He internalized full blame for the stress it caused between Mark and Trenton, and then he worried about Mark more than about himself. The more a person tips toward the 0 on the scale, the more that person worries about other people.

Tuck was so much like me.

By Tuck Taylor

"Dear God, what have I done?" I said into the mirror.

It was Saturday again. It had been six days since Trenton had believed to have discovered his two best friends in bed together, and now he was being quiet, which was better than the alternative. Trenton could be a highly emotional—and very annoying—drama queen when he wanted to be. Several times during the week, I'd tried to tell him that Mark and I were innocently sharing a moment, but I am aware of how it looked. But Trenton typically interpreted the world to be what he believed the world to be. Simple. So he spent the week punishing us both with the silent treatment.

At 2:00 p.m., the phone rang.

"Hello?"

"Hey."

"Hi, Mark. How's things?"

"Fine."

The next moment of pause was different. He'd called me every day since the massage, but all of our conversations were strained and shallow. I was guilt-ridden and not handling it well. This was the first long dramatic silence, and it was breaking through my own ego and drawing me in to his. I pictured the scars on his wrists from when his family had cast him aside. A sense of worry overtook me.

"Mark, are you really fine?"

"Hhhhhh." A loud exhale spoke volumes. He was not fine. "Everything's fucked up now. You only talk to me on the phone, and Trenton won't even do that."

"I know," I mumbled. "I'm sorry about this."

"What are you sorry for? I'm the one who screwed up. I should'a never come over last Sunday."

"You didn't do anything wrong."

"Yeah, well, how do you know I wasn't hoping to?"

"It was just a massage. I was there. Remember?" Making him feel better meant everything to me just then. I was sharing in the blame. Maybe by feeling enjoyment at being admired, I had actually led him toward thinking I liked him in a different way. But I wasn't the one with scars on my wrists, so I had to make some fast choices about what to say next. I knew I could survive this, but I wasn't so confident he would. I would never, ever be able to live with myself if this hurt him in any permanent way. "I deserve as much blame as you do for what Trenton thought he saw."

"All you did was let me in. I was the one who came over. I was the one 'scantily clad' remember?" He paused again "I was the one that talked you into letting me give you a massage."

"Yeah, well...I...." It was time to say something he needed to hear, whether it was the truth or not. "I don't regret it."

Another long pause told me he hadn't expected to hear that.

"Mark?"

"I'm still here. It's just...if you don't regret it, then why haven't I seen you in a week? You're not even calling me, I'm the one doing all the calling."

"I know." Nerves made me chatty, "I know. I know…. But…I still don't regret it…. I just—"

"You just don't want it to happen again."

This time, I was the one giving the long pause. Could he handle this conversation right now?

"I'm right, aren't I? You don't want it to happen again? I got too close. I scared you. I should'a kept my hands to myself."

"It wasn't like that, Mark." Then I quickly added, "It was just an innocent night of two introspective friends sharing our difficult stories. I still want to be your friend. I still think you're a great guy…."

"But we're two different kinds of people, Tuck."

I wasn't sure what he meant by that. Was he letting me off the hook? Or accusing me of not being what he needed? I had to make this right.

"Do you want to come over?" I blurted out.

"Now?"

"Yeah. We could catch a movie or something."

"Why? Because you feel sorry for me?"

"Because I value your friendship."

"You 'value my friendship'? You sound like a shrink now. Do I owe you fifty bucks?" His protective sarcasm seemed out of character.

"I like you…" I restated to make it sound less sterile, "a lot. You're my friend. And I feel sorry for *me* as much as I feel sorry for you. Trenton's making my life a living hell right now." I chuckled quietly. "I'm sitting here alone too, you know."

Herbie Rides Again

Mark ultimately agreed to a 3:30 matinee. We saw a new movie, *Herbie Rides Again.* It was funny enough. I had seen the original *The Love Bug* when I was younger, and I thought I'd enjoy the sequel as much. I guess I'd gotten older, though, because it wasn't quite hysterical. We both laughed anyway, and then I took Mark out for pizza afterward where we remained at arm's length from each other and neither spoke a single word of what we'd done a week earlier. The tension was still there. We were both having a good time, but we were also both obviously reserved and avoidant. It seemed like we were together all day, but I ended up getting home fairly early, at about 7:00.

So since it was early, and the long distant rates were at their lowest, I did what I always did when confusion overpowered all my senses. I called Ronnie.

A call for help

"Hello?"

"Aaaaargh!" I groaned into the phone.

"Oh, I'm fine. How are you, sweetie?"

I laughed. "How'd you know it was me?"

"Not many people growl at me over the phone." She laughed back. "Only you."

"I guess that's a good thing. Phone growlers can be bad."

"Hang on a second, Tuck. I'm going to switch phones. I get the feeling this call might be one I should take in private."

Ronnie and I shared a lot of phone time over the years. She had moved to Washington, DC to marry Donald Donovan when I was thirteen. He was a law student who eventually scored some sort of a job in the government. I think she'd actually shaken President Nixon's hand on at least one occasion. Her world was definitely different than mine would ever be. But regardless of our class difference, she was more of a mom to me than Mom was. She was six when I was born, and I grew up on the family stories that she took full ownership of me when I was a toddler. I think I somehow bonded with her more than I did Mom, and the bond stuck. Whenever I felt utterly alone and in need of a family connection, it was usually Ronnie I reached out to. She was always available to me.

I heard a familiar series of clicks and clunks on the phone.

"Okay, I'm back. What's making you growl tonight?"

"I've done something terrible."

True to family, true to self

My introduction was half-hearted. The words were attention-grabbing, but my delivery was somewhat joking. It was the most my comfort level could take. I really wanted to tell her everything, but I also wanted to respect my fears and apprehensions.

"Oh, I doubt it was that bad."

"Sis, I may have led someone on. I had an…encounter last week, and…well things in Tuckland aren't going so well right now."

"Ugh. Dating. Okay, so which one of you doesn't want to continue?"

"Me. And it isn't really dating. Just an 'encounter'…sort of."

"Gotcha. Can't you just not call her? We ladies are used to guys not calling later. We hate it, but it happens all the time. We get over it…usually with ice cream and a little time."

"I wish it was that simple. We're like…friends. And this encounter's not very…how do I put this? This one's not very typical."

"Why? Is she pregnant?"

"Oh, God no. Nothing even remotely like that."

"Crazy?"

"Anything but." I took a deep, deep breath. I didn't have to say anything right now. I could let her go on thinking what anyone would think. But she was Ronnie. I needed her help, and she needed to know the truth. "It's complicated by the fact that…she's…a…a *he*."

The phone went silent for about an hour. Actually about four seconds, but it felt like an hour.

"His name is Mark." I broke the deafening stillness.

"I'm…sorry, Tuck. I'm just…trying to…figure this out."

"Okay. Good. Now you know how *I* feel."

"Did he rape you?"

"No! It was nothing like that. We didn't…even…go that far…but Trenton thinks we did. It looked bad when he walked in on us. We were both stoned. Both lonely. Sharing our deep secrets. One thing led to the next and…who knows, maybe we *might* have been on our way to doing it…. I don't know. I'm more confused than you can believe."

"So you wanted it to happen, but Trenton caught you first."

"Uhhhh….noooo." I moaned like I was sick.

"You *didn't* want it to happen, and Trenton *saved* you?"

"No, I didn't want it to happen. But…I *did* like the attention he was giving me…and…I don't know. I just don't know what to think."

"This is because you hang out with Trenton and his friends, *isn't it*?" She had said this to me before.

"No…yes…okay…*technically*, he's one of Trenton's friends."

"Oh, Tuck."

"But he's *my* friend too. This wasn't Trenton's fault."

"I wish you'd find different friends. Your own friends. I wish you'd get back some of that energy you had in St. Paul. You were such a popular kid. We both know you have what it takes to make your own friends. All kinds of friends with all kinds of interests. Right now, you have all your eggs in one basket—and it's not ever your basket."

"I know, you say that a lot. But making new friends isn't as easy as it was in high school. Frat house keggers don't do it for me, and Trenton and I go back too far for me just to cut him out of my life because he is who he is."

"I'm not saying to 'cut him out.' But he's *not* you. His friends aren't you….are they? Unless…they are. Tuck? Maybe I'm just not grasping at what you're telling me. Are you calling to tell me you're gay?"

"No, I'm not calling to tell you I'm gay. I'm calling to tell you I'm a fucking train wreck. And you're right. I have been kind of pushing people away lately. A hot girl I work with wants to spend time with me and I just keep avoiding her. I haven't slept in weeks and this deal with Mark has made it worse. I'm lonely. I hate Texas." I plopped down on the couch. "I'm calling to tell you that I've lost control of the dream. Everything's unravelling. I'm falling into pieces. I don't know who I am anymore. I'm not myself. And I'm worried about *him*. About Mark. He has scars. I never wanted to hurt him."

"Sh-sh-sh-sh...Tuck. Tuck. Calm down. You should be more concerned with yourself right now."

"I'm sorry. I just...am so confused."

"You don't think he'll get over it?"

"He has scars."

"You, little brother, have scars too. I'm as worried about you as you are him."

"Thank you for that."

"For worrying?"

"Not many brothers could tell a sister what I just did. Mark sure as hell knows that."

"Are his scars *really* worse than yours? Has he been where you've been?"

"Probably. But you can't see mine."

"His are...*real* scars?"

"His wrists. Because of his family."

"Oh...." She paused politely. "Well, I'm sorry for whatever has happened to him. I also want to remind *you* that you're not from *his* family."

"I know. And I am a lucky, lucky man."

"Tuck, please think about yourself for once. Even if you're going to stay surrounded by Trenton and his friends...at least don't give up who you are because you're worried about someone else."

"I just don't want him to hurt himself."

"I know you don't. You're a kind soul, and everyone can see that."

"I don't know how to handle this right now. How to handle him."

"I have no doubt that you'll handle him just fine, so I'm not worried about him. But, Tuck, if you give up who *you* are, you will end up not helping him *or* yourself."

38

New Nightmares

On an outing with my grown siblings, I saw a future that scared the living shit out of me. While listening to them discredit our parents behind their backs, my perception of the adult world's moral fiber began vaporizing like a lifting fog. All of a sudden, I came to see that adults were no more honorable than the smartass thirteen-year-olds from my school. Now the light at the end of my tunnel was burning out as I came to understand that in four years, my high school graduation was not going to come with an inauguration into the world of people who respected each other, but more or less just older versions of the messed up jackasses I was in school with now.

Mom hated Krieg behind his back, but she treated him with respect to his face. Dad invited Daniel to move back home, and then he made snide remarks to others about him living there. These were adults! By watching what they said about each other, I had to wonder what they really said about me when I wasn't listening.

When I misbehaved, I was told to "act like an adult," and I now wondered what that even meant. Adults were just as unpredictable, petty, and childish as any of the worst teens I knew. This sudden new awareness gave a severe blow to my illusion of the world I was headed into. Like with a virus, disillusionment can spread quickly through a person. My values were already compromised, and so like the Complex in Complex-PTSD indicates, the complexity of my inner world was only getting murkier. If adults weren't better than teens, what the hell kind of future had I been hoping for all my life?

By Kyle Rickett

The next morning, we went to church as a family—Mom, Dad, and me—but conversation was minimal at best. At the pancake house afterward, Mom criticized her fellow parishioners while Dad quietly nodded.

"Mrs. Wright seems to think she's still young."

I hadn't spoken all morning and couldn't find the energy to start now, but my expressive face gave away my confusion at her comment.

"What? You didn't see that ridiculous outfit she had on?"

Nothing was different with Mom, but because *I* had changed, this normal Sunday gossip-fest was now very different for both of us. Normally, to be my normal chameleon self, I'd have smiled and agreed with each word until I could think of something to say that confirmed I'd been her ally against the crazy old Mrs. Wright all along. It would have been one of the many bonding moments where I joined in as her gossip-partner at someone else's expense.

But Fran and Daniel had somehow turned on the lights and shown me what it looked like to be two-faced. I changed my answer this time.

"I thought you liked Mrs. Wright." My voice was hoarse from lack of use. "You talked nice to her in the parking lot just now."

Dad's eyebrows fluttered only once as if he'd heard something that surprised him. When Mom answered, Dad's head shook in disgust so gently that no one saw it but me, and that's only because I was intently watching his movements.

"I was just being nice." Her voice carried a hint of annoyance.

"If you hate her, why were you being nice?" I stopped looking at them and smoothed syrup across my pancakes with a sticky fork.

"Because we were at *church*. And I don't *hate* her."

I didn't respond, but I glanced upward quickly and saw her give Dad a poisonous look as if his silence were offensive to her. He focused all his energy on his own pancakes to try to remain invisible.

It seemed I was changing the chemical properties of my family. Not being Mom's sounding board meant Dad could no longer idle in neutral through the conversations. Now his aloofness wasn't invisible anymore, so Mom would either have to start talking nicer about Mrs. Wright or find a new ally.

I don't remember much else from that morning.

Retreating into my head

Connor's short and wonderful visits, which had been happening since Wednesday, had saved me from soaking into the floorboards of my room or vanishing into the cracks of the ceiling altogether. The hours without him were spent alone, quietly listening to Mozart and John Denver records, or to Papa Louie's accordion tapes. Those tapes held a great amount of joy for me. I often fingered the end of my bed as if it were a keyboard as I hummed with all the notes. I also caught a few flaws he'd made with his fat fingers and mentally noted how to fix them when I'd get my time with a real accordion in my next visit with him.

While listening, I focused all thought on creating small Lego worlds at the foot of my bed. In my miniature stories, I was safe. Trust was easy—I knew what each of my characters was thinking, and what they were saying behind my back. Life downstairs with the Ricketts wasn't like that. I didn't know what any of them thought of me anymore. As much fun as I'd had with Fran and Daniel a few nights before, I'd seen how much secret anger they harbored for Mom and Dad and wondered how they *really* felt about their little brother when they were drinking together without *me* listening. It wasn't just them anymore either. Since I'd caught Jayne eye-rolling me from time to time, I knew I really *didn't* know what was *ever* being said in my absence.

The sleep disorders begin

Nightmares became a constant occurrence. Nightly, beneath the sleeping noses of my "normal" rural family, I lived in a world of ever-increasing restlessness. The three-sided paper and the three secret lives it exposed would not leave my mind. It's like I could hear it breathing in my sock drawer. I'd dream of being unable to run from threats; first, I'd realize I'd forgotten to shred my letter and would wake up in a sweat believing Fran had found it; then I'd lay back down and live through another bike accident that really did cut off my boy parts. Then monsters from the inside fold, covered in black hair, would push open my bedroom door to devour *Home Kyle*—which was me. Then I'd feel Dr. Krieg's hands, and finally, trees growing up inside me. I'd hear actual voices in my room saying, "Don't forget to breath." And I'd jolt awake.

The nightmares seemed to be fueled by the fact that all Krieg's evil wasn't behind me yet. I was not out of danger. I couldn't relax knowing I still had to have my stitches removed by him. I was agonizing over the decision whether to ask for a pill first, or go in awake like I had the last time. I couldn't stay asleep for longer than two hours without having to get up—sometimes shaking—to pee or vomit. Afterward, I'd sneak quietly to the kitchen for a cookie or some milk to settle my burning stomach, then, unnoticed by anyone, climb back into bed and pretend to fly out into space to grab another two hours before the nightmares woke me up again. In total, since the accident itself, the drudgery of this quiet tension went on for eight solid days. But after dinner on Sunday, the last evening of June, Connor came by and gave me something that settled my stomach: his unbiased, unwavering cheerfulness at just being with me.

39

Connor's Plan

When a friend steps up to help. Well, there's just no feeling in the world like it.

By Connor Mason

I couldn't take it anymore. I had to help the poor bastard. Kyle had been cooped up for nearly two weeks, and it was changing him. I kept loaning him books, but he was becoming strangely quiet. It seemed like his whole bubbly personality was just…going away. Fading out.

When he asked me if I'd go with him in a week to get his stitches out, I agreed to it if his mom would let me. I'd never had stitches, but I can't imagine I'd be as screwed up as he was by the idea of having them removed. I've heard it tickles more than hurts. Why was such an easy doctor's visit bugging him so bad?

I knew I couldn't control what Mrs. Rickett would allow. I'd never seen anyone ever convince her of anything, so instead, I thought about things I had control over.

I need to say here, though, that Mrs. Rickett wasn't a bad person, mostly just a nervous one. Sure, she controlled Kyle too much, but she had a big heart for who she saw as her friends. My brother's twenty-first birthday was coming—July 1. Each year since his death, Mrs. Rickett always took my mom out to lunch to distract her until my dad came home from work to be with us into the evening. I usually clung to Kyle during the day while our moms were out. Luck was on my side this year when I found out that on this July 1, our moms were going to take an all-day trip down to Seattle and do some shopping. I personally didn't want to wallow at home alone in self-pity, so when the cat's away, right?

I knew exactly how I was going to get myself and Kyle both out of our slumps this July 1. Disaster Island to the rescue!

40

Disaster Island Respite

Since the bike accident, I couldn't pretend life was simple anymore. The crash cut open both my leg and my denial. It led me to the night I wrote the three-sided paper. Now I knew that even if I closed the Dr. Krieg's side of the page, it was still there. Whether I pretended he didn't exist or not, he still had access to me. No more blissful ignorance for me.

Distractions: They're healthy. When denial doesn't work, we use distractions to avoid focusing on problems we can't solve. Since we can't solve world hunger, we just don't think about it, right? A traumatized person uses distractions also, but sometimes, he goes too far with them.

Like a daily dose of pain killer, Connor Mason came by day after day, providing a much-needed distraction as I analyzed the world from a more critical new angle. Not only were the dark times more isolating, but the bright times with a friend were more bonding. Connor's steadfast integrity glowed like no one else's. My friendship with him was maturing. I now knew that I loved him more than I did my own brother.

Would History Repeat? The problem is that I had once loved Andreo too. My relational brain, which helps me learn quickly, was instead undermining my trust. Could Connor's brotherly friendship explode with the same disastrous results as did Andreo's—and Daniel's?

By Kyle Rickett

"It's the thirtieth, Kyle." Connor whispered like a spy while sitting on the floor, leaning back against my bed.

Propped against the wall, I faced him. With my straightened legs rhythmically tapping a foot against his hip, and both of us in cutoffs, our knobby knees looked like four small coconuts lined up.

"I know," I responded secretively. "Disaster Island, issue forty-one …tomorrow at the Island Dime Store." I leaned forward. "I can't wait to find out if Inspector Carlen will finally announce that Klaus's connection to the country club is so he can get the map to the old smuggler's caves beneath the *bank vault*."

"I bet you're right." He leaned forward also, as if the secrecy of our predictions mattered to anyone. "And you know what?" He excitedly shook my red canvas sneaker. "We've never missed a single issue."

I was so glad he'd come by that I laughed. My cheerful chuckle wasn't from being touched, but from realizing I'd become truly important to someone who, unlike family, wasn't obligated to love me. Man, it felt good to laugh. I knew that tomorrow was Merrick's birthday, but Connor was in such a cheerful mood, I held back any reference to it, at least for the moment.

"We're always, *always* first." Connor's animation built as our monthly shopping trip became a spy mission. "Mr. Hansen even helps. He's our secret connection."

"Our secret connection?"

"Yeah. He saves two for us every month."

"He's an undercover agent that helps keep our record of being first?"

"He sure is. Hey, you know what?—The bank vault's not important now!" He slapped my knee. "Our *reputation* as collectors is at stake."

No spy left behind

"I'll give you money!" I looked straight into his oily face and pretended not to notice more pimples than normal on his chin. He never picked at them like I would have if they were on my face. I admired how physical flaws didn't seem to bother him. "I'm sure Mr. Hansen will sell them both to you—he's always been nice to us."

"No way, Jose." He looked me straight in the eye. "I'm not going without you."

"Hey. Desperate times call for desperate measures, right? Our reputation rests on you, my friend." I pointed a finger into the air and nodded slowly, then dramatically whispered, "We shall be first again."

He smirked. What did he know that I didn't? His eyes intently scanned back and forth into mine.

"What?" I asked.

"You, my good man, are in the dark." His smirk grew to a full smile. "You obviously don't know how this is going to go down. *Do* you?"

"What do you mean?"

"Kyle...our moms are going *shopping* together tomorrow!" He poked at my shoulder several times.

"*What*? Not just lunch, like usual?"

"How could you not know that?"

"No one told me." I was dumbfounded. "I did *not*..." I sighed. "Never mind." I suddenly knew why. "So where are they going?"

"All the way to Seattle. My mom's driving."

"She *is*?" I couldn't believe my ears. "That's fifty miles!"

"That's all morning!" he proudly reminded me. "They'll still go out to lunch, but far, far away."

Thoughts raced back and forth between feeling offended at being kept in the dark, to being excited that my captor wasn't going to be guarding the door.

"Are you telling me that we get the whole morning alone?"

"*Lunch in Seattle,* Kyle. Didn't you hear me? We get the *whole day* alone."

"Why didn't my mom tell me?"

Connor drew his head back, raising a single eyebrow.

I roared with laughter. Connor and I were releasing the stress of my parents' control the same way Fran and Daniel had done the night before—by laughing critically behind Mom's back. Normally, I defended her if Connor accused her of being a control-freak, but I had now taken a new and improved look at his point. Bonding closer with him—or *shifting my alliance*—gave me new release from her controlling ways. She wouldn't trust me—a kid who had *earned* her trust by *never* sneaking out. Instead, she was playing out a strategy by not "divulging" that I was going to be unsupervised for a whole day. It's like she thought she was raising another Fran and wasn't going to tip her hand by giving me information with which to preplan a day of mischief.

I'll become what you say I am

"Let's plan a day of mischief!" I joked, while boiling up *a brand new desire to become exactly what she thought I was* and to push my boundaries to *spite* her. If she couldn't trust me even after I'd proven myself trustworthy, then why the hell should I keep trying? I'd already been punished for it, right?

"Yes!" He laughed and lifted his hand for a high-five. "You definitely need to get out of this house."

I slapped his hand and looked down at our knees. Our legs were pressed together tightly. I tried to lift one leg to drape it playfully over his, but a stabbing pain stopped me.

"Ow!"

"What?" His eyes were big.

"I can't ride, Connor. I have no seat, and this scar hurts bad."

"Bullshit! I'm *not* going alone!" he reprimanded with a finger pointed in my face. "Screw the bikes; we can walk it. We've done it plenty of times."

"Hello! Thirty-six stitches. Still in there!" I pointed to my crotch. "It might take us a while."

"You're so *negative*. Who cares?"

"Oh, that is just so easy for *you* to say. You don't have stitches."

"Stitches, shmitches! It's only a mile. After forty trips, you are *not* going to miss out on this because of a little old scratch."

"A scratch?" I laughed.

"Yeah. A lucky scratch—you still have your wiener, don't you?"

I laughed again.

"Scar or no scar…" He leaned in to shake my shoulders, "we get the *whole day*, Kyle."

We stared blankly at each other as the incredible power of two thirteen-year-old brains conjured ideas. While teenage brains can be bad-idea factories, at least it was fun to feel my gears begin to churn up some schemes for the first time in several days.

"Your eyes are starting to get bright again."

"Huh?" I smiled with only half a mouth.

"Just now. Your eyes. Before the bike crash, they used to be bright like light bulbs. All of a sudden, they're starting to get that way again."

"How…long have you—?"

"How long have I noticed that about you?" he interrupted. "Ever since Merrick's funeral. I guess I'm…just…you know…glad to see it again…that's all." He shyly looked down at his fingers and began nervously tapping the wooden floor.

My smile didn't fade while I gratefully soaked in his willingness to say something so personal.

"Oh, I know!" He looked back into my eyes and broke my trance. "I have a *wheelbarrow*!" he belted. "And a pillow for your sore pussy."

"My sore *pussy?*" I grabbed my gut and laughed so hard my scar hurt. My laughing made him laugh hard enough to slap the floor and grab at his own gut.

That was *not* the sort of joke Connor would normally say, nor was pussy a word I'd ever been allowed to utter, so this moment was extra funny. It had been a long time since I'd laughed that much, and now the release of tension made us rummy. We probably spent about three minutes just trying to catch our breaths and settle back down again.

"We *shall* be first again!" He poked once more at my shoulder, and with a much more sober demeanor, he nodded like a Shakespearean actor. "Indeed, we shall be first again."

"I'm…" I paused for effect, "*in!*"

Evidence destroyed!

After the calmest night's sleep in a week, I got up at about eight-thirty. Mom was gone. A note read, *I'll be back soon.*

"Sure you will," I chuckled.

A few minutes later, I hummed lightheartedly while carefully scattering my sock-full of confetti into the blackberry thicket beyond the back lawn. As I hosed it down to begin the process of rotting, my burden of shame lifted. What a weight off my chest to have that evidence gone from the physical world. From the curse of the sock drawer, I was finally free.

"It's a glorious day." I smiled.

Monday morning with Connor

The phone rang as I finished my cereal.

"You rrrready?" came through the gravelly voice and the rolling r's that Connor had made up whenever he'd read Inspector Carlen's lines aloud.

"Ready."

"Your rrrride is here. Meet me out frrrront."

"Roger that." Spy movie music played in my head.

As Connor appeared in the street, I carefully descended the staircase to the driveway. I wore bright red and white to celebrate feeling vibrant; red running shorts; white socks with red stripes; my red sneakers; and a white undershirt. I was suited to handle a leisurely, warm one-mile wheelbarrow ride, especially after Connor lifted and displayed a couch cushion that he'd borrowed from his rec-room. This was going to be easy and painless—for me anyway.

The first five hundred yards or so were the most fun. Connor ran and jostled me about, *nearly* dumping me three or four times. Normally, I'd have been too embarrassed to be seen in a wheelbarrow, but because I was with my ally, Connor, and together we were sharing in the fun, I didn't care what passing motorists might think. And I have to admit, I'm still surprised to this day that scrawny Connor Mason was able to wheelbarrow me a full three-quarters of the way to the dime store. That last quarter mile, normally the easiest on bikes, was a gentle downhill slope. But his spindly arms ached so badly by the time we'd reached it that he couldn't go on. So the genius plan was already failing by its first leg.

"I can't push you any more, Kyle."

"But I'm only eighty-seven pounds. And it's all downhill from here."

"*You* carry eighty-seven pounds for half an hour and then say that." Then he had a second thought, "And downhill's not an advantage, man. What if I can't hold on? What if I let you go?"

"Okay." I laughed. He was right on so many levels. If he'd have let me go, it would have been a disaster. "I never want you to let me go, Connor." I don't know if he ever got the inference, but it felt good for me to say it aloud. "We're almost there. I can walk downhill."

"You have to, man." He draped an exhausted hand over my shoulder. "You have to."

We abandoned the wheelbarrow in the ditch, kept the pace slow, and I did fine. *I had to.* Failure was not an option: At the end of this morning's journey was the forty-first installment of more than a three-year-long unbroken record of Connor and I being the first in the community to get our hands on the next piece to our flawless collections. We always knew how many months we'd been friends—forty-one on this day. Neither of us was going to give in. This mattered to *both* of us.

Mr. Hansen's welcome

As we limped into the dime store, Mr. Hansen smiled and pulled two fresh copies out from below the till.

"Glad to see you two," he announced.

"Hi, Mr. Hansen," I greeted.

"Hello, sir," Connor added shyly.

"I have an extra surprise for you boys today."

"A gold GTO?" I blurted out.

"No-ho-ho," he laughed. I'd hit him up for that same car every month. "I only get a few toy deliveries, and I don't get much say in what packages they leave here." He pointed toward a pile of cellophane packages of frosted pastries while with the other hand he wiped a tiny bit of sweat off his thin, pointy balding head. He was taller than most older men. Not strong-looking like Dad, but a substantial presence nonetheless.

"What?" I asked, looking toward where he was pointing.

"Those are about to expire…so if you're hungry…."

Connor and I exploded in excitement, looked at each other, and high-fived. We were thirteen-year-old boys. *Of course* we were *hungry*.

"Mr. Hansen, thank you very much!" I smiled brightly while Connor started for the breakfast. Then I lowered my voice and said to Mr. Hansen, "This is really nice of you. Connor's brother's birthday is today. He hasn't said anything about it, but…."

"I know." Mr. Hansen patted my shoulder and spoke softly enough for just me to hear. "His mom was in a few days ago. She reminded me about Merrick's birthday. She said it would have been his twenty-first. It's not the only reason I'm feeding you two, but I confess, it gave me the idea to offer it *today*. And, it's not just because of him; Mrs. Mason speaks highly of you too, Kyle. The way you're watching out for him now, it's not hard to see that you're easily worth at least a donut." He chuckled and patted my shoulder again.

"That's what I'm worth? A *donut*?" When my face lit up to laugh, so did Mr. Hansen's. His V-shaped smile validated his words. We were being welcomed by friendship and not as a trick to try to sell us something or get us to do work for him.

"Think nothing of it, Kyle. I like both you boys." He lifted his voice loud enough now so Connor could hear also. "I've watched you both grow up from little squirts. I look forward to the first of the month as much as you do. You two gentlemen are the most polite kids that come through here." He waved toward the milk case. "Grab yourselves each a milk."

I froze and stared into his face. All those years of putting forth my best behaviors may not have worked so well at home, but it was paying off at the store. An adult person liked me *because* of it.

"For free today." He chuckled.

I smiled again. He'd always been nice, but this extra-personable interaction was a surprise.

"In fact, I need a break. Grab one for me too."

"You're going to eat *with* us?" I excitedly blurted out.

"Yeah." He laughed. "I didn't get this big by not eating."

Connor scooped an armful of pastries, and I excitedly collected three half-pints of milk and three straws while Mr. Hansen pushed stools to an empty shelf we could use as a makeshift breakfast nook.

Connor and I normally previewed the material before heading home, but on this day, we set the comic books down and gave all attention to the man who'd sold us our every issue.

To our surprise, the man-to-teen conversation was absent of the usual "*So what grade are you in?*" bullshit. Instead, he opened himself up and told us stories about his boyhood right there on this island. We each got chances to tell stories of our own—from the bike accident to our ideas of building a floating project for Seafair. He didn't lecture us on what a dumb idea it was, but instead listened as if we were interesting people. It felt like it went on for a long while, but all told, I think we burned less than an hour of his morning.

Eventually, he had to get back to work, and Connor and I had a long walk ahead of us. But that was okay because I was suddenly feeling stronger—and *taller*—than an hour before.

The first quarter mile would be uphill, and the rest of the journey had a wheelbarrow that needed dragging home. Mr. Hansen laughed at both our ingenuity and our tenacity for getting to the store with my scar being where it was, and he apologized that he couldn't drive us home.

We left in a good mood, on a beautiful July morning, and with a whole new appreciation for what it felt like to have had our first true conversation with an actual adult. Neither of us cracked open our comic books. We could do that later in my room—when it was time to be kids again.

Dad's shocking return

It took us a half-hour to walk up the hill, and without a breeze, both of us were sweating. The gravel took about a month off the lifespan of my right shoe. My gait sounded like it was from a monster movie; clop-swoosh-clop-swoosh. Connor retrieved the wheelbarrow, but even though I didn't get in it this time, his arms were still sore, so eventually, I relieved him. A short while farther, he mustered up the strength to take it back. By the time we'd made it halfway home, we'd been reduced to Connor hoisting one handle, and I the other. That's when I heard a familiar sound coming from behind.

"Oh, sssshit."

"What?"

I looked at the ground and kept walking.

"*What*, Kyle?"

"That's Dad."

"How do you know?"

"I recognize the engine and the knobby tires." It was true. I could easily discern the difference in engine noise between a Chevy, a Ford

300

and a Dodge, and my dad drove a Chevy. During the winter, Dad and I had installed an aftermarket exhaust system, making his Chevy truck louder than most; plus, he had traction tires on the rear to keep us from getting stuck in the woods; and a rattling spare tire carrier on the grill. On this island, Dad's was the only Chevy truck bearing that exact combination of a rattling spare, rear tire-whirr *and* dual-exhaust rumble.

"Whoa!" Connor chortled as Dad drove past, slowing. "I knew you were good with cars, but I can't *believe* you know your dad's truck by *sound*!"

We stopped walking. As I watched the white backup lights illuminate, I thought about ducking into the ditch, but it was too late. He'd obviously identified us both or he wouldn't have stopped. The truck had a unique gear-whine it made only in reverse—reeeEEEE. It sounded like a police siren chasing me down.

"This could be bad," I mumbled.

"Why? We aren't doing anything wrong."

"I don't know. He just…hasn't been himself lately."

"EEEEeer." The truck stopped. The engine silenced. Backup lights darkened. The emergency brake ratcheted. Rrrt! The door opened. My heart sank.

"What the *hell* are you two doing out here on the highway at noon?" Dad was wearing his coveralls like this was a trucker's roadside service.

"Hello, Mr. Rickett." Connor wasn't afraid of him, and I shouldn't have been either. But I couldn't read him anymore and had no way of knowing how much trouble I was in. "It's the first! We needed our comic books."

"How many were you planning to get?" Dad pointed at the wheelbarrow.

"Noooo!" Connor sang out playfully. "That's so I could give Kyle a ride."

"But…Kyle's walking," Dad teased. "In fact, he's carrying half the wheelbarrow."

"I know. It seemed like a good idea earlier. He's heavier than I thought."

Dad laughed and shook his head, which he seldom did. We must have really looked funny. "Well, that's why I was coming home."

"What?" I shrieked. My face warmed.

I don't know who he is...but I'll take it

"It's the first. That's why I was coming home," he announced while helping Connor load his wheelbarrow into the bed of the pickup. The couch cushion fell onto the tailgate. Dad grabbed it, shrugged, and tossed it into the truck bed, shaking his head like he thought that was funny too.

"To give us a ride to the dime store?" I smiled—I almost cried.

"Mom's gone for the day. I know Mr. Hansen saves those for you."

"You *do*?" I asked. "You *knew* about that?"

"For crying out loud, Kyle, you've been collecting those for years."

He slammed shut the tailgate and we all headed for the cab. I ignored any confusion about his apparent secrecy around knowing things about me. My relief turned to euphoric excitement so fast that my whole body went numb. I had my *dad* back.

"Well...did you know..." I slid into the middle seat before Connor could, "that Mr. Hansen was born in the house he lives in now?" I excitedly wanted to share everything I knew with him.

"Yeah. I'd heard that. His father built it."

"And..." Connor joined in, "that he has three sisters who are also still here?" He raised both hands questioningly. "Still here! Who *stays* on an island?"

We all laughed. Connor twisted to face us, which pressed his leg tightly against mine for the short ride home. I liked it so much that I pressed my other leg into Dad's. All three of us, now connected, continued to rattle off the things we knew about Mr. Hansen and his family. It turns out that Dad knew both me and Mr. Hansen better than I thought he did. The best part of this whole journey for me was the act of sitting between my now-talkative dad and my newly-appreciated best friend—all of us engaging in "guy talk" in a way I'd never experienced before.

If I looked directly ahead into the rearview mirror, I could see into Dad's eyes. He'd glance at my reflection every so often, and once, he even winked. I counted discretely on my fingers the nine days that had transpired since I'd felt like he could even see me. Today, he thought Connor and I were funny, he came home from work to take me someplace that *I* wanted to go, and he *winked* at me. I pinched the underside of one wrist to make sure I wasn't dreaming, and I was almost surprised that it hurt. As Connor and I each clutched a comic book, I then almost asked Dad to take me to Seattle to scour toy stores in search of the coveted signet gold GTO, but I didn't want to ruin the momentum by pushing him too far.

Dad dropped us off at home, saying he needed to get back to the shop. Connor and I thanked him energetically and then headed to my room to spend the next couple of hours holding our private book club, taking turns at reading each page aloud, impersonating the characters, and making comments all the way through. We were so right. This *was* the issue where Inspector Carlen finally exposed Klaus's big plan to heist the bank through the lost smuggler's tunnel beneath the vault—but he still hadn't discovered Klaus's secret identity as the owner of the bank on the other island. Maybe that would be in next month's issue.

The struggle for sleep

That night, Dad was on time for dinner *and* was his old self when we watched TV as a family. Nobody addressed the change in him. I didn't understand it, but I was thankful for whatever had turned him "normal" again.

At bedtime, my scar reminded me that Krieg still had one more day with me. I spent the next hour staring out the window—nerves fraying as I obsessed over the choice of being drugged first or not.

Thoughts wandered. I chuckled into the pillow at Connor, calling my scar a sore pussy. But then I wished I hadn't recently told Daniel what Krieg had done. The information leak was a constant regret I had to live with now. It was still possible he'd forgotten I'd ever said it, but how stupid of me to have trusted him.

As great as the day had been, I couldn't trust the future at all. Just because Dad was fun today, what evidence did I have that he would be happy in the morning? I didn't know why he'd changed nine days ago, why he'd changed today, nor when his next change would come on. How could I trust someone whose reactions I couldn't predict?

As I meditated on the possible reasons he'd suddenly become himself again, the only rationale I could settle on was that it had been nine days since anyone had mentioned that his friend and I had done something shameful together. Perhaps my family, who handled problems by ignoring them, had ignored this one long enough that its shelf-life had expired. Like Mr. Hansen's pastries, maybe our problems had an expiration date.

Now I needed to make sure that we kept it "expired" so Dad wouldn't have to struggle again with whose side to choose—his best friend or his son's. All I had to do was not talk about any of it so we could move on. I had to muscle through the next doctor's visit without going crazy again. My relationship with Dad depended on me being strong and taking what I had to take, like a man.

Even as a boy, I saw how my actions affected others, so I took a lot more ownership of the world around me than I probably should have. Essentially, through my amazing ability to keep problems private, I saw that the whole family's peace, in general, was *my* responsibility. I could give them the quiet life they wanted by keeping my mouth shut.

Was I normal or not?

The problem on this night would be that I still had the same question: Did doctors do this to all boys? Because if that were true, then I wouldn't have to feel so isolated and singled out. Maybe I was normal and my stress was moot. But if not, then maybe something was horribly wrong with me. Something that made Dr. Krieg think I was the only kid on the island who deserved—or *wanted* his "extra" attention. He had, after all, said that I'd started it by looking at him with my big, bright eyes. That confused me even more because Connor liked my eyes too, and Mr. Hansen responded to them with respect and a free breakfast. So were bright eyes a good thing, or a bad thing?

To keep from going completely insane, I needed to know how similar or different I was from everyone else. Was I normal or not? Most evidence was stacked against me since my sister, her daughters, and my classmates had been making it abundantly clear over the years that I was a high-maintenance, clumsy freak.

As I lay with my eyes wide open, I recalled Connor's story of how when he started seeing Dr. Krieg, he and his mom both hated him. He'd casually labeled Dr. Krieg as a common bully who used his power over people simply because he could. "Bully" was a word I'd never examined. Applying the word to a college-educated doctor—my dad's best friend— a World War II POW survivor—led me to contemplate the true meaning, as was given out by Connor's mom. He uses his power over others, *because he can.*

Was that all this entire shitty summer was? A stupid, meaningless *bully attack?*

My thoughts tangled into knots. My stomach hurt. I was definitely headed toward another long, sickly night. Thinking about how much I loved Connor reminded me of the love I'd once had for Andreo. Again, I fell into my agonizing obsessive wondering about how Andreo could have turned on me the way he had. We were having such a great friendship when…*bam!* He just switched it off. What had I done to bring that on? I needed to know so I wouldn't do it again to Connor.

A Scooter visit

I rolled off my side and stared straight up at the ceiling again. Fear and confusion weren't the only things keeping me awake that night. The first of July was gone, so there was only one day left before Agent Scooter McBride would arrive to spend five full days celebrating the Fourth. Joy mixed into my grief as I began to realize that he just might be the person to fix all of this. He was older, wiser, and hopefully, knew what doctor's visits were really supposed to look like. I couldn't *wait.*

41

Karmic Collapse

I believe the friends we make when we are small children stay with us in heart and soul. Scooter and Andreo were my two earliest childhood friends. I now loved one and hated the other, but neither would ever be erased. Tuck was experiencing the same phenomenon with his friend Trenton and his lost love, Shannon. Both there since childhood. Both burned indelibly into his heart. Both causing him as much pain as mine were causing me.

By Tuck Taylor

"You coming with us tomorrow?" Trenton sat cross-legged on the couch, snacking on a small bag of chips while using a hand to shield his lap from crumbs. It was the first invitation to go anywhere with him in over a week.

"Do you really think that's a good idea?"

"Tuck," he sighed, "let it go, will you? This is getting old."

"*Me?*" I scolded. "I'll *happily* let it go if *you* will."

"Whatever." He rolled his eyes like a teenage girl.

"Don't roll your fucking eyes at me. You haven't talked civil to me in a week. Now you're acting like *I'm the problem*? We both need to figure this out, Trenton. *Both* of us. How do I just 'let it go'?"

"I don't know." He ate another chip. "But just do. I've lost my best friend."

"You've lost your…*which one of us are you talking about?*"

Trenton looked embarrassed. As well he should. That little Freudian slip addressed a hot-spot in my mind that, up to that moment, he'd had no knowledge of.

"*Which one of us* are you saying was your best friend?"

"Tuck…I didn't mean…." He backpedaled. "You both are."

"Not helping, man. We're *equal* in your mind? You've known Mark for a year and he's now your best friend? Jesus! Seventeen years of loyalty just…uh!" My explosion had been brewing for a long time. "When the hell were you planning to tell me I'd been replaced?"

"Re-*placed?*" Trenton's pent-up drama was exploding as quickly as mine. He stood up so he could wave his arms. "Re-*placed?* Is that what you think is happening?"

"All I know is I bust my hump for you, but all you want to do now is housebreak me and make me be nice to your new best friends."

"That's *you* being *nice* to my friends? By taking them to *bed?*" He wildly shook his head and held his hands up. "Christ, Tuck!"

"I didn't take him to *bed!* Even if I'm not being replaced, I'm being turned into a fucking house pet. You said it yourself a few days ago."

"That was a joke. And by the way…fuck you!" he shouted and plopped back down on the sofa. "You're not the one here who can't figure out what the fuck is going on. You're the athletic, handsome, Mister Straight-Guy, blessing my pathetic lifestyle by being nice to my misfit friends…. You're so pompous and proud of your benevolent self and your token gay friends. And now *we're* not even good enough for *that*?"

"*Token*? They're my friends too! They're good people. I'm always nice to good people."

"I see that. Next thing I know you're bangin' them behind my back."

"Whoa!" I held up my hands to stop him. "I'm not *bangin'* them behind your back. Mark and I...." I plopped down next to him. "I have no idea what the hell happened that night."

He set the chips down and stared into my eyes for a moment.

I stared back, but my mind went blank. "Don't ever call yourself 'pathetic' to me again." I mumbled blankly. "You've been my best friend my whole life." All of a sudden, I couldn't place where I was in my life.

"I'm sorry. I was being...sarcastic." His angry face softened. "Are you okay?"

"How the hell am I supposed to know if I'm okay or not?" I dropped my head onto his shoulder. "I live in a world that's so goddamned complicated that I don't even know how to know if I'm okay in it or not. I wish we were little again. We used to have so much fun together."

He grabbed a hand and squeezed it hard, then broke silence. "You know this is karma, right?"

"Karma? I'm being *punished*?"

"Oh, for crying out loud! You're so full of yourself." He teasingly nudged my knee with his. "I'm not talking about you, asshole." He squeezed my hand again. "I'm talking about me. I'm getting the chance to pay back a debt."

"What debt?"

"Six years ago. In your bedroom."

I paused to think for a second.

"Remember?"

"Were we sitting just like this on my bed?" I asked.

"Yup. That fateful night I told you I was gay. I was so sure you were going to hate me for it...."

"Oh, come on. You know me better than that. I couldn't hate you for anything." I shook my head slowly. "But yeah…you were real scared."

"I didn't know you as well as you think I did then. You were a pretty macho teen before you got sick. As far as I knew, you were going beat the shit out of me for telling you. So I had a plan B."

"A what?" I lifted my head off his shoulder. "What sort of plan B?"

"My family had already gone nuclear over it. I didn't think they'd let me come home that night. I didn't know if I could trust you with this, but you were all I had left."

"You were going to be totally alone?" I whispered.

"No. I couldn't be alone. I didn't know how to be alone."

"So…what was your plan B?"

"My dad's gun was loaded and sitting on the back porch."

"*My* back porch?"

He nodded yes.

"Shit," I droned. "Just like Mark. Why do so many gay guys commit suicide so young?"

"What do mean, why?" Trenton appeared genuinely confused by my question. "I just told you *why*. When our families love us and are proud of us for a thousand different things, and then find out only one thing about us, and then tell us that nothing can fix it, and they will never be proud of us again for *anything…and* that they don't even want us in their lives anymore…."

"I get it." I sighed. "From family member to completely alone in two stupid little words."

"I put it there myself. The gun." His fumbling words came slowly with a shiver to them. "I was going to do it in the tree house your dad built for us…but then I didn't have to…. You saved me."

"I did all that just by sitting there?"

You showed me something no one else had ever shown me."

I silently waited. But my heart warmed with emotion as I recalled Mark saying that someone had saved him also, and that he fell apart every time someone didn't save one of his friends.

"I knew you didn't know how to handle that I was gay. I didn't know how to handle it either. But you showed me support for something you didn't understand. Instead of pushing me away for it, it felt like you got closer to me instead."

I stared, still in shock.

"There's no gun on your back porch…is there…Tuck?" His ever-softening voice proved our fight was over and he was now concerned.

"No." I shook my head. "Mark had the same worry last week, and I told him the same thing I'm going to tell you. I'm messed up right now, but…no. I have no plans to do any such thing. I would never do that to you or to my family."

"Good. Because I love you."

"Thanks. I needed to hear that." I laid my head back onto his shoulder.

"It's true. I love everything about you. I love your pompous athletic ass, and I don't care why you're good to my friends. I guess I can just trust you that you and Mark weren't bopping the bologna that night. I just…." He noticed my head slumping downward toward his arm. "What?"

My mouth contorted. Out of nowhere I began sobbing into my hands. "Who the hell am I?"

"Oh…my god, Tucker." He softly slid both his arms around me, pulling my head into his chest. "Yup. Definitely Karma. This is exactly how you kept me from exploding off the earth that night. You held me down. You never let me go."

I jumped and jolted as I tried to hold back sobs.

"What can I do to help?"

I slid my arms around him in return and escalated from sobbing to bawling. "Just don't ever let me go."

42

Lost Alliances

Tuck had a friend who understood the value of support. I had Connor and Scooter. I was learning the same truth Tuck was. But because I had less allies and more bullies than he did, my lesson wasn't going as well as his.

When you are bullied by one person, you learn to distrust that person. But when so many people turn on you that you lose sight of who is on your side and who is not—when nobody seems willing to support you—then you learn to distrust everyone—including yourself. And some studies have shown that when you are bullied at school and at home, well...you're in the deepest shit.

Mobbing *is the act of using lies, gossip, and racist or sadistic humor to turn a large group of peers against one person. Mobbing is meant to isolate and surround. People search for strength wherever they can find it. Bullies who don't feel strong alone build strength in numbers by tricking others to join "their side." The victims, whether they deserve to be* *defeated or not, are so overwhelmed by sheer numbers of bullies that they have no choice but to see themselves as outcasts. Once a person learns he is outnumbered, he reacts. He fights back, runs away, withdraws, or takes his own life. No matter how he deals with it, he is changed. Nothing can ever be the same for that person. Mobbing should be a punishable crime. If it leads to suicide, it should be called murder.*

Learning to distrust everyone can be difficult to unlearn. When I add together the individual components of this story, I see an unavoidable disaster in the making: I was damaged by an accident, which led to a crime, which led to feeling betrayed and unsupported by my family, which disillusioned me about how life worked, which began to open my eyes to how cruel my world had always been, which gave me nowhere left to hide. These were new realizations I could never again un-know.

The only two people I still had on my side were two young boys I felt I could trust but who couldn't help: Connor and cousin Scooter. What could two little boys do to help answer such enormous adult-level questions as those churning in my gut? Nothing. Luckily, because of the power of friendship, just being my friends was all I needed from them.

By Kyle Rickett

The white Ford Galaxy Country Squire station wagon pulled into the driveway at about noon. While any kid loves fireworks, cotton candy, parades, and truck-trailer circus rides, the week of the Fourth of July always *belonged* to Connor, Scooter, and me. For whatever reason, it was the holiday when we kids were given unlimited freedom to roam alone.

We usually began the day laughing it up with the families and filling up on a huge sausage-and-pancake breakfast hosted by our dads. Then the three of us would bike to the parade, and then from there, wander off. We were each given a ten-dollar bill to spend on anything we wanted. Some years, our families wouldn't see us again until the last fireworks fell from the sky at almost midnight. Yes, sir, the Fourth of July was *our* holiday.

I had already set up my sleeping bag and a stack of Scooter's favorite comic books in the rec room downstairs, and I had cleared the spot for him to sleep next to me. I could almost smell his cologne, which made me chuckle a little because he was the only boy I knew who ever really wore the stuff, and he'd been doing it since he was thirteen. He used to say, "It makes me unique." For me, it just added to my admiration for how he never seemed to let being different be a problem. The Fourth was on a Thursday that year, and the McBrides were planning to stay until Sunday before driving home. God, I was happy to have a friend I could hang out with and trust. Between Scooter and Connor, this was going to be round-the-clock companionship. I threw open the screen door with a crash.

"*Kyle!*" Mom yelled as she always did when I opened the door too violently.

I jumped down the first four steps and onto the landing below. "*Ow!*" I yelled. I'd momentarily forgotten about my healing scar. I hobbled the fifteen feet of level sidewalk and jumped off the six steps to the driveway. "*Ow!*" I yelled again. I landed with a crash of rolling gravel under both feet. From the crouching position, I jumped straight up into the air, yelling, "*Great Scott*! You're here!" My scar stung horribly. I grabbed at it with one hand and unashamedly moaned, "*Ow!*"

The disappointment

Doors opened all around the massive vessel of steel and fake wood-grain paneling. Voices filled the air. Auntie Maureen was driving, but there was no sign of Uncle Eddie—which was odd.

"Hi, sweetheart!" she said over the car roof.

The passenger's door gave up Brian, now a much taller and lanky nineteen-year-old home from college. "Hey, stinker," he said. He ruffled a hand through my hair as he walked around me toward the back of the wagon to unload sleeping bags.

Mike, now twelve, and my height, ran around the car from the driver's side, right up to me and grabbed me around the waist. "*Hi, Kyle!*" he squealed.

Theo, also tall but a tad pudgier than his twin, was also home from electrical repair school. He emerged from the passenger's side backseat, and in his normally reserved way, quietly nodded at me as he headed for his luggage. By this time, Auntie Maureen was standing directly behind me. She had some explaining to do.

"Kyle, honey, Scott wasn't feeling well this morning, so we left him home to stay with Uncle Eddie."

My heart sank—no, it caught fire—no, it sank. Oh, hell, I didn't know what it was doing in there, but I didn't have words. Auntie Maureen seemed shockingly bothered at how I'd nearly begun to cry.

"Honey," she said. "Sweetheart…it's okay; he told me to tell you hi and that he's sorry."

I bit at my bottom lip, pointed up with my eyes but down with my face, and mumbled. "It's okay. I'll just…." I didn't finish. Mom was coming down the steps now. She and Maureen connected and hugged for an especially long time. They mumbled things to each other as though they had important business no one else knew about.

The boys busily brought their sleeping bags and suitcases up the steps to the house, and then they traipsed back down the hallway stairs into the rec room to set things up. I followed along behind.

"What's wrong with Scott? Is he okay?" I asked all three at once as they rolled out bags in their own usual spots.

No one answered me.

"*Is he okay?*" I demanded.

Mike and Theo pretended not to hear me.

"Oh, yeah," Brian answered, "I think it might have been the flu or something. He had a bad headache this morning. He wishes he could be here."

I didn't believe him. Brian approached and put a slender hand on my shoulder.

"Hey, it's okay, Kyle. He's really sorry he couldn't be here. I'll make sure you have fun, though." He gently punched at my chin. "I'll do some fireworks with you."

"Boys!" we heard from upstairs. Mom had prepared lunch to be waiting for them so they could eat as soon as they arrived. The McBride kids ran up the stairs in single file. Now alone in the shared sleeping room, I felt really, really, *really* alone. I sat on the floor where Scott's sleeping bag was supposed to be, raised my pillow to my face, and cried uncontrollably into it.

The Fourth of Ju-LIE

I fell asleep in my spot on the floor that first night, but by the time the three cousins woke up, I and my sleeping bag were gone. Upstairs, I hid behind my closed bedroom door.

On the Fourth, I waited on the porch for Connor and snuck him away while the family ate pancakes. I didn't even ask for my ten-dollar bill. I ignored my nieces, which I never did, and I spent the entire day with Connor doing my best to pretend I was okay. He could tell I was upset about Scooter, so he treated me extra-kindly. He only once asked what else was "up my butt." As soon as I told him I had no way of knowing if Scooter was okay, he unconsciously grabbed at Merrick's dog tags, said, "I get it," and dropped the subject altogether—like a true best friend.

We walked home at 10:30, but as soon as he went inside his house, I wandered like I was homeless person, back toward the ballfield where the fireworks crowd was still lighting off their private collections. I couldn't shake the hollowness in my chest, so I half-pretended to look for someone there who'd teach me how to smoke pot in hopes it would help me forget the self-torture at least for one evening. I didn't look very hard, and I didn't find anyone.

I did, however, find myself accidentally entranced by a particular tube top, pink with white stripes, bouncing nicely on the front of a girl who was probably two years older than me. I didn't realize I was staring until she nudged her girlfriend, pointed toward me, and giggled. I turned fast and ducked into the crowd to put some distance between us. The problem was that there were a lot of young tube tops and bikini tops

walking around that year, and so I couldn't help but feel a little like a—
I'll just say it—a horny thirteen-year-old.

I spent the last hour of the night sitting on the ground, leaning against
the back wall of the public bathroom shed, watching the crowds and
listening to their conversations. At one point, I conjured a memory of the
three-sided paper I'd shredded. Which page was I looking at now? I
wasn't the cute little shit now. I wasn't "Homo" at Catholic school now.
Who was I? The emptiness in my chest wasn't getting better. I had the
most bizarre desire for Dr. Krieg to come by so I could go into the
bathroom with him and be his favorite boy for a few minutes. I shook
my head in disbelief and tried like hell to forget the thought had ever
visited.

I didn't return home until almost midnight and after my cousins had
gone to bed. It may have been the fact that my parents, who rarely drank,
did so on the Fourth, but for some reason, it was the only day, every year,
that I could come home that late and not be met at the door by a worried,
angry parent.

Alone again, naturally

I slept in on Friday and Saturday. I played Matchies alone for as long
as I could get away with it. Papa Louie's accordion played quietly into a
pair of headphones so only I could hear him. I didn't come out of my
room until nearly eleven o'clock both days. Normally, Mom would have
pounded my door open, demanding I come out and entertain my stupid
cousins, but for some bizarre reason, everyone gave me space this time.
I didn't even go on the traditional summer boat ride with Daniel and the
boys. I rode bikes with Connor instead.

The visit lasted for the full four days, and no one told me where
Scooter really was. He was sixteen, so I had been hoping he would be
allowed to drive me to the dock shop for grape licorice in Auntie
Maureen's wagon. I had made all sorts of plans, including a fishing trip
on the dock at Bottle Beach. I had imagined the spot we were going to
stake out to watch the community fireworks, and I had planned to tell
him what happened with Dr. Krieg—word-for-word, believing that big,
strong Scott would finally tell me what I was supposed to think about all

of it. I needed someone to talk to so badly that I felt like I was going to burst.

None of it happened. The visit ended Sunday morning. My aunt and cousins loaded the station wagon while I pretended to sleep in again. I didn't say goodbye. I could feel that they were all lying to me, and I did not want to stand in front of them and let them play that game. If they couldn't tell the truth about someone who was so important to me, then I didn't feel like I wanted to hear a single word they'd have to say about anything at all.

After I watched their car cruise away from my bedroom window, Mom walked into the room. I kept staring out.

"Kyle," she scolded, "you could have come out and said goodbye. It took me some clever excuses to keep your dad from hauling you out there by force. It was pretty rude of you."

I wanted to say, "So is lying about Scott," but I knew that would only infuriate the anxiety of Hurricane Mom, and no matter how right I was, I would eventually end up apologizing to *her* for having an opinion of my own. The punishment for ignoring her would be less than for confronting her, so I acted brain dead.

Internalization as rationalization: It must be me

"Honey, come here. Sit down with me." I did as I was told and sat on the edge of the bed. But she stayed standing by the door. "Scott's going to be seventeen next month. He's got other things on his mind. You need to get over this."

"Why didn't he come, Mom? I just talked with him a couple of weeks ago and he was excited about the Fourth."

"Things change. Scott's changed. He's not the same person he was then."

I only knew one thing that had changed as of late and that was *me*— thanks to Dad's friend. I lost all expression. Mom's contradictory comment, "Scott's changed" was a far cry from "He has the flu."

"What do you mean he's *changed*?" My voice progressively weakened. "How could that have happened so quick? I just talked to him. Just before school ended."

"Kyle, I'm serious. You need to let this go. Something's happened that's far too complicated for a little man like you to understand right now."

"*What* happened?"

"You don't need to know that."

Of course I needed to know what had happened. I had the right and the need to know. The problem was that I already knew she'd never give it up. So I asked the next most important question.

"Is he okay?"

"He's fine."

"Good!" I said, but I wondered why, if he was "okay," he didn't ride along in the wagon.

"But you have to trust me. Scott's changed. He's not interested in you anymore."

My heart stopped. A wave of hot panic bubbled up my neck and filled my head. Andreo had once lost interest in me too. Had someone told Scooter about me and Dr. Krieg? My thoughts attacked: *Oh, my God. If he's fine, then it had to be me who was bad. I'm the one who's not "fine." He knows my secret and hates me too. Like everyone else.*

"He's sixteen, almost seventeen, and has different friends now." Oblivious to the terror that was filling my chest, she blabbed on, "He's getting an after-school job. He's...oh, please, honey, remember him how he was and get over it."

How he *was*? You mean when we were friends forever? There was nothing left for me to say. I'd been instructed to "get over" the person I'd shared a room with as an infant. I couldn't ask more questions because it was obvious she wasn't going to answer with any truth—and if it was because he'd found out what I was, well, then my heart couldn't handle hearing it said aloud. *Ever*!

I angrily closed my mouth, stood, and walked to the window to look at the dirt directly below. Dirt that was too soft to kill me if I jumped. I was stuck there. In hell. Death wasn't even an option. At least not then and there.

I only had to wait a few seconds before hearing the door close. I stood for nearly half an hour, shaking atop weakening knees, almost vomiting from the fear that Scooter had come to find me repulsive—*and maybe that I'd deserved it.*

Maybe Connor

On Wednesday, the tenth, Connor was allowed to visit after dinner for a few hours. He'd become my favorite—and only—distraction from the private head-games I was falling into. On that evening, we had set up a Monopoly game on my bed. I was feeling casual again, wearing underpants and sitting cross-legged across the board from him.

"Whoa! That's a big scar!" he exclaimed. "Threads are hanging out of it. Ooh! It makes me cringe."

I looked down at my crotch. The elastic leg band of my briefs had pulled away with the leg, exposing everything. Even my dirty parts were partially escaping onto the bed. Once upon a time that would have embarrassed me, but with a deep desire to share my confusion with someone, I did as I'd done with Daniel and slid my junk off to the left to show him the scar.

"I got lucky it didn't cut anything important."

"I know. I can see it. It's all still there." He pointed at it. "They're right about you short guys," he teased. "You've got a bigger you-know-what than me."

"Oh, gross!" I laughed. He was probably being nice rather than honest, but the comment was funny enough to cackle at either way.

"Well, you *do*." He laughed quietly with me.

"So now you know I'm still a boy, and you'll never have to carry my books to school for me, eh?"

"I can't believe how close it came to…." He leaned in to whisper, "Can you still get a boner?" Then he reeled back and laughed louder.

"Yes! God! How rude." I scolded through a big grin.

"How do you know? Have you gotten one this week?"

"*You're* a boner." I turned red, grabbed my underpants, and pulled the elastic back to hide the scar and body parts. "Did that make you horny?" Then kidded, "Boner?" still laughing.

We played a little longer, but I turned serious. I wanted this off my chest. Letting him see my privates was a good opening move to discuss what was keeping me up at night.

"Speaking of boners, have you ever..." I thought for a second before continuing, "ejaculated?"

"I don't know. I'm not sure if I did once or not." Connor could have been lying politely, to avoid disclosing. He quickly became uncomfortable, cleared his throat, rolled his dice, and counted out his move. This suddenly reminded me of three years prior, when Andreo had tried to engage me in sexual conversation against my will. I wasn't going to do that to Connor. I compassionately went for the main point so he wouldn't have to feel as violated as I once had.

"Okay, then you didn't." I rolled my dice and counted.

"You have?"

"Yes," I said, and then I felt an urgent need to share the most bizarre thing that had ever happened to me, but to fudge a little with the truth so it wouldn't feel quite so creepy. I leaned forward, which triggered Connor to lean in as well, and then with all the seriousness I had in me, I said, "Kathy Melenick made me do it when I was getting stitches."

"Whoa!" Connor said slowly. "She was my favorite sitter."

"She's *my* favorite now!" I laughed.

He got it and howled back. "Good one!"

"Thanks." I was lying about the *who* but not the *what*. It felt good that someone *cared*. I went in deeper. "First, she cut off all my clothes. She stripped me naked."

"You're kidding." Being stripped naked was the scariest thing in the world to Connor, who, not too long before, had admitted to me that he was nervous about showering in gym class the next year.

I wasn't ready to tell him that it was creepy old Dr. Krieg who had done it to me, so I combined all the events of the clinic visit into one story and let him think it was Kathy who had done all the touching. It was partly true. Sure, the details were manipulated, but the story was still what I needed help with.

"It made my whole body wiggle, and I breathed really hard."

"Whoa." Connor exhaled slowly.

"Dr. Krieg and her held me down, and he made her wipe my thing with wet towels 'cause a the blood. There was lots of it. All over my…you know. My everything."

"I'm glad I don't see him." Connor's eyes were saucers, which looked funny through the magnification of his dark-framed glasses.

"I tried to think of other things, but it didn't work and I got a huge boner."

"Oh, no."

"And she didn't stop cleaning."

"No waaaaayyyyy."

"When it happened, it felt really—"

Dad!

"Ahem!" resounded angrily across the room.

What we boys had forgotten to do was close the bedroom door. My supposedly absent father then stepped into the room.

"Connor, it's time for you to leave," he commanded.

Connor and I both snapped to attention so quickly that Monopoly pieces flew every which way. My breathing went into almost hyperventilation. I'd blown it. Dad had forgotten about the expired event, and I'd now thrown it back in his face. I stared silently in terror at my father because I knew that once he'd reached these tones, he couldn't be reasoned with.

Connor wisely scampered out of the room quickly, without saying goodbye or anything else. As soon as he had gotten through the open door, Dad turned his eyes straight onto mine.

"What the *hell* kind of talk is that?" He was *Angry Yelling Dad* now. His voice went into its stern, accusatory, scolding mode where at least one word in every sentence was emphasized three times louder than the words around it. "That's the *last* time you'll *ever* talk about that nonsense, do you *hear me*?" He paused.

I nodded in a cold sweat.

"*Do you* hear *me*?"

"Yes, sir," I squeaked through my anxiety.

"You need to stay away from Connor the rest of this summer." Then as quietly as he'd entered, Dad left me to the loneliness of my dungeon.

I continued to stare out through the silent, open door. I couldn't believe what I'd heard. Dad almost never helped with disciplining us kids, but when he did—when he told Mom to enforce punishment—she did it. I knew Connor was gone for good.

I stared blankly through the now empty doorway. Daniel, who'd many times been on the receiving end of that same angry voice, quietly snuck past as though he'd been listening to the entire scolding. In fact, he may have been the one who'd tattled on my conversation in the first place. No matter how old my brother got, he never outgrew being a snitch. That goddamned scar had now cost me my last friend, and the only honest ally left alive.

I wanted to cry, but worried that Dad—or Daniel—would be back to make sure I didn't. My chest was hot and my face flush. I choked back tears while slowly collecting Monopoly pieces, and carefully, methodically, placed each in its little bag and back into the box as though the game were still brand new. I tried to make the cleanup process last as long as possible so I could have something to do through the loneliness until bedtime.

43

Heartfelt Summary

Isolation is a powerful force that leaves an individual unable to interact openly with cohorts (allies). Without the opportunity to interact, the isolated individual cannot know what the cohorts are thinking.

Mob-bullied, gaslighted, isolated people often fall victim to a false perception that nobody loves them anymore at all. They learn to distrust friendship itself. Overwhelming evidence seems to have proven that everyone hates them. Then when Complex-PTSD becomes a factor, the sufferer adds complexity. All-or-nothing thinking can creep in to every aspect of life. "If they don't love me, then they hate me." "If they love me right now, life is excellent. But when they turn on me—which they will—my entire life is horrible." Many of them will go through the rest of their lives continuing to believe this. They won't realize it. They just know that friends can be more dangerous than strangers.

Connor was a good guy. I knew I loved and needed him. But I had no idea how much he loved and needed me. All I knew was that he, like every friend I'd ever made, was gone now too.

By Connor Mason

"I wish I could fix this," I whispered at his chimney. It was the only part of Kyle's house I could see from my bedroom window through the trees. "If I really *was* Inspector Carlen, I'd save him right now."

I'd been having a lot more thoughts about Merrick lately. I think it was because Kyle's accident woke up some fearful part of me that was awake back when Merrick died. I've never told anyone this before, but Kyle was the only reason I had made it through the funeral. I had wanted to get up and run so bad that day that I had to keep squeezing his hand tighter and tighter to keep myself in the chair. He just sat there and let me do it. He never said a single thing about it. Not ever.

"He is *so* cool," I whispered as I softly, nervously pounded a fist against my windowsill like I was slowly beating a nail into the wood.

I didn't squeeze his hand to keep myself from running away anymore, but during those years after the funeral, I still got a lot of strength from him in other ways. He was always so happy. He kind of made me stronger just by being who he was. I forever wished I was as happy as him inside.

My biggest worry that night was that Kyle's dad was beating him up just beneath that chimney while I was sitting alone in my safe, warm room staring at it through the trees. He looked so scared when his dad walked in.

But Kyle really, really, *reeeeeally* loved his dad. Sometimes he'd stop playing with us kids just because he'd hear his dad's truck start up. And he never had any bruises or scars, so I wasn't sure enough about any abuse to start trouble by accusing Mr. Rickett of that. Maybe Kyle wasn't getting beaten up right now.

"I need to stop worrying." I kept pounding on my invisible nail. "Kyle is Atomic Ant. He can handle anything. He's a fucking hero."

I flashed back to the bike accident. There he lay, practically paralyzed with pain, bleeding all over the beach and laughing at my worry. "Come on, Connor; don't make me laugh," he'd say. All the while, it hurt *me* just looking at him.

My mom liked Kyle the most of any of my friends, and she was right to. She always talked about how different I was after he started coming around. A bunch of pictures went through my brain his taking me to ride his sister's bike on the day I moved in, and showing me his best, private fishing spot; His holding my hand at Merrick's funeral; His comforting *me* while *he* was practically bleeding to death; and the way he talked like an adult to Mr. Hansen.

The darkness of night was making the chimney impossible to see when all my thoughts and worries added up to a summary statement I'd never considered before. I'd known for a long time that I really loved Kyle. But on that night, while worrying myself to death over him, I trusted on his strength and realized he was more than a friend.

"I need you, Kyle. You're my official role model."

44

Day of Reckoning

By this point, all my "fun moments" at home were done. Life really had become miserable around the clock. The summer of '74 was a perfect storm, meaning that the events leading to my demise were not a single chain, but a random spattering of coincidences. Like an earthquake happening at the same time as a downpour, a high tide, and a car accident, multiple disconnected events added together.

For what was probably two unrelated reasons, my two final friends were now gone. I'd spoken too soon. I had no allies left on earth, and my disillusionment with life was complete. I didn't just feel alone; I really was alone. All that was left now was Dr. Krieg, who was about to get another chance with me in his cage.

By Kyle Rickett

On Monday, July 15, three long weeks after the stitches went in, the dreaded time had come—like a slow moving, but unstoppable steam roller—to take them out. My final decision was to go without a pill and tough it out like a man. On one hand, my tortured mind wanted to hide from what was about to happen. But on the other hand, morbid curiosity wanted to break through the mystery memories of Dr. Krieg and the Island Voyager Scouts. Those half-baked memories were hiding somewhere inside my head, and I wanted them exposed. If any of it had really happened, I wanted to face it.

Or did I? *Maybe hiding a little longer would have been better.*

I was becoming more nervous by the mile as Mom drove toward the clinic. Too late to take the pills now.

Other than that, it was a beautiful morning. Sunlight flashed as we glided beneath massive tree branches as big as trees themselves hanging over winding island roadways. If only one would gracefully break from its own weight and crush my side of the car, making my death so much easier for my survivors to explain than if I'd jumped off a bridge of my own free will.

All windows were down, letting in the aromatic, freshly cut grass of a rural American summer. I remained silent. I'd been silent a lot lately.

"Whatever happened to my jabber-box?" Mom tried to engage me. "How come you don't talk my ear off anymore?"

I couldn't think of a single honest thing to say. And my sense of humor was gone altogether.

Mom slowed the car. I locked my gaze onto a sprinkler-head hissing its spray onto the rich, green, recently mowed lawn as she steered us into the clinic parking lot. I studied the scene to keep my mind busy. Mower tracks lined the lawn lengthwise like stripes, making it obvious it was mowed by machine. Shadows from trees and the building lay across it in multiple patterns. This was part of why I got Ds at school. I stared at lawns and sprinkler heads through the windows instead of engaging with the monsters in the classroom. Damn. With all my friends gone, my home life was starting to look like my school life. Not only that, but I was minutes away from being Santa's favorite boy for another show. My three secret worlds had been colliding a lot this summer, and they were all about to explode again.

"Are you going to go in with me," I asked with a hoarse voice, "when he takes my pants off?"

She shrugged off the question. "We'll let the doctor decide."

"Great," I mumbled.

Now that we could see the building—and we'd come out from under any heavy branches that could kill me, I couldn't put this visit out of my mind any longer. This was where all my problems had begun—probably as long as eight years before. The place suddenly smelled like death. But I couldn't keep the stitches in forever. This had to happen. My heart pounded as I closed my eyes and chanted silently, *I can't wait until this is over*. Saying that in the clinic parking lot made me feel like I was nine years old again. Why wouldn't these goddamned triggers go away?

Mom parked the Oldsmobile in the spot closest to the door and beneath the cherry blossoms.

"Damn fruit trees," she said, wrestling to pull the keys out of the dash. "Birds are gonna poop all over it now."

"Then why'd ya park here?" I asked in a monotone, *who cares* voice. But then I wondered why I'd bothered to put out the energy.

"You need to be close to the door."

I couldn't tell if that was a compliment or a dig. I sighed and pretended I had driven there alone in my signet gold GTO.

Disaster on the clinic lawn

We followed a concrete sidewalk that split a freshly mowed lawn in two. Mom moved on ahead. I felt so alone all of a sudden. I had originally asked for Connor to ride along so he could hang around the waiting room for support. Secretly, I'd hoped Dr. Martinson would see him and make a public display so Krieg wouldn't feel so free to mess with me behind the thin door. But by wanting to share my life with Connor just twelve hours before, I had ruined those plans for good. So now every lonely step toward the door was harder to take than the one before. I also began to panic, regretting not taking a pill. Reality struck—*I didn't want to remember anything.*

At about 9:15 a.m. and almost halfway between the car and the door, I had to stop and catch my breath.

"Do we need to go slower?" Mom stopped to look back. "Do your stitches hurt?"

I meant to answer her, but when I opened my mouth to say, "Sorry, Mom," my lungs couldn't push out words, and I tasted the chemical of fear. I tried to walk another step, but my legs wouldn't obey.

"Kyle, for God's sake, don't do this to me now!" My mother's anxiety could rise faster than anyone's on the island. If things didn't go right, no matter how big or small, she would freak out. In fact, it seemed that the smaller the problem, the bigger her episode. And it didn't matter whose problem it was; she always complained that people were doing it *to her*. I started to catch only bits and pieces of her words. I heard "Behave yourself," and then, "You're embarrassing me." Then Krieg's raspy voice in my head said, *"It's show time."*

The ground shook and shifted a foot to the left, knocking me down. Thankfully, my face missed the concrete. Was that a real earthquake? I tasted grass, sat up, and hugged my knees. I reached for my mother's arm, but I wasn't sure where to aim. She was spinning around me, and when I looked up, my stomach suddenly, and with no warning of any kind, gave up my morning cereal. I vomited too quickly to point my face downward. Milk, orange juice, and half-digested pieces of cereal and banana covered my chin and shirt on their way to the ground. "Ow!" I groaned. Vomiting hurt like a knife wound to my sternum. It had been this way since I started taking antacids every day—about three years now.

Would an ally-turned-bully-turned-ally turn bully again?

I couldn't make out what Mom said next, but before long, I felt the embrace of someone who still felt warm and soft, from out of the world of those who'd gone cold. Kathy Melenick had stepped out to see what the commotion was about. She put herself between me and Mom, hooked her forearms under my armpits, and helped me to a standing position. I still hated her for what she had done to me three weeks before, but also, she was Kathy, my favorite babysitter. And I kind of knew she hadn't wanted to do what she had done. But damn it, she was still Krieg's nurse, and she was probably going to strip me again in a few minutes. How confusing! Did I like her? Did I hate her? I think the answer was yes to both.

"It's okay, Kyle." She walked me back to the Oldsmobile and leaned me against the headlights so I could half-sit on the bumper. "Oh, Kyle," she said sweetly but quietly enough that Mom couldn't hear her. "I'm so sorry for what happened here last time. I don't blame you for being…nervous." She ran her fingers through one side of my thick, but short hair and consoled, "You little sweetheart." She kissed my forehead like she used to do when I was little. I couldn't bring myself to look into her face, so I have to assume she was being sincere.

I wished I knew exactly what she was apologizing for. I knew what I *wanted* an apology for, but I still wished I knew, in *her* words, what she believed happened that day. I didn't seem to know what anybody meant by anything they said anymore.

She left me leaning against the car, holding both shaking hands over my burning chest. My queasiness began to ease, but my forehead still felt cold as I watched the two women talking in the distance. Kathy then disappeared into the clinic. After a quick minute, she came back out and handed Mom a towel and an envelope. She turned toward me in the distance and waved. I didn't wave back. She went inside.

"Are you okay, sweetheart?" Mom returned to the car a bit calmer.

"I'm sorry, Mom." I shrugged while looking at the ground.

"Well…it is what it is. Let's clean you up. Raise your arms for me, okay?" She toweled off the second coming of my breakfast, starting with my face and then rubbing my shirt. It hurt. The towel was as soft as burlap, and Mom was scrubbing like the vomit had already dried into glue. She wasn't being mean; she always saw cleaning as a chore that needed the usual amount of elbow grease. I air-dried alone while she brought the towel back to the clinic.

"Okay," she said as she returned and walked past me. "Don't worry, honey-bunch. We aren't going to do this today."

"Well, then when are we going to do it?" I asked on my way back to my car door.

"Let's worry about that later," she said kindly. "Let's go home, sweetheart. I'm sorry this was so hard for you. I promise we'll find a way to make this as easy as we can."

I liked it. Her respect for my fears seemed to come out of nowhere. It was nice.

The rest of the day was deafeningly quiet. Daniel and his truck were gone and Dad was planning to come home late again, so I ate dinner by myself in the kitchen. I asked Mom why I couldn't stay up and eat late with her and Dad. She said that since I'd thrown up my breakfast, she didn't want me to starve that long. I finished at about four-thirty and then went into the living room to watch TV.

45

Earthquake?

If two people connect but don't see it, does that mean the link never happened? Or is it like a single ocean wave that is born somewhere out at sea, travels inland for its entire lifetime, and then dies alone on a beach amid a billion other nameless, forgotten waves, a daily event that happens to waves billions of times a day, but no one witnessed it? Perhaps two people can be connected but they just don't realize it.

By Connor Mason

I wanted so bad to go with Kyle when he got his stitches out. He was too scared to do it alone. I'd always heard it was an easy procedure, so I was just sure his mom would at least let me sit next to him while Krieg did whatever he needed to do.

At exactly 9:16 a.m., Kyle called for me from outside my window, so I ran to it and jumped into the window box, holding my full body weight on my straightened arms while my legs dangled and kicked at my bedroom wall.

"Kyle!" I shouted, so happy to see him.

No one was there.

"Wow." I dropped to my feet. "I could swear I heard him call my name."

Then an earthquake shook my body, but nothing in the room moved. I guess it was just a dizzy spell. Maybe from allergies.

"I must have gotten up too fast."

46

The Devil Makes House Calls

Evil itself cannot be explained to me. I absolutely, positively, cannot grasp or understand or connect with true evil. I wonder if any person who has a fully functioning conscience can comprehend the actions of those who don't have one.

Even today, my mind has no way to understand how Dr. Krieg could so easily tromp through my family's trust, taunting our values the way he seemed comfortably able to do. It's all I can do, even today, to accept that this kind of evil—which makes no sense to me—happens all over the planet, half the time right under all of our noses.

By Kyle Rickett

I woke up in bed, hands on my forehead, mumbling, "What the hell?" My tongue tasted funny. "Yuck. I feel awful." The sun was up but the shadows in my room were angled wrong for early morning. I looked at my clock. 11:30 a.m. already. I didn't remember going to bed, but I did know this feeling. Why I was experiencing it was the mystery. I distinctly recalled choosing not to take the pill. I stumbled lazily into the bathroom. When I pushed my PJs down to my knees, I noticed my briefs were on backwards.

"This is getting creepy," I mumbled. I stood at the toilet, and as I touched myself to aim—"Ouch." Rawness. Again. Like Voyager days. I skillfully ignored it, figuring I'd coat it with ointment after my shower like I used to. I gave the tub faucet a twist to warm it up, and then I stared at my ugly self in the mirror while stripping. Some days I thought of my reflection as a kind of good-looking young man. Other days, I saw an ugly, small, albino freak.

"Freak." I waved my middle finger. Today, I wasn't good-looking.

I got into the water and washed my hair first, then my body according to the rules of gravity. Face, neck, shoulders, chest, back, and tummy. Then the tender spot. For the past three weeks, I'd taken special care to wash carefully around the stitches.

I sat down in the tub, spread my legs, brought a washcloth in for the gentle cleaning, and stopped.

"What the...?" Water had blurred my vision. I shook my head and wiped my eyes. I looked again. The dark discoloration, the scabbing, and the black threads...were *gone*.

"Oh, my God," I said slowly while remembering Kathy handing Mom an envelope. Was there a pill in it? Mom's words rang through my mind: "We'll find a way to make this as easy as we can." I then remembered that I did *not* remember anything since dinner. I certainly didn't recall putting my pajamas on. My dick was raw. "Oh, no—" I wanted to cry, but I couldn't. This was apparently the way life was. Someone had either carried me down to his clinic and delivered me to him, or.... "Oh, no. She let him in my room...while I was *drugged*."

I sat for a long time. Steam rolled around me. I shivered like I was freezing as hot water pounded the top of my head and fell from my hair into open eyes. The water tickling my skin proved I wasn't dead, but I was almost too numb to feel it. Staring at the faucet, inches from my face, anchored me to the moment. Hiding in the steam and the loud spray of water against porcelain soothed my nerves and blocked the world beyond the shower curtain. I wished this moment alone would never end.

Shaking my head slowly, I recapped all that had happened.

"They drugged me…and he did it again." The reversed underpants were another private message from him to me. A calling card from that other world, once hidden across town in his office and inside the folded paper that I'd taped shut, but now infiltrating my home. My own *room*. It was all real. Not a dream or an irrational fear. His words about how my white hair was going to make me a star soon wedged into my brain as if he were saying them to me right then. "What does he want from me?" Then I gave in, "Oh, why the hell do I even care?"

I crouched in defeat. The shower that pounded my head and flowed over my body kept me from disappearing until I'd used all the hot water, making it too cold to stay. I shut off the faucet but sat, face pressed hard into my kneecaps, shivering from the cold water I'd at first been too paralyzed to leave. Eventually, I stood, dried off, and stumbled across the slippery tiles to look back at the ugly face in my mirror.

"They're gone." I was poetically referring to the stitches *and* my friends with one comment. "No one can save me now." I looked up toward the heaven that I had once believed in and sneered. "Good one, *God!* I asked for someone who could help, and instead, you took away the only people I could trust. You couldn't just send someone…could you?" I focused back on my face. "Well, Jack. Wherever you are…I guess I'm going to come be with you soon."

Somehow that comment gave me a morbid sense of comfort. Wherever I was headed on my journey through all this summer's crap, was going to have a kindred soul there waiting for me to join him. Whatever awaited me, at least I wouldn't be so alone with all this anymore.

In the mirror, I was uglier than I'd ever been. So was the world.

"Maybe there *is* no one to send. Maybe I'm the only one who thinks it should be better than this." With a heavy, intense stare I burned a look into the eyes in my mirror. I was looking at my own eyes but seeing Jack's. For a brief moment, we were now the same person. "No one saved you, did they, Jack. No one's saving me either. No one ever saves anyone."

I walked back to bed, naked, and crawled in to warm up. I fell quickly into a dream in which I was the one who'd wandered into Daniel's room and sat on the end of *his* bed. I once again asked him for help, and when he ignored me, I grabbed his wrists and tried to pull him toward me to get him to listen to how much pain I was in. After all, he was my brother.

"Daniel!" I screamed.

I pulled and pulled on him again. How could he just sit there ignoring me? I needed someone I could trust. A dad. A friend. An older brother. Anyone.

"Daniel!"

47

Mystery Calling

Psychopathic Dr. Krieg, being pretty much a common pedophile, had indeed realized my greatest fears and had indeed taken advantage of my parents' blindness one more time—and in my own room. He was becoming bolder. Psychopaths do that. The more they get away with, the more sick confidence they build. If people like Hitler could do what they did and not feel bad about it, then I guess Krieg could do what he did the same way. I couldn't comprehend it, but I at least needed to accept it as true.

Rock bottom was coming fast, and like riding down a mountain on a sled with no brakes, I was learning it as the way things just were. All seemed lost at the time, but since I hadn't met Tuck Taylor yet, I had no way of knowing that he was somehow being prepared for a calling he didn't know he was answering. Somehow, and I absolutely cannot explain how, but somehow, Tuck and I were dreaming the same thing at the same time...again. It seems that miracles, whether real or imaginary, are one thing that absolutely cannot be predicted or even fully understood.

By Tuck Taylor

"Tuck!" Somebody shouted and grabbed my wrists.

Oh, God! I tried to scream. But I couldn't open my eyes. Paralyzed between consciousness and sleep, I couldn't defend myself. They were trying to pull me out of bed.

Oh, shit! Oh, shit! I strove to yell, but I couldn't wake up. My eyes were stuck shut. My hands were glued to my chest. Panic filled me from head to toe. They tugged and I couldn't stop them. My spirit thrashed, hoping not to be killed by whoever had broken into my apartment, but my body lay vulnerable, paralyzed as if I was drugged or already dead.

"Tuck!" the voice screamed again. What the hell was happening? Leave me alone!

The whole world started to shake like a locomotive was coming, bearing down on me. Things were getting worse. Terror! A crow cawed so loud that it sounded like a woman's scream. "Save him!"

"*Jesus Christ!*" My legs jerked. My arms broke free and shot straight up to break the attacker's grip. I opened my eyes and gasped for air. The room was out of focus. Where were they? *Who* where they?

As light started to form into shapes. I became able to see my dark bedroom door. My desk. The window.

I was awake.

No one was there.

"What the fuck was that?" I panted and pushed my palms into my eyes to rub the crazy out of them. Then I scanned the room one more time to be sure I was alone. "Jesus *Christ*! What the *hell* was that?"

Listen to the dream

Confused and relieved, I was definitely alone and thanking my lucky stars that the crow had woken me from the trap of the nightmare. Three times that summer I'd dreamt of being in The Place Without Shadows. Why was this dream different? It was the first to end in violence. And who was it that kept calling my name?

It was stress-induced, no doubt. I was sure no one was really crying out for help. These psychotic nightmares were proof I needed a change in direction. The clock said it was 1:00 p.m. I knew it was Tuesday.

I'd been on call all night at the hotline. I'd only gotten three hours of sleep since breakfast and needed more. So I lay still and as my breathing calmed, somehow I dozed back off.

I immediately faded for the fourth time that summer into The Place Without Shadows, but this time, I was not alone. Above me flew the white dove from years before, once again speaking riddles without moving its beak.

Show me trust.

"What?" I asked. Everything vanished and it seemed I was suddenly standing face to face with it, in a place of absolutely nothing else. Just me and the bird. "I show everyone trust."

Show one like me.

"One like you?"

Show one like me.

"You mean a bird?"

It's time to go!

"But I'm not done with school. I don't know—"

You know enough!

Again, my legs jolted. "HUH!" I woke up again, exhausted and now also frustrated.

"God!" I shook side to side. "These fucking dreams are driving me *insane*!"

I calmed down and stared into the ceiling. Whether these stress dreams were self-induced or some sort of guidance from The Place Without Shadows, the message was the same. Get up and move on. I still believed about 80% that they were a psychologically explainable self-induced stress release. But that other 20% of me was becoming more and more curious about the bird. Was he a messenger of some kind?

"I should have asked the bird for clarity." What the hell did *one like me* mean? A bird? I was supposed to teach a goddamned white-feathered bird how to trust me?

Then frustration built again as I wondered whether this was a natural subconscious dream or a mysterious otherworldly message. Either way, I had to decode it. I sure as hell didn't know "enough" like it said. Look at the mess I'd made with Mark and Trenton. Had I proven I could be trusted when I stirred their lives into a tizzy? I had been in college two years and had only begun to explore the ways and depths in which people suffer from inside. I hadn't learned how to administer therapy on anyone, human or fowl.

"This was just a stupid dream." I squeezed the top of my nose and rubbed my eyes with a thumb and forefinger. "Don't fall for it, Taylor. Don't give in. This is all just natural stress."

A new plan

I stumbled sleepily into the bathroom. "I know enough," I huffed. Then I kind of laughed at myself. "Oh brother." Still suffocating in the sweltering afternoon heat I looked into the mirror into baggy, dark eyes. "Oh God. I look as bad as I feel." My long, thick hair was greasy and tangled from sweat and sleep.

"Stupid bird."

A shrill caw snapped my head toward the window. It must have been right outside. It was the same scream that had woken me up by sounding like a woman screaming, "Save him!"

"Save *who*?" I grabbed my hair with both hands. "What in Sam Hill is going on?"

I walked to the window to look for the crow and put an end to this insanity. I was right. He wasn't but six feet from me on the telephone line trailing from the building. As I silently stared, several more landed, one after the other next to him.

"God, I'd love to get a picture of that." Like dominoes, the angle from my vantage point was fascinating. The lighting was perfect for a dramatic black and white, if I could catch them before they flew off.

I kept a camera loaded and ready for lucky shots. This was a good one. By tiptoeing and staying quiet, I was able to snap off three good shutter clicks before the birds took flight in turns. I got three more shots of their departure.

I lowered the camera, feeling rejuvenated. Somehow, seeing the crow that had been a part of my dream made the whole thing less crazy and more explainable as just a crow. "I must have dreamt about a bird because I could hear birds outside my window." But also, as simple as it was, taking the pictures like a photographer was more satisfying than anything I'd done in days.

The answer is a click away

I held my camera up and rotated it slowly, looking intently at the front, top, and bottom. It seemed to be a living part of my waking life. A friend who shared in my greatest joy and who helped me document everything I saw. It helped me to artistically and effectively express how I saw the world, one snapshot photo at a time. Then I glanced over at my cold, dead college textbooks. Then I positioned the camera back up to my face and scanned the room through the lens. I liked looking at the world through a lens. Somehow it made everything more meaningful.

"I'm leaving," I said aloud, putting down the camera.

Saying those two words lit my face into a smile such as I hadn't expressed in months. So I uttered them again. "I'm fucking *leaving*!" I felt an even deeper cleansing in my soul.

"Oh, my God." I held my camera up to speak to it like a friend. "I love you." I looked back at the textbooks. "I hate you." I smiled again and headed for the bathroom mirror.

I put the camera down so I could talk directly to my reflection, which looked brighter and less exhausted than a few moments before. I smiled excitedly into the mirror.

"The dream's right. It's time to go. Time to get the fuck out of Texas." Another smile lit across my face. "I can't go home, though. All my friends are gone." I gooped up a toothbrush and began scrubbing my teeth, back and forth, back and forth. Just like my decision to go or stay, go or stay. The rhythm of the brushing brought my mind to the summer before when my grandfather had taken me to a grange hall so we could listen to his next-door neighbor and best friend, Louie, play accordion at a town celebration.

"Grandpa!" I shouted. White foam ran down my chin and splattered on the sink. "I guess I coooooould…" I held the toothbrush still while I pondered the thought, "go stay with Grandpa for the rest of the summer!" The idea seemed to come out of nowhere. It was a fresh idea. One that felt good as it cleansed the confusion out of my body, heart and brain. "Why didn't I think of this before?"

I cleaned up. Feeling this good had to mean I was on the right path. I picked up my beloved Cannon camera and winked into the mirror.

"Fuck Texas!" I blurted out and then gazed back into my eyes in the mirror. Was I being ridiculous? Back and forth, go or stay.

"I can't." I watched my own shoulders droop. I put the camera down on the countertop. "Everyone wants to be done with college. I'm just…being normal. I've come this far. I should finish what I start." Then I looked back into the mirror to make a final statement to the disappointed face. "But, oh, man…if I had the guts, Duluth, Minnesota would be a perfect change."

48

Telephone Demon Stalker

The thing about rock bottom is that you don't know how far you can drop until you finally stop dropping. I apparently still had a tiny bit farther to go. Just when you think things can't get worse…right?

Catholic school, while out of mind for the summer, still existed, and I still had a full year of it left. Andreo still had a vendetta on me, and I still didn't know why. Occasionally, he liked to remind me of it by injecting a dose of disruption into any peaceful moments he feared I might be enjoying. On Tuesday, July 16, he must have been bored with his own life and felt the need to mess with mine, so he paid an unwelcome visit. How is it so easy for some people to kick a guy when he's down? Why the hell was he so obsessed with me?

By Kyle Rickett

Papa's festive accordion harmonized with mine at the grange hall in Duluth, Minnesota, while we played my best song, "The Johnny Oslo Schottische" for a delighted crowd that danced and waved at me.

At high noon, the phone rang.

"Kyle! It's for you!" I crash-landed back into my lonesome room on Torano Island, where dancing with my fans was only happening in my head. My catatonic, still naked body was lying flat on the bed; the music was a tape player, and no one was celebrating my talent.

I sighed and pulled a pair of neatly folded PE shorts out of a drawer, not caring whether I *fell out of them* or not, and thumped down the stairs, cynically wondering why it mattered that I even *take* the stairs. Why not let someone throw me off the balcony—maybe drug me and strip the shorts off first for some pornographic pictures?

I crossed through the living room, too numb to speak. Fran was visiting *again*. Her girls were playing in the corner with a dollhouse Mom kept for them. The women stopped their mindless, gossipy couch conversation to look, but I kept to my quiet shuffle to the kitchen.

"Well, *that* was certainly quite *rude*." Fran made sure I heard her comment to Mom.

"Yeah!" Jayne shouted in her usual henhouse agreement.

"Yeah, Uncle Kyle. Don't be a rude dude!" chimed in BJ with a four-year-old toothless lisp and a giggle.

The wall-phone receiver was lying on the kitchen desk. I carefully held it to my ear for a second.

"Hello?" I hoped it was Connor.

"Hi, Homo!"

My heart tightened in my chest. God was angry that I'd stopped praying. I hadn't thought things could get worse, but they just had. My defeated body awoke to a more terrified panic as I felt a volcano of black, oily blood squeeze out of my heart and push its way up my throat. My secrets were unraveling. Enemies were in the living room. Enemies were on the phone. My friends were all gone. I pictured again my folded paper.

These two worlds weren't supposed to blend. I looked out the kitchen window at the beautiful summer leaves, which the icy death of St. Tiberius school wasn't supposed to merge with.

"How's Homo-Boy?" he attacked again. I slowly, carefully, without creating a scene, hung the phone back up. I looked down at my chest and could see my heart beating erratically under thin skin. My hand shook as I drew it back.

I realize I should have shouted at him. I had been taught from birth to be bully-bait, so that's what I was. I should have called him a prick and threatened to beat the living shit out of him at school. But that wasn't me back then. If I had been the kind of kid who knew I could stand up to him, he wouldn't have called in the first place. In fact, he just wouldn't have been so obsessed with me at all. He was the bully. I was the bait. He was as trapped in this toxic scenario as I was. I had a lot to learn about standing up for myself, but there and then, I had no one to teach me how to do that. In fact, since I hadn't met Tuck yet, no one would have even allowed me to learn it on my own.

I wished I could have thought of something to shout back at him, but no matter what I'd have said at that time in my life, it would have only enraged him further. He apparently hated me a lot more than I hated him. Besides, my mind went blank when he attacked. Hanging up seemed like the most power I had. Thoughts then raced shamefully to my vulnerabilities.

When you live your life with secrets, *those secrets own you.* Was my secret out? Who did he tell Mom he was? Did he ask for me by name? Whether he was tactful or not, he proved he could reach my family by telephone—and could tell them anything while I lay helpless in bed, foolishly listening to happy music only a few feet above. I looked around the kitchen to make sure no one had heard the voice or had seen me hang up.

These phone calls came usually only one or two times each summer, and like a naïve idiot, I never expected them. I knew it was Andreo making the calls. But for the love of God, I still didn't know why.

Silently, I wandered back toward the stairs.

"Who was that?" Mom asked while Fran pretended to be preoccupied by leafing through a magazine that had sat on the coffee table for weeks unread.

"I don't know." I stared at the floor and kept my pace. I almost said, "A producer wants to hire me as a porn star." But, instead, I answered with a different lie, "There was no one there."

"Phh." Fran huffed arrogantly and kept pretending the magazine was more interesting than I was.

"Huh," Mom commented.

I slunk all the way to my room, where I imagined myself at midnight, swimming beneath Andreo's boat with my dad's antique hand-operated drill and sinking his hateful ass in his sleep, solving my problems once and for all.

Trust

The day dragged slow and quiet until Fran and the girls' goodbyes loudly announced their leaving. As soon as the front screen door closed, and the voices moved to the driveway, I came back downstairs to lie on the couch. Fran's two-year-old Dodge Duster sounded bad, backfiring and smoking up the place. Mom came back in and closed the front door, shaking her head in disgust.

"Why doesn't she tune that thing up?" I asked. "I could tell it was misfiring the other day, too."

"Because," as she disappeared into the kitchen, Mom sarcastically commented, "she knows Dad wants her to."

My parents never figured out that in order to get Fran or Daniel to do anything, they needed to use reverse psychology. Both siblings had the tendency to bite off their noses to spite anyone who gave them advice.

Where are my stitches?

I waited a minute, trying to work up the courage to ask her a question that I wasn't sure I wanted the answer to. I was still off balance from the residual trauma of Andreo's phone call, so all-in-all, I was not in a good place for a stressful confrontation with my mother. But I really wanted to know where my stitches went. Finally, I worked up the courage to enter the kitchen, quietly and humbly.

"Mom?"

"Yeah?" She was sitting at the table reading the morning paper.

"How did my stitches get taken out?"

As I've mentioned before, Mom's anxiety could rise quickly. She became obviously nervous and addressed me with a tinge of anger, as if I had accused her of something. "You needed them out, Honey. We talked about that."

"We did?" I honestly didn't remember us talking about it.

"Well, I told you we would find a way to make it easy for you."

I turned red, not from anger, but horror.

"You wanted them out, didn't you?"

"Yeah…but…did you watch him do it?" My voice weakened. "Was it Dr. Krieg? Were you in the room with him?"

"Of course it was Dr. Krieg. Who else would it be? And there was no need for us to be in the room. You were already in bed. Daddy and I stayed downstairs."

"Why?"

"What reason would we have to watch? Anyway, he told us it was best if he did it alone."

"Why? What would make it best for him to be alone with me?"

"Oh, Kyle. For crying out loud. He's your *doctor*. You wanted your stitches out. He took them out. What…is…the…*problem*?"

I became too weak to talk. I suppose if I'd been a fighter I'd have screamed "because he raped me!" But I was not up for a fight. She'd have just called me a liar. Then she'd tell Dad and Fran that I'd falsely accused the honorable Doctor of something too horrible to mention. And worse yet, the mere mention of his actions would have meant that I'd willingly taken my own tape off the three-sided page and opened it up for the world to see. I would be announcing the existence of Santa's favorite elf, which, in and of itself sent sheer terror through my mind, body *and* spirit. She was already irritated. I knew I couldn't take that terror on.

I mumbled a sound that resembled the word "okay," turned around and quietly left the kitchen.

Relentless worry

Forty-five minutes later, as I lay on the couch, staring at the edge of the coffee table through one open eye, the phone rang again. I sat straight up so fast that the room spun. As my dizzy head settled, my heartbeats became almost too loud for me to hear Mom answer.

"Hello?"

"Oh, my God," I whispered, but nearly vomited. That's when I realized I was gripping a cushion so hard I was nearly damaging it. Instead of releasing my fingers, I focused all consciousness on listening through the kitchen door and inventorying my body, wishing I had shoes on in case I needed to flee for my life if Andreo told Mom what I was.

"Oh, no, no, no, you're not interrupting anything…. I've got time to talk now. Sure."

My gut started to hurt.

"Oh…no." She responded while someone was telling her *something*. "You're kidding." She spoke with a dramatic moan.

My fingernails started to hurt from my grip.

"Oh…noooooo," she droned again. This could be bad.

Then she laughed.

"Oh…God." I moaned in relief and released the cushion.

"Not much here," she continued. "I've been caring for my little guy lately." After a short pause, she answered, "No, he just got bumped up on his bike a little. He'll be just fine in no time."

It was one of her friends. The circulation of blood restarted moving so freely in my face and neck that I almost overheated from relief. I lay back down and closed my eyes. "Thank you, God."

Get on with life

After about fifteen minutes, I heard the loud goodbye, and then Mom appeared in the doorway. She saw me lying dead on the couch and sighed from obvious annoyance that I had been there since Fran had left.

"Kyle, honey, why don't you go out and play?"

"With who?" I asked in a monotone voice I had to force out. My mind was almost not in my body as I obsessed over how fragile the boundaries between all three of my worlds were today. Maybe I should have just completely given in, stopped fighting for my life, and blurted out what the rest of the world was threatening to tell her: *I have sex with Dad's friend and I'm a homo—whatever that is.* Then she could kill me and it would all be over with.

"What about Chad?"

"Huh?" I snapped to again. "Oh, Chad plays with Connor, and I'm not allowed to play with him."

"Oh, c'mon, Kyle; there are a lot of kids on this block. This has been going on for weeks now." Mom then used words that sounded suspiciously like something Fran would have fed her. "You've gotten to be such a moody teen. Why aren't you yourself anymore? Is life really that bad?"

Is life really that bad? Was she stupid? Was she 100 percent clueless as to who I even was?

I had no way to respond. After spending nearly fourteen years proving to her that I loved Scooter McBride, she apparently couldn't see that his mysterious disappearance just might have hurt me so badly that I could barely breathe. I had told her in plain, un-coded English that Connor was my very best friend, and yet she didn't seem to see how it would have any impact on me that he was banned from my life now.

Is life really that bad? Mom couldn't see past her own nose. To me, life was indeed that bad, but every time I tried to share the grief with someone, it only got worse, so what could I do but stay quiet and not make eye contact?

"I'll ask Dad again about you and Connor. I can't promise anything, but…." She motioned me to the kitchen. "C'mon, honeybunch; even if I can't get anywhere with him, summer will be over before you know it, and Dad'll forget all about all of this. Then you can talk to Connor again and you'll have your school friends back."

My *school friends*? Was she completely blind? Outwardly, I'd become distant and silent, but the world inside my head was filled with voices screaming insanely. She *knew* I hated school. I had *begged* her so many times to let me out of St. Tiberius because *I had no friends there*! She had never heard a word I'd said, had she?

I'd been reduced to secret voices shouting in my head. I'd been reduced to Fran's level by sending a behind-her-back eye roll! I couldn't take her on openly. These covert, unsent retributions became the only voices I had anymore.

"Let's have some ice cream. I'll be your summer friend."

Mom's version of a solution: ice cream

I got up as instructed but with posture drooping and head tilted. My hair was beginning to curl out at the bottom by my neck and ears. Mom didn't usually let it grow that long. For some reason, she'd missed the July monthly haircut.

I went where she pointed, sat where I figured she'd wanted me to sit, and placed my hands politely on the table. I sighed heavily, wishing I was at the shop with my dad, working on tractors with him. Instead, I sat in the kitchen waiting for a breakfast bowl filled with whatever she would dish up. My bare feet swung slowly back and forth.

She served a white bowl piled with three rock-hard scoops of vanilla ice cream stacked like a pyramid. Vanilla was her favorite. She turned away to dig out a helping for herself, then looked back and gasped when she caught me carefully lifting the scoops with my spoon and two fingers, looking for any pills that might have *accidentally* fallen into it.

"What have I done?" she whispered.

I snapped a glance toward her. How much more confused could I possibly become? She obviously knew exactly what I was looking for. But…who *was* this woman? Was she actually feeling *guilty*?

49

Sound Advice

It seems that everyone struggles. No matter where you look, people are dealing with pain, physically and emotionally. Today, I speak in public a lot about the different ways people respond to it all. Some ignore life's complexity by memorizing football scores and beer flavors. They learn nothing and help no one, but at least they themselves don't suffer. Others become the agents of change, taking arms and fighting to make the world better for others in the same boat. By turning their pain into a mission, they feel victorious and free. And still others succumb to the suffering and become defeated or self-destructive, maybe alcoholic, drug-addicted, or suicidal!

As I study the world's most successful people, biography after biography shows only one truly common thread: The good people who change the world for the better are from all backgrounds, all races, both genders, all sexual orientations, and all classes. Some were raised poor, others rich. Some were healthy, others sick. The one thing I see in success story after success story is that in almost every powerful change agent, someone in that person's past was on his or her side...no matter what.

By Tuck Taylor

Who was I kidding? I wasn't going to leave Texas. As badly as I wanted to, no one anywhere *needed* my rescue. My reserved nature was stronger than my impulsive side. I wasn't going to quit college to take pictures of crows. I had one reason to leave: I was unhappy. I had half-a-dozen reasons to stay: 1) Mom and Dad were proud of me for what I was doing, 2) I was going to become a doctor and couldn't let them down, 3) College is always the right choice; isn't a formal education always good? 4) I was young, so I could easily put a few years of hard work into myself and then start living a good life in my mid-twenties, 5) What friends I still had in life were all here, and 6) The crisis clinic needed me; it was shorthanded and I made a difference there.

A voice of reason

At 3:00 p.m., the phone rang. Usually it was Mark who called around that time. His calls were diminishing in frequency, but even though it had been a couple of days since the last one, it could still be him. I grabbed the phone, but I didn't pick up. I gave it a third ring so I wouldn't sound excited to talk.

"Aaargh!" A female voice tried sounding like a pirate.

"I'm fine, sis." I politely chuckled. "How are you?"

"Fine. I just thought you deserved a growl. Paybacks, you know."

"You're not very scary, though. I can *hear* you smiling."

"Oh, I can be scary when I want to be."

"Boy, that's for sure." I politely chuckled. "So, is everything okay?"

"Oh, yeah. I was just thinking about how much I love you...and...."

After a very short and conveniently placed pause, I interrupted, "There's more to it than that. It's three o'clock. You're paying the higher rates. What's on your mind for real?"

"I talked with Mom."

"Oh...no...." Jesus, this was only going to get worse. I was having nightmares, and now Ronnie was telling my mom about my stupidity with Mark.

"No, no, no. Don't worry. I didn't tell her about you and Mark. That's up to you to do, and frankly, little brother, I don't see any reason you would ever need to tell her and Dad about any of it."

"I told you nothing really happened."

"And I believe you. But they worry about your friendships with Trenton and his friends even more than I do."

"Do they think gay is contagious?"

"Cut them some slack. They're from a simpler time. They don't know what to think."

"So I'm not being dishonest by keeping secrets?"

"What good would come of it? I mean really. It's not technically a secret. You don't tell Mom about the girls you sleep with, so how's this dumb little massage so different?"

"I suppose." I rolled my eyes to heaven in a thankful expression that she was totally on my side. "I'm flattered that you think I sleep with a lot of girls though." I laughed.

"Don't you?"

"Sure, in my mind. Out in the real world, I'm focused on school, work, and crisis lines."

"My point stands. It would just make them worry all the more. Trenton and his friends have to deal with a lot of hatred aimed at them just for being who they are, and Mom would just worry incessantly that it was happening to you too. So why put her through that if it isn't a real issue anyway?"

"Good point."

"There is something I do worry about, though."

I silently waited for her to tell me what it was. I picked up a pen and started tapping a rhythm on the kitchen counter.

"Depression," she finally said.

I sighed. If she'd known about the dreams I'd been having, of being pulled out of bed and scared half to death, she'd really be worried.

"After you hung up the other day, it hit me. Tuck, college is stressful. You're away from home. You're hanging with friends who don't share your interests…. Why are you voluntarily adding that crisis clinic to your burdens?"

"I don't know. It's for credit."

"There are other places to intern."

"They need me there. And Mom and Dad are proud of me for it."

"Mom and Dad are already proud of you."

"I know, but—"

"They were there…remember?"

"Remember what?"

"Cancer. Losing Micah. Losing Shannon. They talk to me about it sometimes."

"Really? They never say anything to me about it?"

"They don't think you want to talk about it. After all you've been through, they admire how you keep going. They think you're one of the strongest people in the world. I visited Dad at work one day. He keeps a photo of me and Don and the girls on his desk next to his phone."

"Well, any dad would do that."

"He keeps *five* photos of you hanging on the wall next to it. He also has a binder next to the phone of the photos *you've* taken with your own camera throughout your life."

"Wow," I whispered. "I didn't know that."

"He shows it to everyone. You're only in your second year of college and Mom already calls you 'my son, the doctor.'"

I laughed. "That is so Mom."

"It really is." Ronnie laughed back.

I heard a kitchen timer go off in the background.

"Time's up," she cheerfully blurted out. "I gave myself five minutes for this long-distance call."

"Okay. Thanks for calling, sis. I really mean it."

"You're welcome, sweetie. You were on my mind. I just wanted to encourage you not to burn yourself out. Your college degree needs to be the main focus of your life right now. All this other stuff needs to be the small things that you don't waste too much energy on. Don't lose sight of your dream, honey. Never lose sight of your dream. Don't let anyone...not Mark, or Trenton, or Mom, or the crisis clinic...or *me*...take it from you."

"Okay, sis. I won't."

"I love you, little brother."

"And thanks for telling me about what Mom and Dad say about me behind my back. It means a lot right now."

50

Insane Accusations

Again, I speak of an evil I cannot comprehend. Nothing can drive a reasonable person crazy faster than trying to reason with an unreasonable abuser who, without any conscience, says whatever he or she wants to say in order to win every conversation. If the reasonable person is a much younger sibling, the practice of rhetoric is better described as an act of absolute balls-to-the-walls bullying in its rawest form. Child abuse. I'm not talking about Dr. Krieg this time. Something I didn't recognize back then was that my problems at home were greater than anything Krieg or St. Tiberius could dish up. My sister, Fran, knew enough of my struggles to know how to confuse, humiliate, and belittle me on a relentless and recurring basis.

So she did.

She knew that Mom forced me to forgive and forget any horrible things she said, so Fran brazenly used my trust and my family ties to her advantage. I couldn't really tattle on her because at only thirteen years old, I couldn't figure out how she was doing it. And any time I tried asking for help, I got nowhere. She always, always, always faked innocence to her allies...my family. And I was always, always, always instructed just to be nice to my sister and turn the other cheek. Apparently, my family couldn't comprehend the evil of a sociopath either, but instead of being confused by it, they simply denied it was possible.

Even if I had proof of what she'd said or done, I was simply called a liar and my proof was dismissed. Mom, Dad, and Daniel usually said, "Let it go. She didn't mean anything by it." So, like a well-meaning little brother, I always, always, always let it go and tried to accept that her words were just another in a coincidental lifetime of isolated "slips of the tongue."

In today's psychology, Fran's technique for driving me crazy is called gaslighting, and it is a long-term strategy intended to water down the truth around somebody to the point that no one, not even the victim, can be certain of what the truth even is anymore. When someone is gaslighted into believing he is crazy, he comes to the place where he no longer trusts his own perceptions and, therefore, can no longer fight for himself. Here's how it feels: 1) Each single incident isn't enough to drive you crazy, but to remember and tell the whole story of a lifetime of small attacks would take hours, and would sound crazy. 2) No one has ever believed you before. 3) So at the mere thought of trying to defend yourself, your brain knows it can't. 4) So if you try to defend yourself, your badly beaten brain spins into a tornado and then blanks out while you're trying to defend yourself. At that point, you look and feel crazy.

Frustration attacks you from the inside while people attack externally. You're outnumbered, and after being proven wrong so many times, even you are not on your own side. You can lose your train of thought before you can prove your innocence. You become as guilty as they've said you are.

By Kyle Rickett

That night, the phone rang at five minutes after five. Our family dinner times tended to fluctuate depending on when Dad could get home from the shop. Some nights we ate before the evening news, other nights afterward. This particular night we ate early, around 4:30. Mom had a firm and standing rule about the evening news, which every person she knew was aware of. She'd watch the news from 5:00 to 5:30, and if anyone called during that half hour, she would not answer. Everyone knew it. So when the phone rang at a few minutes past 5:00, I answered, but with a cautious finger ready to push the cradle down if it was Andreo.

"Hello," I cautiously droned.

"Hi, Kyle," bellowed Fran's cheery, faintly slurred voice.

"Oh, hi." I dropped my hand away from the cradle. "You know Mom can't talk now."

"Yup!"

"So why'd ya call?"

"To talk to you!" she announced cheerfully. "Sometimes it's just nice to talk to my little Buster."

I smiled slightly. That was nice. She hadn't called me Buster in years. It was a nickname from happier times.

"So…what'dya want to talk about?"

"You-ahh!" she laughed boisterously. "Mom says you're kind of down, so I thought I'd call. We've all been worried about you."

"You all have?"

"Oh, yeah. You know we all love you, and we want to make sure you're happy."

"Oh. Okay."

"So…why have you been so moody lately?"

"I'm not *moody*," I protested, and then I felt defensive. "If you talk about me all the time, then you all know why, right?"

"Well, we want to hear it from your own mouth. C'mon. What's got you so mad at everyone?"

"I'm not—"

"I've been wiping your nose since you were born. I can read you like a book. We all can. And we can tell you're mad by the way you carry yourself. You're at that age where you're clumsy and can't control your emotions. I remember when Daniel was like that too—but then I guess he's still that way. Ha ha ha!" she laughed arrogantly. "Boys aren't mature enough to be good teenagers. Plus, you were always way-hay-hay too emotional to start with. There's nothing dumber than a boy with too much emotion. You're mad. No one deserves you being mad at them, so I figure you must be depressed or something."

"I'm not depressed," I stated.

"Then you're mad…and I was right. Wasn't I?"

"I'm not *mad*!" I was starting to feel twisted like a pretzel.

"Well, you sound mad now."

"You're making me mad by telling me I am already!"

"See? I was right. I mean, it's not that any of us really care. We know we didn't do anything wrong. So it's your problem, not ours."

"So why are you calling to talk to me about it then…if it doesn't matter?"

"We think you need help to get things straightened out."

"What *things*?"

"This is about Scott, isn't it?"

I was trying to keep track of where she was going. It felt like she was all over my mind, grabbing at anything she could get a thought-twisting finger on. She wouldn't let me process a full thought before moving to another question, driving me deeper into a confused whirlwind. And what the hell did she know about Scooter?

"You know I love you, right?" she asked like she already knew the answer. "I bought you that little car, and a movie and dinner…."

"Yeah. I know." I immediately regretted letting her take me out and buy the two-dollar car for me.

"Then you need to forget about Scott. He's not your friend."

"*What*? He is *too* my *friend*! He's my favorite cousin! I like him better than all the rest of them put together." My stomach soured. What if Scooter hated me and I was too dumb to know it?

"Yeah, I know. Mom told everyone how rude you were to them last week. And if you made an ass out of yourself all because of Scott, then you really blew it this time. He's *not* your friend. Trust me."

"Trust you?" Did Scooter hate me? I couldn't think. What had I done that would make Scooter hate me? Or maybe he knew I couldn't make friends at school and could finally see why.

"You still there?" she checked in a cold voice.

"Mom—" I murmured. "Mom tells people about that?"

"Not that she needed to. We all saw it."

"I…" I whispered softly as I lost a bit more of my ability to think of any reasonable response.

"You what? You hate me? Is that what you were going to say?"

"No," I mumbled.

"Good. Because you need me too much. I'm helping and you know it." She laughed arrogantly. "You need to let me ask you something."

"What?" The kitchen began to fuzz over as my eyes lost focus, like I was…*trancing*…or something.

"What sorts of things did you and Scott do in that sleeping bag you always slept in together?"

"Uhh…*slept*."

"You sure about that?"

"Sometimes we talked…about my nightmares." My face was turning red. What was I was being accused of *now*?

"Oh, what *nightmares*?" she scoffed. "You don't have nightmares! And everyone knows that boys don't sleep together in one bag, unless—"

"Scott and me have been doing that since we were babies! He's my cousin…my friend." Or so I hoped. "He protects me and buys me licorice. He was *supposed* to be here for the Fourth and take me for a ride with his new driver's license."

"Scott likes boys—not girls!" Fran shouted.

I have many memories of her being the one to make the juiciest announcements. It was her most exciting competitive tactic in life…to be the whistle-blower whenever she could be. But what the information did to me at that moment confused me more. For about three seconds, I felt shock. Then for the next three, relief that the separation really *was* about Scooter and *not about me*. But on the seventh second, it moved to fear. If this were true, how could it be undone? Did this mean he really was gone forever?

After a long silence, she again asked, "You still there?"

"No, he doesn't."

"Yup, he sure does."

"How do you know?" I quietly asked.

"What do you think? I'm lying? Is that what you think?"

"Noooooo." Frustrated, I defended my response—*again*.

"They caught him."

"Who caught him? What the hell are you talking about?"

"I'm a Christian, so I don't deserve to be sworn at, Mister. Certainly not by a snotty-nosed, overly emotional, moody teen."

"Who caught him?" I corrected. "And what are you talking about?"

"Auntie Maureen caught him and another boy from his football team making out behind a fence." She then added a footnote that seemed important to her. "But I have to tell you, it didn't surprise me one little bit."

"So what?" My mood changed quickly as I instantly transformed from victim to savior—Scooter was in trouble, so it was my turn to step up for him. My shoulders went from sagging in defeat to rearing back for a fight. I was now beet red. What did she mean it didn't surprise her? Scott was awesome. This was unbelievable.

I didn't care what he was being accused of, and I also didn't understand it. I had never met a boy who liked boys before. Those were called *funny boys* back then, and Scott wasn't one of them. We islanders thought of them as big city people, who talked with lisps and let their hands hang limp on their wrists. Scott was a tennis champion, football player, softball team captain, a track team superstar, and a goddamned fine man. He was handsome, tall, and as manly as anyone I knew. Scott protected smaller kids. He was "Agent McBride at your service." I replied to her accusation by making sure she knew she hadn't shaken my friendship. It was the moment I began to see that I could fight like a man if it were for someone else. I just couldn't fight for myself.

"I don't care what you say he is!" I said, but then I recalled her report that he'd been caught red-handed kissing a boy. If it was true, it didn't matter, so I added, "And I don't *fucking* care *who* he kisses. He's my favorite cousin and nothing will change that. Is *that* why he didn't come to see us last week?"

"You think Mom was going to let a pervert like that sleep in your sleeping bag with you again?" She puffed loudly into the phone, ignoring my latest swear word.

"Mom did that?"

"She needed to protect you. You know as well as the rest of us do how bad you are at protecting yourself. You are so lucky we are willing to love you despite how much work you are."

"He's *not* a *pervert*! You're *wrong*! I *love* him like he's my *own brother*! Stop saying mean things about him!" I was getting more confused by the second. Not only from the news about Scott, but that my own mother—the woman who'd always thanked him for protecting me—had taken him away.

"A little advice?" Her anger seemed to have transformed into a tone of wisdom. "You need to stop saying 'love' when you're talking about him. People are all going to think you like boys too…. *Do you?*"

"*What?*" I almost dropped the phone. What the hell was she talking about?

Mom stepped into the kitchen. It was only 5:15, but she could hear me yelling and knew exactly what was going on.

"Give me the phone." Her chin wrinkled in anger. I handed it over and stepped back two paces. Mom took it from there.

"Fran Marie Rickett, what the *hell* is the matter with you?"

The two women fought for a minute or two. Mom noted, "You've been drinking!" and asked a series of ridiculous, unanswerable questions. "What made you think that was a good idea?" and "Who do you think you are?" while I went upstairs, pulled my bathrobe off the first hanger, sat on the floor of my closet, slid the door closed, and hid beneath the robe.

Insanity begins

The closed darkness of the wardrobe closet soothed me slightly. The world had gotten too big and too crazy. There in the dark, I shrank the world down, contained the sensory overload, and felt a tad more in control of my own brain. There, her fingers weren't inside my head, stirring my thoughts into a whirlwind.

"Oh, my God. Oh, my God. Oh, my God. Oh, my God." I rocked back and forth, feeling tears falling down both cheeks.

"Who am I? Who am I? Who am I?" I cinched my eyes tightly closed to stop the tears.

"Why am I here? Who needs me? No one. No one. No one needs me here. I don't need to be here." My scar started to hurt, but I didn't care.

"I have no friends. No friends. No one loves me. Oh, my God. Oh, my God. Oh, my God. It's not just me. It's really happening. It's really happening. It's really happening. I'm nothing. Nothing. Nothing."

I tried and tried to cry, thinking that if I could just wail it out, I'd feel better. But I couldn't. I could only chant, "Oh, my God. Oh, my God. Oh, my God," and feel tears without the wailing.

I did this for forty-five minutes before I began to feel silly under a robe in my closet. I feared Mom coming in and catching me in tears. So I hung the robe up, dumped my box of Legos on the floor, sat cross-legged, and stared at them. The way they fell, a pattern emerged of Dr. Krieg's angry face. I stared in an empty trance for the next two hours.

51

The Taylor Articles

As my mind was falling apart, Tuck's inner torment was building also. Both of us were short on sleep, riddled by dreams, and confused over who we were to those around us.

Trauma victims often write. Inner torment comes to life when we're alone or undistracted. Writing with ink on paper, as I've mentioned in an earlier chapter, puts body and texture to otherwise loose, un-tethered emotions and thoughts. Writing is like putting a leash on an otherwise formless thought and pulling it into the natural world so we can see where it goes, and maybe even control it for a few moments.

We both wrote, but in different ways. I wrote and destroyed so no one could know what was going on in my insane head. Tuck had no secrets. He wrote to control cancer and loss, but to him, words were a waste of paper if someone didn't read them. But in all fairness, Tuck could trust the people who read his words.

By Tuck Taylor

Up to now I haven't told you about my journal. Mostly, I suppose, because it wasn't technically a journal. It was a series of magazines I'd made myself with colored pens, photographs, and tape. I called the magazine *Taylor*. I wrote my own articles, photographed and developed my own pictures, and taped or glued it all together whenever I had enough to fill a whole issue. I was nine when Trenton and I wrote our first article entitled "Dinner Time." We wrote it like we were the dog. All our photos were taken from the dog's level, of my mom pouring food into his dish. Trenton didn't keep writing articles, but I did. When I left for college, I counted sixty-six issues stored neatly on a shelf over my bed—nearly three hundred short articles, spanning twelve years of life. Mom said she would never, ever allow anyone to destroy them because they were such a special report on the history of our family as seen through the eyes of "an important little boy."

It was a clever hobby I'd had ever since I'd been in that car accident with Shannon, and my parents let me use their typewriter when I was seven. I practiced it so much that by the time I was nine, I could type like a secretary. Remember, we didn't have computers back then, so my ability to type was a highly unusual skill for a boy to have developed.

With my dreams turning to nightmares, and my worry that maybe history (cancer) was repeating itself, I probably should have started journaling again. It might have helped ease my inner turmoil.

Never lose sight of your dream

Ronnie's call had come at a good time for me as I waffled on whether to stay or go. I was really starting to hate school. I sort of wanted to write an article about the crows on the phone line and how my camera was calling for me to leave Texas. Mark's poems were taking on a brighter theme again. He was starting to move forward again with his life. Trenton was acting more and more like he wanted to move on also. A decision had to be made soon.

The words Ronnie had said at the end of the call, "never lose sight of your dream" rang out in my mind over and over again, causing more confusion through guilt because she meant for me to "stay, stay," but I was hearing "go, go." If I were to take her advice all the way to the molecular level, then never giving up on my dream would be the opposite of what she'd intended.

By nightfall, the loneliness of that apartment had gotten me so depressed I almost couldn't stand my own company. I was also worried that everything she'd said about me being in the wrong place at the crisis clinic was going to change my mood when I showed up for work that night.

I feel sorry for people who rely on family for advice, but whose family uses that advice to constantly hold them back. Ronnie was always on my side, and I had only the highest respect for her advice. Even when I didn't agree completely, I always saw *something* in her wisdom that could change or guide me forward.

She was right about me needing a more positive internship.

I guess I didn't have to quit everything. I could go about it slowly, trying to bring myself back to balance without overcorrecting and making a whole new mess. I could quit the crisis clinic without quitting school. I could acclimate myself to new waters slowly. As badly as I wanted to leave, common sense, or…fear…kept making me stay the course just a little longer.

It was 7:30 p.m. when I lay down to get a few hours of sleep for my upcoming midnight shift, and I decided, as I fell asleep, that I was going to rethink everything. The clinic was short-handed already, but I needed to start preparing my coworkers for my eventual early retirement. I figured I'd tell them that night that I was quitting next week to give them time to adjust the schedule, and give me time to adjust my thinking and be ready to leave on my last day.

52

Escape Plan

What I learned from the activities that summer was that I had no proof my life was going to work out if I stayed my course. So I began to think that maybe I needed to change that course. Just like getting into a cold pool slowly, changing who I was at the core could be done if I allowed myself to move forward one inch, accept the new temperature, and then move forward another inch. "Evolve" rather than "change." I wanted to stop pretending I could leave my family in an imaginary gold hot rod. I wanted firm proof that I could leave them for real if things got any worse.

By Kyle Rickett

I came out of my trance and scooped the Legos back into their box. Then I wrote a letter to Scooter. A short one. All it said was that I loved him and I hoped he loved me too, but I wouldn't blame him if he didn't.

I planned to steal a stamp from Mom and mail it the next day. But I had no idea whether anyone would let him see it. At least I'd have tried.

By nightfall, I had isolated myself deeper into my head than ever. I was mad at so many different things that I had to scream about something.

"She fucking *drugged* me!" I shouted into my pillow. "Argh!" My own anger frightened me because it felt as if I were about to go completely insane and explode into a zillion pieces. It actually hurt my chest and stomach. I needed to love Mom, so to calm myself down, I had to search my brain for reasons to forgive her. I knew how much she herself relied on medications to get through life, so I guessed she wasn't doing anything to me she wouldn't do to herself. And I believed that it was Kathy, the medical professional, who'd guided her into using them on me, probably by saying that she was doing me a favor by being humane—like drugging a nervous pet before a long car ride.

I closed my eyes, but I felt the eyelids shivering, and whispered another chant, "I love Mom. I love Mom. I love Mom."

Family peace was my job

As the next few days slipped past, it was impossible for me to tell whose side Mom was on, actually. On one hand, I could tell she felt bad for me, but on the other hand, Fran had told me that Mom was the one who took Scooter from me. And I never overheard Mom try to talk Dad into letting me have Connor back like she'd promised. I loved her, but she was confusing me in other ways too. She was letting my hair grow long, which was something I had wanted for years. I didn't ask her about it for fear she'd remember it was supposed to have been cut. And for whatever reason, I'd found myself with more permission to go farther on a bike and stay out later past dinner than per the normal, long-standing rules of the house. Daniel's bike seat was still detached, so I pulled Fran's old girl's version out of the shed. Some minor adjustments were in order because the last person to ride this relic was a nine-year-old version of Connor from the day I'd met him. Adjusting the seat height from his position to mine hurt a little in my heart. But at least I could now ride all the way to the Torano Island Library, as long as I continued to stay away from Connor.

I was once again obedient like a family dog, especially since I knew Mom really did love me. I'd gotten lucky when I snuck out with Connor to buy that Disaster Island issue, but I never would have considered sneaking over to Connor's house after the way things had turned out. If I'd gotten caught doing that, then whatever was going on between Mom and Dad, and Fran and Daniel, would only get worse. My keeping to myself annoyed all four of them, but it also kept them calm. Any disobedience or questions from me seemed to light firecrackers between all of them—firecrackers that would burn *me*. My obedience was the key to keeping them as calm as possible—which, in turn, kept me from rocking back and forth on my closet floor. If they were calm, I was too. If Mom was giving me extra room, then she was at risk of being scolded if I abused it. As usual, their peace seemed to be my responsibility, so I handled it conscientiously.

The problem with being as obedient as a family pet is that sometimes pets run off when the gate is left open, and I was starting to understand why they did. Each day, I would ride my bike as far as she'd said I could, all the way to the library. The farther from home I got, the calmer I felt inside. My heart was usually hot, like it was on fire, but hollow at the same time. I did only what was allowed, but I no longer cared if I stayed safe. I'd ride right across the street without looking for cars, daring one of them to put me out of my misery. One day, I almost got hit. When the woman blared her horn, I flipped her off. I immediately felt ashamed and mouthed the words, "I'm sorry," but she flipped me off in return and sped away.

Who was I becoming?

Another inch forward: the youngest trucker

If the half-mile to the library brought me a certain level of peace, imagine what a thousand miles would feel like. My thoughts were of escape. I imagined riding all the way to I-5 and then pedaling north—or south—until I was somewhere else for good. When long-haul sleeper cab trucks rolled into town for grocery and gasoline deliveries, I'd stare in through the windows, imagining myself behind the wheel, especially while they were heading *off* the island. That's when I wanted to be the driver—when they were wheeling toward the interstate. Maybe that's why Daniel became a trucker—so several times a month he could live the fantasy of leaving the island. I wondered why he kept coming back, though. I wouldn't.

Sometimes, while standing on the roadway alone when no cars were coming, I'd rehearse putting out a thumb to see what it felt like to hitchhike for real. I'd scout the brush for a secret roadside hideout where I could begin slowly piling critical belongings over time so that on any given night, I could get on my bike and ride away without anyone knowing I'd already packed. Stockpiling possessions wouldn't be as scary as actually running away, but it would be a physical move in the right direction. If one night I actually had to do it, I'd be prepared. I'd be a hundred miles away before they'd find my bike and figure out I'd left.

I remembered those words from my dream, *go with him*, and pretended they were an instruction from God, or some wise overseer to get into one of the rigs—to go with one of them and never, ever come back. I hated fantasizing about it and slowly wanted to make it real. I tried to make out their faces and wondered which trucker the voice would tell me to go with. I wanted a friendly one.

The fantasy began picking up a sense of realism as I rehearsed my thumbing moves alongside the hard, paved road. The practice was so realistic that I'd dream about it at night. In some of my dreams, I'd actually get in the truck. It felt amazingly real. In both worlds, awake and asleep, I started to wonder if I should *really* hitchhike and go. I knew that if I wanted to commit, all I had to do was not withdraw the thumb when I heard the next truck coming. It was that easy. I was literally one thumb away from becoming a bona-fide runaway. I'd put on my best smile, let my eyes sparkle at the truck drivers, and would get picked up eventually. No more fantasy. Like immersing into the pool slowly, I'd just find myself one day totally on my own.

Sometimes while riding Fran's bike toward the library, I'd pretend I was heading to the onramp to hitch a ride off the island once and for all. In an effort to turn my imaginary moves into real ones, I wouldn't even motion toward turning into the parking lot until I was almost too far past it to succeed. Then I'd wheel it in hard, cursing under my breath for not having the guts to keep going. Perhaps by practicing the real moves enough, I could edge a few inches closer each day until I slipped into being ready to follow through.

One thing I couldn't figure out was what a trucker would want from me in return for the ride. How could I convince one to let me stay? I had no money and was legally too young to get a job. Maybe I could cook for him and become his personal mechanic. I knew how to give good backrubs. I could relax him in the sleeper cab, then disguise myself as a grown man by sitting on a phone book and wearing a cowboy hat and sunglasses so I could drive the rig while he slept it off. I knew truckers could use this service because my brother always had a sore back from the road. He said my hands on his neck were worth a million bucks. He once whined that he wished someone would drive the highways for him for a few hours when he couldn't keep his eyes open. Dad had taught me already how to move big trucks around the yard. I could even drive a clutch. Small or not, I was already trained and *perfect for the job.*

Back to fantasy...for now

But who was I kidding? I wouldn't break the rules...ever. Each day, I'd ride as far as I was allowed, veer into the library, get off my bike, and sit by myself for as long as Mom had told me I could. I'd go to the far back corner of the parking lot, almost into the woods, where there was practically no sound. I was developing a love for dead silence. In fact, loud or sudden noises were starting to make me jumpy—another lifelong symptom in the making.

I'd toss rocks into the sand a few feet out. Draw pictures in the dirt with sticks, and erase them with my feet. Then, with exactly enough minutes left on my new curfew, I'd ride back home, avoiding routes that could take me past neighbor kids cheering and playing in the street or on a front lawn.

Sometimes I'd bring Matchies in my pocket and play quietly in the sand at the edge of the parking lot until it was time to go home. Each Matchy represented someone I knew. The blue GTO, Camaro, and Maserati were me, Scooter, and Connor. The crappy cars were family members and Andreo. Once I even assigned the flowered VW hippy-bus to the girl in the pink-and-white tube top and had her invite me in for a few minutes. (*That was a new thing for me. I had never had one of those dreams Andreo said he'd had, but unwanted erections were becoming a recurring event*). There in the parking lot, usually out of sight from the general public, I'd live out my little half-hour roadway scenarios in the dirt streets I'd made with a flat stick. I'd speak for my characters under my breath. Me, Scooter, and Connor would drive together on pretend roadways, away from school and Torano Island.

Then I'd eventually get bored and toss the cars that I'd taken meticulous care of over the years like they were the rocks. Every day, I missed riding bikes with the guys, going to the dock, or just hanging out with Connor. Every day, I missed Scooter more than the day before. Each day, my imaginary worlds became stronger, and my real identity out in the world became more of a mystery to me. Who the hell was I?

The sweetness of solitude

I didn't know if this extra leash was a permanent change or some sort of a trap or tease. I figured I'd be reeled back in when Mom decided. I didn't care. But I had more boundary area for now, so I figured I'd use it while I had it. By doing so, even for only the few days until my birthday, I'd made the glorious discovery that when I was completely alone, bathing in total peace, my stomach would settle and cool. When no one judged me, corrected me, or raised an eyebrow at how I moved an arm, or which side I parted my hair on, or how I answered a question or even positioned my body at a desk or table, that's when I could feel free to think what I wanted to think. Alone I felt safe. Creative. I began to like that.

53

Depression

Depression can strike anyone. In a healthy life, depression is okay if it brings about a change or allows its host to process loss. My depression was more about hopelessness, but Tuck's was more complicated. His long-term depression wasn't healthy, but his recent increase in depression that was being driven by his dreams and his Trenton situation was probably a healthy version. He needed to understand that it was time to move along. This depression could have been nature's way of showing him he had outstayed a time in his life.

By Tuck Taylor

My plan to quit the crisis clinic went more smoothly than I'd hoped. I promised one more week, but they said that when a person announces intention to quit, it's best to let him go quickly. Rhonda, the clinic head, believed that people who were burning out proved to be ineffective at helping callers. She let me go two nights later on Thursday.

By the following Monday, July 18, my loneliness had gotten far worse. It seems that when I'm completely alone for hours on end—days on end—that memories of Micah, Shannon, and all my high school friends, even Trenton, danced around with more excited force my head and made the real, grownup world seem sooooo alone.

Sleeping at night wasn't working as well as I'd have liked, so I was napping by day also. It was kind of a vicious cycle. I'd nap by day, which would make me less tired at night, so I'd sleep less, then need another nap the next day.

I think my level of depression was spiking also. I had lost sight of two of my favorite routines, which were swimming and running. The crisis clinic had somehow broken my routines, and for some reason, I had either forgotten how good it would feel to go for a long run, or I was too depressed to want to get started again.

Even when I was awake, I was half asleep. Dreams seemed as real as reality. Reality felt like a dream. Trenton was almost never home anymore, and I was starting to wonder whether he and Mark and all the other guys had realized what Ronnie had realized—that I wasn't really *like* them. It seemed they were moving on without me. I felt like I was being left behind.

I felt the way I had felt when Shannon left. Utterly and permanently alone. Or like when I had cancer. Erased.

Still conflicted about whether to stay and feed my brain or go and feed my heart, I was starting to fail at seeing myself continuing in this as-is situation much longer.

54

The Worst Birthday Gift

I've come to understand there are a few different ways by which people drastically change. One is by hitting rock bottom. It's when you've exhausted your options, and you've taken every hit you can possibly take, and then someone hits you one…more…time. It's the last straw that breaks a back. There really is no such thing as 110 percent. Once a balloon is 100 percent full, another percent bursts it. I was at 100 percent. Not one more puff would fit into me.

But the explosion is not always the end of everything. Sometimes the end of one story is the beginning of the next. Rich farm lands emerge from volcanic ash. Personal freedom follows the bloody wars of defiant revolution. A boy becomes a man when his childhood is destroyed and he can't go back. (The word "destroyed" means "damaged beyond repair.") When he ultimately gives up the hope that things will get better on their own, he finally takes action. We're survivors. We do or die. Or as Papa Louie would often say, we "shit or get off the pot."

So, finally, before my spiraling life turned around, which I'm excited to tell you it did, the last truly bad thing that happened—my rock bottom—was my fourteenth birthday. It is recorded indelibly on my heart as my own personal day of infamy. The final straw. As you read my tale, you'll be tempted to think I made it up. But be aware: Reality is often stranger than fiction. I couldn't make up this stuff even with my wild imagination. Depending on my mood now, recalling the events of that unbelievably bizarre day either sends me into laughter or draws tears. No other single event could showcase the insanity of each member of my family better than how we'd interacted on my fourteenth birthday—the day my illusion burst beyond repair.

By Kyle Rickett

I pretended Connor was in the chair to my left. Something in Mom's eyes told me that she felt terrible about his absence, which didn't bring him back, but felt validating. Each time she'd pass behind my chair, a motherly hand would rub my shoulders. She and Dad still had some sort of tension going on between them, so I guess I didn't blame her for doing what she needed to keep the peace with him. My fingers fiddled with the puka shell necklace Connor had given me the year before. It now dangled between the buttons of my Western shirt that had once been Daniel's. I imagined turning to my left and thanking Connor for a Hot Wheels car wrapped in flashy paper, like it was the crown to the kingdom. He would have picked the perfect car, too, because *he* knew which one it was. The signet gold, Pontiac GTO.

Mom surprised me by giving me a model kit of the exact Kenworth truck I'd been wanting to build. I wanted to paint it the same dark blue color as Daniel's real truck and even paint his name on the side. I hadn't expected her to remember which truck I wanted, but once again, she proved to be impossible to read, *and* willing to give a little extra effort while simultaneously keeping me captive. I received a card from Scooter in the mail. It was nothing special. It only had his name signed in it. No note. No message. No phone call. The standard dime store card was pinned to the corkboard next to the wall phone, taunting me with its impersonal greeting. *Happy Birthday to a fine young man.*

That's not what I wanted to hear from him. I wanted to hear the truth—in his words—not Fran's. I had no reason to doubt that they'd caught him kissing a boy, but I didn't believe their bullshit that he'd changed and had lost interest in me. They were the ones who'd changed. Our whole family had turned crazy over the concern that Scooter might not take a *girl* to the prom. For all we knew, he had been that way his whole life. I didn't know what to think about it because up until that point, I honestly hadn't believed those kinds of boys were real. I thought "gay" was an insult meant to make someone feel like an outcast. But now that I knew a real gay person, and he was the coolest guy ever, I couldn't imagine what all the fuss was about. There was nothing bad about Scooter. Nothing. My biggest worry now was that they might be telling him the same lies about me not wanting to see *him* anymore. Fran would definitely do that. Now that his secret was out, did he know that I didn't care about it? Had they given him my letter? This wasn't him. It was them. I hoped he knew the same in return. While Mom cut cake, I pondered the notion of making sure the first truck I'd choose to hitch a ride in would be on its way to Portland where I could pick up Scooter.

Dad was absent too. It was Friday and he couldn't leave the shop. We always accepted that work came first, so this wasn't unusual. I missed him, but my anger blended in, so I couldn't make heads or tails of what I thought of him anymore. My father had been a First-Division Marine, the toughest of them all. He relaxed by felling timber and hauling it out of the mud so we could chop it, stack it, and sell it. He was a man's man from head to toe. Was he *really* hiding from his little son because he couldn't face what I was going through?

I missed Connor so much I could barely stand what Dad had done to him. Did he even know why he was uninvited to my birthday party? Connor had never said a cross word to me. How could they be treating him like this? And what were people telling him about me?

With both knees in nervous tremor, I closed my eyes. *Dear Lord, Please tell Scott and Connor how much I miss them. Please.* Then I remembered there was no point in praying to that useless god. So I tried to connect with them psychically to transport the words "I'm sorry" into their heads.

So the only people at the party were me, Mom, Daniel, Fran, and the girls. Daniel's hair was greasy like he'd been up all night or hadn't showered—or both. He was eating cake and telling me about how he was going to buy me a birthday present when he got his next paycheck.

"What do you want?" he asked.

I hadn't smiled a full-face grin since five seconds before Connor was thrown out, so I shrugged and lifted a corner of my mouth once to indicate I didn't know. But I did know. I wanted life to be simple again.

"You're not too happy for a birthday boy," he remarked.

"That's for sure," Jayne quietly added and then rolled her eyes.

My fork was poking at the cake, but it was not moving anything to my face. I mapped out in my mind a direction to run from all of them, and I wondered if I could hitch a ride in a semi before they could catch me. My eyes lifted to look through my eyebrows at Daniel for only a second, then dropped back onto the cake.

"You shouldn't slouch like that," he instructed.

I sighed and wiggled my shoulders slowly, then slid my butt back so my body would appear more erect in the chair. I thought, *Four more birthdays and I can live alone. Then I can sit how I damn well want.*

Fran seemed to have brought her own problem to outweigh my little birthday thing. She was wearing her extra big redhead wig. She said she had done it to be funny, but no one could know for certain what she was truly trying to say. So today, on my special day, she was as flamboyant as she could be, dressed to the nines in a white miniskirt and a flowery black and silver silk top tied off above her tummy. Her cleavage was pushed up and out, and that huge, oversized, long red wig topped the whole outfit and screamed, *Look at me! Look at me!* She looked hot actually. Wigs were popular back then. It seemed like every woman had at least one. Fran was sporting a typical 1974 "go-go-girl" look. She was a knockout when she wanted to be. I now know we Ricketts have always been a good-looking family. She looked exactly like the pictures of Mom at that age, but Fran was usually dressed in a more risqué way.

Fran had borrowed her neighbor's Pinto to attend the party. She hadn't remembered to buy a gift—unless the blue GTO had satisfied the requirement for her—but she did want to borrow Mom's Oldsmobile.

"Why can't I borrow it for a week, Mom? You don't need it."

"It's *my* car Fran, you have your own!"

"Yeah—when it's *running*!"

All aboard the crazy-train

"Your father has told you over and over again to keep it tuned up. It's your own fault it's down now. And you knew Bob was leaving town long before you got into this mess."

"Oh, how do you know that's the problem?" Fran's indignant tone filled the kitchen "Dad doesn't know *everything*! It was running fine a few days ago. Dodges are terrible cars. This is a new problem."

"Dodges are perfectly good cars!" Mom responded with her own rising tone. "And you're not borrowing the Olds. I need it!"

"Oh, you do not. You have neighbors who can drive you to your little grocery stores. I have *work* to get to."

"Don't you tell me I don't need my own car."

"Why can't Kyle come take a look at mine then? Maybe it's something simple. Dad taught him everything he knows about engines. It's a Duster. How hard can it be? Kyle can handle that."

"It's a slant-six, Mom. Those are simple engines—" I perked up. My spine straightened. Fran was bragging about me to Mom.

"It's Kyle's birthday," Mom answered Fran rather than me. "I'm not sending him to—"

"I'll do it Mom," I proudly interjected. "It's okay. She needs me."

"She doesn't *need* you, Kyle. She can hire a mechanic."

Fran quickly jumped in, "I'm saving money to buy the salon as soon as Dumb-Dumb Doris loses it to the bank. He's *offering* to do it."

"She's my sister, Mom—I'll do it, really. I love her."

"Oh, he's a little boy." Again, Mom spoke to her and seemingly ignored me altogether. "He's not going to tune your car with no tools in an apartment building parking lot on his birthday. And Doris isn't losing the salon to the bank. Where do you get this nonsense?"

"I opened some mail by accident—she's behind on everything."

"You opened her mail *by accident*?" Mom looked like she was about to pull her own hair out.

"I thought it was junk mail."

Destination reached: Crazyville

"You thought her...bills...." Mom shook her head in disgust. "Uhhhh!"

"Why do you baby him like you do?" Fran changed the subject and kept control of the argument.

I tipped my head. *Baby me*? How did *that* relate to borrowing a car? I put a forkful of birthday cake to my mouth slowly.

"Uncle Kyle's a *baby*?" BJ giggled.

"*What?*" Mom yelled back at Fran with a look of indignant surprise. Her eyes squinted as she tried to find reason in that sentence.

"He has the easiest life of anyone I've ever known!" Fran exclaimed.

"What?" I asked.

"Dad teaches him how to take care of himself and you protect *him* instead of me." Did that really make sense? Even to Fran?

"I don't believe what I'm hearing!" Mom replied.

"Jesus Christ, Mother. Open your eyes. You baby him the same way Aunt Maureen did Scott."

"Don't you *dare* go there, Fran!" Mom looked toward BJ and Jayne. "And not in front of the girls."

"You've given him way too much freedom. After all those years of playing with Scott in that sleeping bag...and where does he go every night on that bicycle of mine? You don't even check up on him."

"I go to the library," I defended.

"*Oh, the library*! Says who? Show me your books!" Then she turned to Mom and warned, "I'd keep a closer eye on that one if I were you. Everyone in town knows he sleeps with Scott. And what about that doctor of his?"

"What the hell are you talking about?" Mom opened the door to the living room. "Girls, go play with the dollhouse. You can take your cake with you."

Both girls obediently grabbed their plates and skipped into the living room.

"Have you gone completely crazy?" She let the door swing shut.

The blood drained from my face and heart.

"He spreads his legs for Dad's friends and you call *me* crazy?"

Shock overcame me. How did she know what Krieg had done?

"You treat him like he's a perfect angel. You don't know what he's really doing on my old girl's-bike every day. Have you checked his drawers for extra money?"

"Oh, he was getting stitches. I was there! You're just talking crazy now."

"Extra money?" I didn't make the connection, but I knew she was accusing me of letting other men do what Krieg had done. It was happening. All my secrets were being dragged out into the open. Was my sister demon-possessed? My shoulders weakened. I gave up any facial expression. I had an urge to rock back and forth like I'd done in the closet. The fork fell from my hand. Cake hit the table. Only the sound of the fork bouncing onto the floor, showering the area with vanilla crumbles, was heard. I looked at the only person on the planet who knew what Dr. Krieg had done to me. I remembered telling Daniel that Krieg had told me to keep my legs spread apart. Daniel looked down at his plate and continued to chew cake and wiggle his fork nervously.

I looked at Mom, who was staring back at me. She was *there*. She *saw* them hold me down. She *heard* me begging her to help *me*, not *them*. Then she drugged me so he could do it again. Why wasn't she saying anything now? How could anybody even *consider* me to be doing *that*?

I looked at Fran. She was looking back at me, then at Daniel. She had a smirk on her face. Fran had a way of laughing with her mouth and body, while sending hate with her icy cold eyes. This was one of those times.

"You *told* her?" I tried to yell at Daniel, but it came out hoarse.

Mom's face turned angry. She swung it back over to Fran, who looked back, square in the eyes like a boxer ready for the bell.

"My God, Fran!" she yelled. "What's the *matter* with you? Why do you have to be so damned mean all the time?"

My heart swelled with sad disbelief. What kind of a stupid question was "Why do you have to be mean?" Fran can't answer that. She doesn't know why she's mean. Why doesn't someone finally *demand* that she behave with some human dignity?

I looked at Daniel. He was now standing, shoulders arched, looking humble. He tiptoed to the sink and set down his plate, still half-covered by a crumbling wedge of white cake. My eyes followed him, but he never returned the glance. He walked quietly, rubbing his hands together like he was washing them in an invisible sink. He walked around the table, cleared his throat, and vanished out the kitchen door. It swung shut. I was alone with the still arguing women.

"Who else did you tell?" I asked Mom in a low voice.

"No one told anyone anything, Kyle!" Fran blurted back. "What? Do you have something you need to share?"

No one told anyone anything? Now she wouldn't acknowledge what she'd said seconds ago. I looked at Mom with desperation in my raised brows.

"Mom?"

Mom was too furious to speak in sentences. She turned back to Fran and blurted out, "*My* car! Get your *own*!"

The *car*? My sister, who was actually dressed like a whore, had just lobbed the ugliest accusation she had in her arsenal at the boy who'd offered to tune her car for free on his birthday, and Mom went back to the *car*? My sister had twisted the truth about my relationships, then said,

"No one said anything," and now she was getting away with it. Mom had fallen headfirst into another trick—*again*!

And then, as if on cue, the kitchen phone rang. Startled, I accidentally hollered, "Ah!"

"Get a grip, Kyle. It's just a *stupid* phone." Fran stomped over and answered it. "It's for *you!* That is, if you think you can *handle* it!" She threw the receiver in my direction, but the cord snapped it back so it hit the kitchen wall with a thud. I jumped again at the thud.

Having no idea who it was, I let it dangle. I watched my mother refocus on Fran and continue screaming mindless questions, ignoring her behavior and accusing her of having an evil soul. I tried to remember the name of a person, anywhere, who was on my side anymore. Rather than defend me or tell Fran that her behaviors were unacceptable, Mom asked dim-witted questions no one could answer, like, "What kind of a comment was that?" and "When are you going to straighten up?"

The chill from within

The icy cold started in my chest. It moved outward, pushing body heat away from the inside, out through the skin. My brain left the room, and I couldn't hear their screaming anymore. I was cold, but I knew a blanket wouldn't warm me. The chill was from inside. *Please let me die now,* I prayed. Death had to be better than being in that kitchen. Even though my own mom and sister were ten feet away, I was now utterly alone on the earth. I couldn't hitchhike now if I'd tried. No way did I have the strength to climb up into a truck cab.

Sound went dead, which was a blessing. The arguing was hurting my brain. It was as if a volume knob had rotated to the left. I couldn't hear, but I could see the women yelling empty, irrational words at each other. It meant nothing. I saw the unattended phone dangling, which was either my broken-hearted best friend calling to ask for an explanation, or my archenemy from that other life, calling in to this one to remind me that I was a homo in need of another beating. Didn't matter either way. I could see my big brother and dad's empty chairs with no cake plates. Crumbs and dabs of melted ice cream where Daniel had once sat. Was this *my* fault for being given more freedom on my bike? For being a homo? For being Dr. Krieg's "favorite white-haired boy?"

The shivering started innocently enough, and my teeth began to chatter. By the time Mom took notice, my forehead was beading with sweat and I was having a hard time staying up in the chair.

"Kyle!" Fran yelled. "Stop pretending to be sick, you selfish little prick!"

"He does this," Mom responded.

I don't remember much after that.

55

Mr. Nice Guy

Tuck and I had both become Mr. Nice Guys. It wasn't working for either of us. How to balance being too selfish (too sociopathic) and too empathetic can be tough to learn. Tuck and I were both experiencing the identical lesson, but we were going in different directions with it.

He had been taught from birth, through the actions, words, and behaviors of his family, that he was worth fighting for. So, therefore, when needed, Tuck could fight for himself. He could stand up to bullies, make people listen to him, and trust in his own motives.

I had been given a different message from birth. The Catholic message was that I was a sinner and now my family's behavior was making me believe it. Andreo's unexplained betrayal and Dr. Krieg's ownership of my body proved that I was to be as strong as an Atomic Ant when putting others ahead of myself, but I was never to think myself valuable enough to fight for. Not even by me.

By Tuck Taylor

"I'm leaving Texas." Trenton stood six inches from me, holding the front doorknob in one hand. His penetrating eyes didn't flinch. He'd been rehearsing this moment and was playing out the live performance.

"*Now*?" I glanced down at his hand on the doorknob.

"No, not *now*." Again not a single twitch in his face. "Next week."

"Why? I thought we were in this together. Four years."

"I know you did." Then he said in a more compassionate tone, "But you have to understand, I'm done. I hate Texas." He paused from trying to look tough long enough to offer, "I'm sorry."

"Well." My jaw dropped slack. I'd had no idea he hated it there. Or maybe he had received some crazy offer to go somewhere else, so he had just decided that he hated it there so he could talk himself into leaving. "So do I…but…I've been…."

"You've been what?" Still speaking softly, his firm words proved he'd thought this moment through and wasn't going to back down. "Holding out because of *me*?"

"Well, that's part of it, yeah. Isn't that what friends do?"

"It's creepy." He moved his hand from the door to my shoulder.

"Creepy? Being honorable to my childhood best friend is creepy?"

"Were not kids in the St. Paul neighborhood anymore. I'm a grown-ass man, Tuck. I don't need a sitter. You choosing to live like this, in my world, may be nice, but it's…well, yeah…it's creepy. It's not at all needed." He removed his hand, shrugged, broke eye contact, and walked past me toward the couch.

"You're my best friend," I said, following him. My heart sank when it heard my own mouth say that. "I made a promise."

"You're changing, Tuck. I'm changing. Childhood promises are meant to be…*reassessed*…as we grow up." Much of what he was saying sounded scripted, like he and his friends had worked together to figure out how to tell me of this new plan.

"How am I changing?" I raised my voice and stopped at the couch while he sat down.

"You quit the crisis clinic. You got naked with Mark. You never leave the apartment. You stopped exercising—"

"Okay, okay." I sat down next to him but at a full arm's length.

"Do you love it here?" he prodded.

"No. I hate it worse than you do."

"But you stay here because of me."

"In part." I shrugged in agreement.

"You know that kind of makes me feel like shit. Like I've been forcing you to live somewhere you hate."

My head shook. My eyes widened. Scripted or not, that made so much sense I couldn't believe it. "I'd never…thought of it that way before."

Mark

Trenton got up and put a Rolling Stones album on the record player. He turned the volume low. He wasn't done talking with me.

"I still love you, Tuck. You're just…such an. .amazing guy. But I really need to get to New York. Life is calling me there. You can come with if you want."

"I'm not moving to New York, Trenton." A little sarcasm tainted my decline of his last-minute offer. "If I leave here, it's going to be to a slower pace, not a faster one. But thanks anyway for the offer." I changed the subject. "Who's going to take care of Mark now?"

"Mark…is also a big boy, Tuck. Why do you think he won't survive without you?'"

"That isn't fair," I said. "Mark has slashes on his wrists. I can't help but worry."

He didn't answer, but I could see his wheels turning behind his eyes. After processing some thoughts, he responded, "Mark's doing fine. You are a good man, Tuck Taylor, and I appreciate your concern."

"Thank you." I gave him a gentle smile to show genuine gratitude for his compliment. "I'm glad Mark's okay. Is he going with you? Out of Texas?"

"No. I met someone and we're going to New York together. Mark's going to finish school and stay surrounded by our friends. Don't worry about him." He slapped both his own knees and got up quickly. "It's just arrogant now if you keep worrying."

Time to pack?

About a half hour later, after Trenton had left to go be with his new friend, whoever that was, I found myself wandering about the apartment pretending to pull my hair out with both hands.

"Oh, shit. What do I do now? What do I do? What do I do? Do I go or do I stay?"

Some decisions are easier to make than others, I guess. I knew I wanted to leave, but in order to put my money where my mouth was, and to make the real-life move, and physically pick up and walk away from college, I now had to commit for real. I knew my inner world was going to explode. Emotions were going to be high. I knew a little of how the human brain worked. With Trenton's sudden announcement, my feeling abandoned couldn't be avoided. But I, too, was a big boy who didn't need a sitter. If staying here was the right thing to do—putting my degree ahead of everything, like Ronnie had advised—then pushing through the emotions was something I could do. If I needed to, I could try getting through it by writing an article about it for my sixty-seventh issue of *Taylor* magazine.

"Why does this have to be such a *god damned hard decision*?" I just didn't *want* to stay. I took a small stack of college books out of my bedroom and put them on the kitchen eating bar just so I could look at them.

"Should I do it? Should I go? Should I stay?" I tapped the textbooks nervously like I was writing to someone in Morse code. "What do I do? What do I do? What do I do?"

56

Abandonment

Looking back at the whole picture now, I can see that reality is in the eye of the beholder. Being alone in the world and "perceiving to be" alone are two different problems—both are real. I was surrounded by people who loved me but were distracted by their own battles, so I perceived I was alone. While it's true that three key villains were intentionally and simultaneously isolating me, the rest of the world unconsciously played along by accident.

Parents can really struggle to know how to handle—or recognize—their children's turmoil. What my mother was about to do to fix me may have been the wrong solution, but in an amazing and complex turnabout, it worked toward my betterment as a man. In fact, it worked so well that I've gone on to say it was the best mistake that ever happened to me, and the worst mistake to happen to her, or to Dad, or Fran, or anyone from that family.

As the moment of transformation approached, my perception of feeling utterly alone was about to get much worse, but soon to end suddenly. Mom didn't know how to handle me, but she knew how to pray. Thanks to some sort of divine intervention, I was about to make a friend she didn't mean for me to meet. But first, I had to be made ready to accept his help. Deeply rooted trust issues were closing me off from accepting assistance, and those issues had to be addressed. In order for me to reach out my hand to a stranger and accept Tuck Taylor's rescue, I would first have to grasp fully how desperate I really was. To forego my automatic distrust of him, I would have to surrender completely and utterly, which is precisely what my circumstances led me to do next.

By Kyle Rickett

For the next few days, no one spoke full sentences. Daniel quietly snuck in and out each day like a burglar. Questions were short and answers were yes or no. Fran didn't come by even once. Usually, she needed grocery money or babysitting, but not anymore. Gone. She simply didn't come by. At least not while I was awake.

On Thursday morning, the twenty-fourth, I got up as usual and planned to live out my day as I had the previous three, lying alone on the couch wishing I was dead. No more of my bonus bike rides. After not defending me against Fran's lies, I figured Mom just thought I was getting into cars with men at the library now. I didn't like wondering if she was picturing me naked in motel rooms. I was tired of defending myself from one Rickett family accusation after another after another after another. Fran couldn't accuse me of being with more men if Mom could see me the whole day, right? Maybe if I stayed in plain sight, Mom would defend me the next time Fran said something so sadistic.

Surprise vacation

The house smelled especially good that morning, like sausage. I hadn't showered in three days, and I was now wearing the same mid-length shorts from my birthday, but I had swapped Daniel's hand-me-down shirt for a plain white undershirt that had been bought for *me*—not *him*. My first lifelong change was that I would never wear his hand-me-downs again. Ever! My longer hair was matted flat on one side, wild on the other. Once I entered the kitchen, I saw that Mom had made a big breakfast, with two eggs, steak, *and* sausage. I loved steak and sausage, and they were both there on my plate. As miserable as I had been lately, I only wanted things to go back to how they were before I had crashed bikes with Connor and found out I was my doctor's favorite white-haired boy.

Seeing the meal placed at my seat almost brought a smile to my otherwise miserable face. Was this an apology? I felt my cheek muscles start to tighten ever so slightly. Thoughts of relief popped in. Perhaps the Ricketts were just having a bad month, and now that bad month was coming to an end. I knew I could forget all about it if everyone would be who he or she used to be. The whole story could be filed away as a dream if everyone cooperated with me in making it so.

"Hi, honey!" Mom turned from the stove with a fresh cup of coffee. Her smile was an obvious fake, but I took what I could get.

"Hi, Mom." I hadn't said much in the past few days, so I had to clear my throat and then say, "That's a big breakfast." I normally would have smiled while I said good morning, but for now, that was still a struggle, so with faint beginnings of one, I continued, "Are you going to eat with me too?"

At Mom's place setting, there sat not a breakfast plate, but some papers and a small stack of cash. My faint smile died away. I slowly scanned the kitchen for more clues. My little blue suitcase with the single red stripe, and my brown canvas duffel bag, both packed, were sitting on the floor by the kitchen door. I realized the house was empty of other people.

"Kyle, honey, I'm so sorry for how hard your life has gotten lately."

"It'll get better, won't it?" I sheepishly responded.

"It will, of course, but this summer has been unfair to you. I'm still mad at Fran for the things she said to you on your birthday. It breaks my heart to see your sad little face every day." She wrinkled her chin to show her most compassionate expression. "And, besides, Fran told me that you said we're hard to live with."

"*What?*"

"When you went to dinner with her and Daniel the other night, she said you told her that we're hard to live with."

I tried to speak. But what could I say? She was right. Fran *had* asked me for a comment, so I *did* say, "They can be hard to live with sometimes," but…it was just a stupid comment that *she* had prompted me to say. Still, I couldn't defend myself; I really had said it. This was another of the millions of acts of gaslighting that they'd been doing to me my whole life. I had no defense. None.

"So…right now, we're not helping by fighting with each other around you. We think it might be a good idea if you take a break from us while we work these things out. Maybe we can become a better family for you when you come back."

A what? A better *family for me*? Was she insinuating that this was *my* fault? Was she taking a cheap shot at putting the guilt for this huge decision onto *me*?

"Granddad has agreed to let you stay with him for a little while."

"Mom?" I noticed she didn't say that Granddad *wanted* me to stay with him. Fear gripped my chest again. Was I literally being punished for the comment Fran had tricked me into saying a week before?

"I made your favorite breakfast," she added, diverting my attention to the plate, and then, as though there were no gravity to this at all, she instructed, "Hurry up and eat, honey; there's a cab on its way to pick you up."

"A taxi?"

"Dad gave Fran my car for a few days. I'm so mad I can hardly stand it. You'll take the train from Everett. Your ticket's on the table."

"I'm going by my-*self*?"

"I think you're old enough, and I think it'll be good for you to get away from us. You've taken that train trip with me three times now."

"Mom, that was years ago. And they closed the train depot in Duluth. How will I get there?" I fell into the mode of looking for reasons not to accept this.

"Kyle, it's going to be fine. They just opened it up again. It's a new building, but it's in the same spot. Papa knows where it is. He'll meet you there."

"Do I still have to change trains in Minneapolis? Aren't you afraid I'll get lost?"

"You're fourteen now. A smart little man. They changed the transfer to St. Paul on Friday night, but signs will tell you what train to get on. It'll be an Amtrak to Duluth. And Granddad will pick you up in Duluth on Saturday morning. I've given you enough money for all the food you can eat."

"Duluth?" I still couldn't believe it. "I'm going to Duluth…alone?"

"Honey, you go there almost every summer."

"Not *alone*. Dad usually drives us all together." My despair had reached a new depth I had never dipped into before. I didn't know a person could feel worse than I'd been feeling. But here it was. I was being sent away—and to a place that had nothing waiting for me. No friends. No Matchies. There was nothing for me in Duluth but an old man. I loved my Papa Louie, but what the hell had just happened? Was my entire life over? Nothing—absolutely nothing—felt right. First they made Scooter disappear, and now I was disappearing too. Mom kept saying this was a gift to me so I could get some rest from their fighting, but it seemed to me they believed all their problems this summer were *my* fault. *They were getting rid of their problem.* I knew it. I couldn't make sense of it any other way. Any hope of regaining my almost-smile dissipated.

I couldn't muster the strength to ask any more questions. Her compassionate words seemed genuine—but she'd proven she could cut Scooter out of her life—and now me? Had Fran convinced her that Scooter and I had fooled around in our sleeping bag? Now both of us were magically unlovable? How could I defend myself if I didn't know why she was doing this? And why ask? After watching how she didn't address the truth with Fran, or even tell her just to shut up and behave, but instead argued with ridiculously unanswerable phrases, how could I trust her information now? The insanity had won. My own mother had become nothing but a politician who'd say whatever words seemed right at the moment. Nothing would ever be the same now. She and Dad were supposed to teach me how to trust people. But they couldn't be trusted themselves.

Goodbye

"There really is no one left," I mumbled.

I didn't ask anything. I didn't eat the meal either. It might as well have been poison. I didn't shower. I didn't comb my hair. I didn't put on a clean pair of pants. Like a once-wild horse, I'd been broken. There was no fight left in me, not even an eye-roll. It was time to go where I was led. Into a small pen with the other broken horses. I grabbed the papers and suitcases and waited at the door for the cab. Mom probably wanted to tell me to go clean up. But I'm sure that my trembling hands, blank stare, and red face warned her not to.

Cabs were rare on the island. They were a city thing. So when a yellow one honked in my driveway, it might as well have had flashing lights and sirens. It drew the attention of whoever was in earshot. With my shoulders drooping, and a small suitcase in each hand, I walked with my face pointed ground-ward down the long, gravel driveway. Daniel's Kenworth was gone. He'd left during the night, and I had either not heard it roar to life, or I'd blocked it from my memory. I kicked rocks and wondered if this was even my driveway anymore. Would this be the last time I'd see it?

Mom walked beside me, trying not to look at the neighbors' houses. She seemed nervous, or scared. She got to the cab door first. The driver had opened the trunk and taken my luggage. She handed him some cash and thanked him, reminded him that the train would leave precisely at noon, and then leaned down to kiss me on the cheek.

"You be good for Granddad, okay? You're a good, good, good boy, and I know he'll be happy to see you."

I didn't look at her. I waited until she was done so I could get in the cab and lock the door.

The cab backed onto the street. Mom waved. Her chin quivered as she tried not to cry. Even though I wasn't sure I'd see her again, I didn't wave back. The cabby shifted into drive and we began cruising slowly southbound toward the highway, and then my eyes caught a half-dozen neighbor kids walking the ditch in the opposite direction, toward the beach. They were escorting Connor and a humongous tractor inner tube, which the seven of them were playfully rolling together with their spindly arms. They were in shorts with brightly colored beach towels slung over their shoulders. I knew the inner tube. It used to lay around the shop until Dad told me I could give it to Connor on his twelfth birthday. Connor, being the honorable guy he was, treated it like it belonged to the whole block and he was merely its custodian. Chad, who had a playful arm around Connor's shoulders, pointed with a shout. Connor saw that it was me in the car. As we cruised slowly past, he gave me a cheerful, energetic wave and a huge smile.

"Cool, Kyle! A taxi!" He put his hand to his mouth to shout through the glass, "Where ya goin'?"

I only had the energy to put my hand on the glass and stare.

"Those seem like nice kids," remarked the cabby.

My habitual deferral to prayer brought a silent plea to a God I didn't think I believed in anymore: *I might as well be dead. You could have helped. But you just fucking didn't.*

I closed my eyes but was immediately startled by a flash of light. Another white dove fluttered quickly from my chest, across my field of vision, and up through the cab roof. Maybe it was my soul. I pictured getting on the train, but I couldn't picture getting off at Duluth. No one was ever going to save me. Nothing was ever going to be the same.

57

Final Call to Action

Prayer. I can't explain it. I can't prove it works. All I know is that between my mother, myself, and Tuck Taylor, something surreal was happening.

By Tuck Taylor

Still struggling between my desire to leave and my commitment to finish college, a flash of light caught my attention. I recalled the dove from my dreams, now in my waking life too. I finally accepted that I was being called—I don't know how else to explain it. But by who? Night after night, with inexplicable urgency, even after I'd made the decision to leave Texas, the white dove brought messages I couldn't decipher. The timing was crucial too. Its presence was becoming more aggressive than when I first saw it. It was the dove that first appeared when I was at the edge of my own death, and when it signaled my return to life. Even though I was saved, my carefree childhood ended at the moment I surrendered to cancer. I was a changed person from that moment on. Something was now connecting me to that surrender—that change, as if I were living in that moment all over again—right at the boundary between clinging to life and surrendering to death. The dreams were becoming less about my stress and more about messages that meant something, but *what?*

With every lonely day that passed, my unrest increased. Trenton was leaving. Mark was moving on with his life. All the suffering I'd done on their behalf was looking more like a clever way to torture myself. What good came of any of it? I was turning out to be their problem, not their savior. Trenton said he'd stayed in Texas too long because of me. I'd carelessly pushed Mark and his wrist scars into a risky position. Apparently, trying to help *everyone* was helping *no one.*

Between night sweats and daytime uneasiness, I couldn't get comfortable. I jittered like a coffeehouse caffeine addict. When standing, I'd want to sit. But when I'd sit, I'd urgently need to stand. When in bed, I'd want to walk around, but once up, I'd be overwhelmed by the need for sleep.

My nightly strolls in The Place Without Shadows came often and lasted longer. I woke up more, slept less, and was losing confidence in knowing whether I was fully present in either location. Though The Place Without Shadows was peaceful, wondering what were the reasons for my visits gripped my attention. Worrying that I might have cancer again harassed my peace and infused my nights with dread. One would think I'd have called a doctor, but I believe I was too afraid to find out I was sick again. Residual trauma sometimes creates a tendency for avoidance as one of the long-term side effects. Besides, all my cancer doctors were in St. Paul.

But I didn't feel the symptoms of illness. So, instead, I hoped I was right about the dove being a messenger, not a dream, and that I'd been chosen as the recipient of a mysterious call into action through some crazy astral connection with my sister, who'd once simultaneously dreamt the same thing with me. I hoped someone I knew wasn't dying. Maybe that's why I was being brought back to it.

Oh, hell, none of this made any sense. I was sleep-deprived and grasping at straws for an impossible answer.

For now, the dreams were *becoming* reality. I didn't know the master plan for where I was to go, but the time had come to respond by leaving *here*. Duluth, Minnesota, would suffice for the time being.

My decision was made once and for all. No more waffling. I was leaving. Now. I couldn't take one more hour in that tiny, hot apartment. It was time to bolt. I'd been preparing for the possibility of leaving for over a week, and it was time to call Grandpa Tucker and surprise my family with the change in my course.

From the distant railroad line, I heard a horn that reminded me of what my dad used to say whenever he wanted to get me into the car. I chuckled as I repeated his famous words.

"C'mon, Tuck; it's time to go. The train has left the station."

PART 5

Complete Surrender:

MY RESCUE AT ROCK BOTTOM

58

The Real Underworld Exposed

Complex-PTSD would remain undiagnosed in me for nearly thirty years as well-meaning doctors, naturopaths, psychologists, and even chiropractors would attempt to cure my neurotic, fearful depressive moods. Don't get me wrong; I've lived a rich and fulfilling life for the most part, but with a vein of complexity woven throughout. On that complexity, I've been misdiagnosed as manic-depressive, bipolar, sleep-deprived, high-strung, hypertensive, depressed, easily distracted, overly sensitive, or having high blood pressure, an addictive personality, or ADHD. For decades, I've been medicated, coached, and criticized—all with minimal and temporary results.

It wouldn't be until I turned forty that I heard the term PTSD, and I was fifty-four the first time I heard of Complex-PTSD. The doctor who diagnosed me did so after reading some recent papers on the topic and then witnessing my face go blank while I was trying to tell him about an argument I'd had with a neighbor. Dissociative episodes had been happening most of my life, but without anyone knowing what they were, I remained mistreated with no success.

At fourteen, after my infamous birthday betrayal, I remained at rock bottom for about a week, mostly in a trance-like state one would, at the time, have called a stupor or a daze. Today, I know I was experiencing my longest single dissociative episode. During the day-and-a-half long train ride to St. Paul, I moved in and out of the dream so fluidly that to this day, I can't tell you how much of the trip I was awake for. It was all such a fantasy.

By Kyle Rickett

The trip was more like a dream. Believe it or not, I actually lost count of how many days it took to get to the midnight four-hour transfer in St. Paul. In reality, it was one day and two nights, but because of how dissociated I was, it felt like six days. I was exhausted when I stumbled from the train at a little after 11:00 p.m. The concrete platform felt like it was still moving with the tracks' rhythm. The muggy night heat proved the *place* was real, but I wasn't sure that *I* was.

I wasn't alone anymore—but that was bad. Somewhere in Eastern Washington, I'd picked up a ghost who followed me around the train, like he was watching from behind. I thought he was a figment of my imagination at first, but the farther away from home I got, the more real he became. He was dark and scary. He even followed me off the train and across the platform.

The air-conditioned station felt good. My armpits were soaked. My bags weren't heavy, but I was tired of protecting them. Hell, I didn't even know what was in them. They'd been packed for me as if I were too stupid to pack for myself.

I saw a bank of lockers and remembered how I used to ask Mom, "Why would anybody put stuff in a locker if they were on a trip to someplace?" She used to say they weren't for people like us who knew where we were going.

I put two quarters in the coin slot of locker number 111. Both bags fit. I twisted and pulled. The tumbler clicked as it released the key into my hand. My heart jumped—*I guess I didn't know where I was going.*

In a daze, I gazed at the closed locker door—a scratched, gray shield between me and the baggage from my old life. I'd just pushed this "adventure" to the next level by trading my two big bags for this tiny key, which was the train station's property. Again, I looked at the locker. As long as that door remained closed, I was detached from everything that had ever been mine.

Stuffing the borrowed key into my pocket, I turned to decide which direction to go. A few yards to my right, a sign pointed toward the *4th Street Exit*, which looked as good as any direction to walk. With that ghost—that dark spirit—still hovering behind, I wondered if I'd ever come back to locker 111 for any of my stuff.

I left the station. I wasn't supposed to. Never had before. I'd broken from the path my mother had instructed me to stay on. I'd stopped following the ancestral footprints that the Ricketts had imprinted between Torano and Duluth.

A new world

The sidewalk on 4th Street was well lit but quiet for a city. The hiss of a freeway not too far off in the distance brought more life to the scene than what I was used to at night. There were cars and people, but not in crowds. Nighttime was darker, and quieter on the island. In fact, I was becoming sure that absolutely nothing ran by the same rules here. I hoped that, too, was a good thing.

I think something in my brain may have snapped. I felt safe, at night in a *city*. I now know I shouldn't have. Even a friendlier city like St. Paul has a district a boy shouldn't be in at night, and train stations are usually in that district. Nonetheless, for the first time ever, I felt no urge to pray, not even for protection from the Dark Spirit. Having come to expect the disappointment of prayer, that it had never brought me positive results, the burden of begging an angry God for help and forgiveness left my chest. With his absence came release—calm and cool. God wasn't helping, but he also wasn't *judging* me as worthless. In fact, no one was here to punish me for anything. My hands, now free from baggage, gently rubbed my shirt. For once, my stomach didn't burn.

"This could be good," I mumbled.

I stood quietly in the city streetlights, confused by how good it felt to be detached. A certain sense of excitement came with the clusters of headlights and taillights traveling past. What few pedestrians I saw ignored me. Busy city people didn't nod or say things to me the way small town people did. Maybe I had become invisible. The anonymity was calming like when I was alone in the library parking lot. My normally shallow breathing effortlessly flowed in and out of my relaxed lungs. Dr. Krieg, St. Tiberius, Fran, and the Rickett family were all gone. The light-headedness from the train had evolved to dizziness as I scanned the overwhelming size of the world around me. Traffic lights changed colors in the distance, and occasional diesel truck engines reverberated off the buildings' walls. This was a different late-night world than any I'd ever stood in. Here I had no guidance and no rules. I could freely choose any direction to run.

It wasn't quite the experience I had imagined when I had fantasized about running away, but it sure felt good to be unchained from Mom, Dad, and Fran. It turned out that I hadn't needed to teach myself how to hold up a thumb because, ironically, my own mother had purchased a train ride out of town *for* me. It was looking like I'd never have to give a massage to a trucker. The problem was timing. If I'd have left on my own, I'd have had a plan to follow: Hitchhike to Portland, find Scooter, and *then* start over with him as my ally. Mom's solution pushed me out for real, but if I were to choose not to catch my connector train, then it left me without a plan—*or an ally*. But regardless of how I'd gotten here, being alone felt as liberating as I'd hoped it would. I figured I now had five good solid hours between trains to decide how far to take this. I shyly glanced over my right shoulder.

The second level to this problem was that I wasn't *totally* alone. I still had "Tall-Dark-and-Scary," my large, silent stalker spirit, following me.

My obedient nature and fourteen years' worth of family training nagged at me to turn back, but my heart reminded me that there was *nothing to turn back to*. Habit was to run to Mom for comfort, but she was the one who'd sent me here.

With all my possessions gone, it was time to leave the boy behind. So, like a man, I walked forward into the unknown. My chest was hollow and I was going to have to get used to it. I felt betrayed and didn't know how I'd ever find a way to trust another person again. I felt physically anesthetized and out of my body—but unafraid, like I had nothing to worry about losing. I shook my empty hands, proving it was true. I had nothing to hang on to or protect. Nothing for anyone to take. Completely dissociated.

"I could get used to this."

You can take the boy off the island, but...

The city was soulless, like a snapshot, except that it smelled of diesel exhaust, like Dad's shop. A Greyhound bus slid past me on 4th Street with its right blinker on. I was free to wander. Having no reason not to, I boldly turned to my right and walked the sidewalk as if I knew where I was going.

In truth, I didn't know where I was going *to*, and I only *thought* I knew what I was leaving behind. I crossed an intersection at Wacouta Street. I'd only been off the train for twenty minutes, but it felt like hours. My heart may have felt hollow, but my skin was electric, like it had been dead for years and was now alive. I was sad and excited at the same time. Not wanting to appear lost, I fearlessly strolled to the next intersection at Wall Street. A darkened farmers' market stood to my left. I wondered how busy it got in the daytime, and how different it was from the island's rural farmers' market, which I knew was only open on Saturdays and only during the summers.

I turned right and walked on Wall toward East Kellogg Boulevard. Seemed like as good a direction as any. I turned right again, thinking I was probably headed back toward the train station, but behind it now. That's when I saw another Greyhound leaving a building a block ahead of me, and heading toward where I'd come from. Apparently, I'd found a bus depot.

I strolled to the bus depot, which didn't look crowded either, but also wasn't as abandoned as I'd thought it would be at night. A dirty-looking man held the door for me. I said, "Thanks," but I veered far away to pass him. I was like one magnet pushing away from another. He'd probably been holding the door for everybody. His scruffy beard and long stringy hair veiled his face. He wore a green fatigue jacket with dog tags on a chain. A Vietnam vet. "One of the crazy ones," Mom would have called him. He held out a hand and asked me for something, but his body odor made me speed up and move quickly past. It was easy for me to curl a judging lip. I hated long beards because I couldn't read expressions through them. But something about him caught my attention, and after clearing the doorway, I was compelled to turn and stare. His eyes and nose looked young. I felt bad that I'd judged him. He was probably Merrick's age. What if he was? What if they'd known each other in Vietnam? What if he had been there when Merrick was blown up? Maybe that's why he was crazy. Maybe he was just a nice kid from an island somewhere too, like me.

"What the hell are you lookin' at?" he demanded.

"Nothing!" I turned and clumsily tromped farther into the depot. He didn't seem like he'd chase, but I memorized the door location so I could avoid it later.

"Hey, kid!" a woman yelled from a distance to my left.

I looked the other way and pretended not to hear. Twenty paces later, I was in a different room. A lobby. My eyes opened wide to soak in the scene. I'd never been anywhere like this before—a strange city bus station at night.

"Oh, my God. What have I done?"

Waking up

I looked back in the direction I'd come from. I'd made some turns on streets I'd already forgotten the names of. I couldn't see him anymore, but the smelly veteran had shaken me up. He looked like Merrick with a beard, which made me miss Connor all of a sudden. My dissociative dream-state started waking up. My rural-born fear of the city exploded in my chest, switching my natural sense of anxiety back on to high alert.

414

"Oh, shit." The dream had ended and I wasn't in my bed, but in a bad place.

"Crap. I'm an island boy," Panic constricted my breathing. "I can't *be* here." The release was gone. I could *never* get used to this. I was vulnerable again. The place wasn't crowded, but for the middle of the night, there were more people than I'd expected—and some of them weren't like me. I put a hand up into my blond hair and suddenly felt *very* rural, *very* white, and *very* small. I re-inhabited my body, as Kyle from middle-class Torano Island, where the only cultural diversity we knew was that guy down the block who still had his Swedish accent.

I patted the front of my pants to make sure I could still feel the key in my pocket.

"I'm sorry, Mom." I looked around, wondering which door would take me back to the train. "Now I know why we never left our stuff before."

My stomach hurt again. My watch said 11:23. I forgot what time that was in Minneapolis, and I'd become afraid to leave the bus depot alone. I frantically looked around at the walls. A clock said 1:23. I had a ticket in my wallet that said, "5:49 a.m. departure." I counted on my fingers.

"Four-and-a-half hours." My eyes closed in relief. "I'm okay. I have time to find my way back."

I knew, sure as shit, that I'd be lost for good if I didn't calm down and get control of my thoughts before running through one more unknown door. I was turned around enough already that I couldn't remember if I was supposed to dart left or right once I got out of the building. And because I was afraid of the Vietnam vet, I really wanted to use a different door to exit, which was making my odds of getting lost even higher if I weren't careful.

"Oh!" Both of my hands grabbed at my stomach. As my pulse settled, my stomach burned. A brief but stabbing pain reminded me I hadn't taken care of myself for days. Maybe with some food, I could calm my stomach and think things through so I wouldn't run in the wrong direction and be lost for good. I could gather my wits, find a safe doorway, and follow the correct sidewalk back to where I was supposed to be.

Or better yet, perhaps if I sat still, I'd wake up in bed on Torano Island where I really belonged.

Regrouping

Ever since I had ignored that lady shouting, "Hey, kid," no one else had acknowledged my existence. That let me feel a little safer and made the whole facility feel calmer than at first. So I strolled to a wall of vending machines and bought a stale sandwich, red licorice, like Scooter used to buy me, and a Pepsi. Food made me think about Mom. How could she let me go alone like this? It was so unlike her. Things between her and Dad must have been bad for her to break her overprotective rules and send her overly-emotional "little sweetheart" on a train alone. Of course, I was the one who'd wandered away from the track—but *still*...! This was her fault. Not mine!

I thought about money. If I didn't get back on the train, how would I eat? Beg at a doorway, like Merrick's scruffy impersonator? Money was limited. I'd already spent two of my thirty dollars and I'd only been there forty-five minutes. Kids can't make a living. Not at fourteen. No matter how confusing my relationship with Mom had become, *at least she fed me.*

"What have I done?" I muttered from a faint heart as I choked down one of the two sandwich wedges. The first few swallows hurt my chest. The hard, chewy licorice and the icy pop sweetened the staleness between bites. I sat on a red plastic seat, bolted to a row of them. All filthy. This was a freaking nightmare. But the quieter I got and the longer I sat, the more I was able to look around and take in the building's atmosphere.

The bus terminal was gross. It smelled of stale cigarettes and gym floor wax, with an overcoat of something that reminded me of urine. The walls were gray and brown, like they were intentionally painted to depress me. But they were filthy to boot. Thousands, possibly millions, of dirty hands had rubbed up against them since they were last cleaned, if or whenever that might have been.

After a couple of buses left, I realized the crowd had thinned a little more.

A poster for a men's mission hung in a glass frame across the lobby from where I was sitting. I stared at its depiction of a white dove taking flight with an olive branch in its mouth. I knew it was in reference to that child's story about Noah finally getting his answer from God when he was looking for a place to land the ark.

Dirty little entrepreneurs

To the right of the poster were the bathroom doors, painted black with badly worn brass push-plates on one side. No part of me wanted to go into the men's room. It looked too dangerous, like the boy's room door at St. Tiberius, but worse. If I held back on the pop, then I could pee on the train later.

Not far from that door, a couple of skinny guys about my age, maybe a shade older, and definitely taller, seemed to have appeared out of nowhere and were now sitting together. They didn't talk. After only a few minutes, a man, who'd wandered in from the street, stepped up to speak to them. After a few words, he nodded his head and disappeared through the black door with the blond boy following. They obviously needed to do more than pee because they didn't come back out for a good ten minutes. When they did, the traveler walked quickly away, but the blond went back to his seat and handed something to the dark-haired boy. They kept looking over at me, but each time, I'd look away. They were showing some interest in me. I wished another bus would roll in and unload a crowd so I wouldn't feel so alone with them. I didn't know whether their interest in me was good or bad. I became more unnerved by the minute.

"Are you lost?" came a voice.

I gasped and turned around.

A medium-sized, sandy-haired man stood before me. He reminded me of the waterbed salesman my brother and I had once talked to in a Seattle shopping mall. My brother had advised me that day never to trust a single word a salesman ever said—all they wanted was one thing: to *make a deal*. This one in the bus station was wearing pressed pants, a pale yellow shirt, and a burnt orange necktie. He stood behind and above me, asking his question through a light brown, bushy mustache.

"No, sir," I answered.

"You sure?"

"I'm not lost."

"Good." He gave a nod. "Because I've got some extra cash on me."

"Some what?"

"Some cash." He glanced at his watch. "And ten minutes."

"Ten minutes?"

"That's all. Ten minutes. Nothing longer."

"Um. Uh. I've got a bus coming." Nerves were making me chatty. "I'm headed to Granddad's house…my Mom's in the bathroom. I-I-I'm supposed to wait here for her…."

"Your mother?" He looked around and appeared surprised. Then smirked. "This is kind of an odd place for you to be waiting for your *mother*."

"But it's a bus station," I said.

"Exactly." A sarcastic laugh came with his answer.

"She'll be back in just a minute." I pointed to the ladies room door. "And…" I needed something to say. I had to think fast. He *looked like* a salesman and had said something about cash. I was stumped but needed to say something, "we don't really have anything for sale."

The man huffed a single laugh, took a drag off his cigarette, dropped his gaze to my pop and licorice, and then looked over at my bare knobby knees. "Nothing's for sale, huh?"

"No sir."

Without words, he focused his gaze into my eyes almost like he was trying to intimidate me into changing my mind about something.

"What?" I was starting to feel some *real* fear. "I'm just waiting for my mom…honest."

"Fine." He looked over at the ladies room door and saw the two boys near it. "My mistake, I guess." He looked directly at my mouth, shook his head once like he'd just lost a deal, shrugged, and said, "Too bad for me."

"Huh?" My nose wrinkled. What the hell had just happened?

"Suit yourself. Sorry to bother you, son." He threw his cigarette on the floor and squashed it with a foot. "Say hi to your mom for me."

To my utter amazement, he simply walked to the light-haired boy who looked most like me. Both boys had watched my exchange with him. The man spoke with them, then pointed at the ladies room, then at me, not caring that I saw him do it. I heard their voices, but I was too far away to make out what they were saying. The dark-haired boy shook his head no, obviously in answer to some question. The light-haired kid didn't look at me, but he scanned the man up and down, then nodded, got up, and went into the men's room. The man looked at me and shrugged again like he was showing me that I'd missed out on something. Then he followed the boy through the door. I snapped off a piece of licorice and swallowed hard. *Why were they all looking at me?*

No sooner did the door settle back to closed than my eye caught movement from the boy stationed outside the bathroom. He was wearing a dirty jean jacket over a white T-shirt. His dark, brown eyes were locked onto me. He was intimidating, but the distance between us was good and he seemed unwilling to leave the door while his friend was inside. His skin was freckled but tight and smooth. He was too young to be outside at night. He looked rough but not athletic—more like an alley cat that shouldn't be messed with.

"Hey!" he shouted. He pulled something from his pants pocket and held it out like an offer to come look. Cash.

I glanced back at his face.

He slowly nodded *yes* while fiddling with the money.

"Me?" I pointed at myself.

He nodded again.

I shook no, but wondered—maybe he only wanted to talk. Maybe I could casually ask what was going on in the bathroom. What I wanted to know the most was: *Is it dangerous?*

The boy moved his free hand, making sure my eyes followed as he pulled a plastic bag from his coat. I knew it was pot. Daniel kept bags like it in his room. "C'mere!" He motioned for me to come over.

I thought about it, but I was startled when I looked behind myself again and saw, to my surprise, the dark spirit still staring—but *bigger* now, and more solid. Like it was not imaginary. What *was* that thing? It was standing a few feet closer than before and sent a freezing cold shiver of fear down my neck.

Panic

That thing is real? I'd had enough. I was too alone and terrified in the big, dark city to spend another second there. Panic finally overtook me. I searched for a door or a portal back through time. Where was the sidewalk to the train station? Maybe I could get back to the island somehow. Maybe my problems weren't so bad, and maybe Connor didn't hate me after all. Maybe I could get someone to let me see Scooter again. *Which way was that door?*

Confusion worsened. How had I gotten here? I wondered if I had made too much of all that had happened this summer—like things weren't as bad as I'd made them out to be. Fran's constantly critical voice rang in my head. "You always make mountains out of molehills." Maybe she was right. And Mom really *was* crying when I left. Maybe she did love me after all. How could I have let myself think those terrible things about my family? What an ungrateful little jerk. Maybe, if I focused, I could calm down, cheer up, and rejoin my life where I'd left it.

"This is stupid," I declared through a lump in my throat. "I'm getting the fuck out'a here!"

I slipped into my natural super-power: escape. It's what I did best. Athletes and musicians trust repeated training and instinct to let their bodies perform without thinking through every move, and when it came to escape, so did I. The waterbed salesman needed ten minutes, which gave me a head start to flee the boy guarding his door, so I lurched from the seat, dropping the half-eaten licorice and spilling my pop. Panic to leave overruled any urge to look for a towel. I vacated the mess and headed toward my only known landmark, but once I passed the vending machines, I was utterly lost.

"Fuck off, you pussy!" I heard from that boy I'd just run from.

"Oh, my God!" Panic exploded in my chest. Escape kept my legs moving, even though wisdom begged me to stop. I scanned left and right but refused to look back. Too much fear. "Oh, please, God. No!" A door led out. That was good. But to where? Didn't matter. Out was better than in, so I left the station. Something I shouldn't have done.

"Oh, God! Oh, God! Oh, God!" Nothing looked familiar. I'd exited the wrong side of the building. The sidewalk air was hot and muggy like before, but the streetlights were in different places. Wedged in the ground-level pathways between tall buildings, how was I to know which way to head? After dashing a bit farther than I should have, I came to a sign pointing left toward *Shepard Road*. To my right *N. Sibley St.* Disbelief hollowed out my chest. Even though I'd forgotten the street names I'd taken when I left 4th Street, I knew these weren't them. This couldn't be real, but it was. How could it be? The train station couldn't have been more than a hundred yards away, but which way? I didn't even see any tracks. If I was to be killed out here, I wouldn't even know where I was while I died.

"Where the hell is 4th Street?" My heart sank. I spun back around to look toward the bus depot. Going back might help me find the right sidewalk. But the ten minutes might be about up, and I couldn't risk running back into a trap. "Oh, God, please, please, please, please help me find my way back." I closed my eyes. "I promise I'll never wander again."

Tracks!" It hit me. A building could hide under bigger buildings, but tracks are thousands of miles long—and engines make noise. "Calm down, stupid," I chanted. "Listen, listen…listen."

A ship's horn blew and it was close. "That's not a train!" How could there be a ship in the middle of a city? "The river!" The tracks were a few blocks from the river. But how far from the river was I? My spinning head wondered which side of the tracks I was on and whether I should walk toward the horn or away from it.

Caught

"What are you doing, young man?" A bold voice from behind sent a wave of adrenaline through me.

I was caught. I was lost and in the city's complete control. My fists clenched and legs readied for a dash, so I turned to see if there were any clumps of people that I could slink into and bolt.

"Stay right there, son," instructed a tall and sturdy policeman. "I haven't seen you around here before."

"I'm not like them." I looked past him toward the bus depot.

His gruff face instantly became the only friend I had now.

"Not like who?" he asked.

"I'm sorry…. I mean…no one…I…." I stammered, ready to vomit.

"What's going on here?"

I could only think of one thing that I could say to him.

"I'm all alone." The stress was too much. I started to cry. "And I've lost my way."

59

The Distant Chimney

When people care about each other, the hardest of times can seem more manageable. But if a person doesn't know that someone cares—well, it doesn't really help.

By Connor Mason

The taxi took Kyle away on Thursday morning. By Friday night, I couldn't stand how quiet the neighborhood had gotten, and that didn't make sense because I had seven other neighbor kids to play with. I liked them all right, and I did spend time with them, but I didn't connect with them as tightly nor as easily as I did Kyle. So in a way I was lonely *while in a crowd*. I played and rode and swam, but somehow it felt empty. At first, when Kyle was trapped in his house, I knew he was there. But now he wasn't there anymore. So the loneliness hadn't really become as big a problem as it was becoming now.

At some point during the middle of the night or Saturday morning, I jumped in my sleep and woke up. "Whoa!" A ghost, or the Grim Reaper to be exact, had flashed into my sleep and scared the ever-loving *shit* out of me.

I almost got up to vomit. These were the kinds of nightmares I used to have when I was getting sick. "It's summer, not flu season," I reminded myself.

I lay still for a few minutes to get over the nausea. The only thoughts I had were of Kyle. Where the hell was he? And why was I suddenly worried about him?

I reached to my nightstand for a tissue to wipe a bead of sweat off my forehead and again I thought about Kyle, who always had a handkerchief in his right front pocket. He was never embarrassed to use it around us neighbor kids. I'm not sure he realized he was the only fourteen-year-old, probably on the whole planet, that carried one around. He had reasons; some minor sinus issues in the winter and hay fever in the summer. If the other guys made fun of him for it, they didn't do it around me. When I set the used tissue back onto my nightstand the way Kyle probably did his handkerchief every night, I sighed. "I miss you, man."

I had gone to bed at ten that night after staring at Kyle's chimney through the trees again. This time, he wasn't ten feet below it, and I wasn't worried about his dad beating him up anymore. But I couldn't get his sad look out of my mind from when the taxi drove off. He had just pushed his hand up to the glass and stared at me like he was being taken to prison.

Unanswered questions

Mrs. Rickett wasn't the kind of neighbor lady who would talk to kids, so on the day Kyle left, my mom offered to find out what she could for me. Unfortunately, that wasn't proving to be as easy as it should have been. For some reason, Mrs. Rickett was being mysterious about it. Even with adults. All she'd tell Mom was that Kyle had been given a surprise vacation to his Grandad's house for his birthday. Mom couldn't even pry a return date out of her.

For me, life once again looked like it did when Merrick first left for boot camp. Now with Kyle gone too, I realized how dependent on him I'd become. There were seven other kids living on this block, but without Kyle at my side, I wasn't ready at first to go out and wrestle with my shyness. If any of them would come to my door and specifically ask if I could come outside, I'd probably go on out. But, with my shyness, books were just easier than knocking on a door that didn't have Kyle on the other side. Loneliness wasn't new, or scary, for me, so I comfortably dug all my old tricks out of the bag and started reading novels again. On this day, Friday, I'd read one cover to cover. Really. A whole book in one day.

Looked like I would be riding my bike to the library a lot more often for a while. My favorite time to ride was morning, right when it opened. It wasn't busy. Usually it was just me in the fiction section, and the librarian, Mrs. Noell, doing paperwork at her desk. I could pick up a few days' worth of books and be home before most of the neighbor kids came out to play. Most days I got several chapters read before anyone came to the door to see if I'd come out to swim or ride bikes. I keep saying I was lonely, but when I look back now, I guess I was mostly just lonely for my best friend.

After jolting awake that night, I couldn't explain away the horrible dread I felt all of a sudden, or why I was suddenly so nauseously sick.

I fell back asleep, sulking about how I wasn't allowed to go to Kyle's birthday, and now I was wondering if I was going to be able to have him at mine.

I hoped to God that he knew how worried I was about him.

60

The Ultimate Surrender

Suicide—what was I thinking? That's a good question. The human mind is programmed to survive. In order to choose not to survive, the human mind must be so twisted as to alter the way thoughts are intended to work.

The greatest human fear is said to be the fear of abandonment. We're social creatures. To isolate a single person from the social fabric of his or her environment...well, that would change the way thoughts are supposed to work. Suicide could actually be seen as a positive option at that point.

By Kyle Rickett

I have no recollection of how I got from the sidewalk policeman to the platform. Absolutely none. It was a total blackout. But I remember standing alone on platform seven. Toes at the edge A resting locomotive layered a distant but heavy rumble into the air. The muggy summer night was illuminated by bright lights that buzzed. I felt tiny. A small suitcase dangled from each hand. My filthy white T-shirt, un-tucked in the rear, smelled of a teen who hadn't showered in days. That was not like me. My matted hair, uncombed and stringy, proved it to be so. I stared straight ahead, not looking at anything. I revisited the dream of the young man with the growling cougar. I wished he'd appear so I could "go with him." Something told me this long, crazy night was about to end. It was the strangest feeling. Trying to plan my next move, I could only see three minutes into the future. Was I about to die?

I still wanted to know what was going on in that bathroom. Or did I? Perhaps I already knew, and now I just wanted it confirmed. The faces of those two boys projected across my inner movie screen. Then the waterbed salesman's eyes staring at my knees and mouth while he said, "Too bad for me." Then I remembered Krieg's "As I recall, you were a screamer." Then I saw the faceless dark, hairy man from my flashbacks. The difference between me and the two boys was that the blond went through the door *voluntarily*. For him, it wasn't a trap.

"Oh, my God, this was what Fran meant when she said that thing about money in my room." Is this what she thinks I do with Dr. Krieg? Willingly?

Questions rang too fast to count. *How much do they make? Are there cameras? Have they learned to like it? Do they want to be there? I wonder if Jack is really dead, or maybe…did he end up here? Will I end up here myself one day?* Oh, God…maybe the words "Go with him" were about the waterbed salesman. And finally: *Was this the life I'd been trained for?*

I was worn down. So far during this trip, I had only faded briefly into light sleep on the train a few times, curled uncomfortably in a seat. Half of the trip had been spent in tears from missing my life. How long had my family been so selfish? I loved them—and *hated them*. From moment to moment, I couldn't tell which of them loved me and which didn't. I couldn't read them anymore. Again I asked myself, *Why does life have to be so confusing?*

It didn't matter. None of them were here now, and I couldn't do anything about any of it. By St. Paul, I wasn't sure how many days I'd been gone. One and a half? Two and a half? Several times on the train,

I'd felt the surprise of my own consciousness returning from random trips out to space.

With a heavy sigh, I stood and wished that Connor had come with me on this trip. Him I trusted. I had earned *his* trust in return, but then my family broke that for me. Having our friendship squelched, just as I had begun to appreciate how genuinely he cared, was blowing my mind. Connor was all I had left. The guy *never* criticized me. Andreo, Fran, and my family didn't seem to have his ear. Connor was a perfect friend. Steady as a rock. How could he have been banished? I hadn't been given a chance to say goodbye to him, and I didn't know if he was even aware yet how far away I was. He could never like me again now, could he? Not after he found out I'd abandoned him. Sure, part of me knew I hadn't abandoned him of my own free will, but I felt responsible anyway. If I hadn't grabbed at his bike on the first day of summer, everything that had taken place between that moment and this one would have been different. I had learned well that it was always easiest just to take the blame for the bad that happened around me.

I snapped-to with a shake of my head, still standing at the edge, but not at all alone. The dark spirit had followed me back and was continuing to grow larger and heavier with each hour, materializing into our world from some other dimension, taking on mass and filling more space with each moment. He was as real as flesh and blood. I looked back to my right, slowly. I still felt him, standing now in reaching distance; he was the Grim Reaper, sure as could be. Like in the cartoons, he was twice the size of a mortal man, and dark black like the hollowness of eternal space. Staring down at me. Watching.

I looked forward again. I can't explain it clearly, but the platform became a strange dark beach. A black sea appeared before me. It was death. My three minutes were up. It was time to die. I don't know why I knew that. The dark sea lapped at my feet, but expanded outward, beyond the horizon. The exact edge of where it began was a slight blur. If I extended a foot forward, I could have stepped into it, it was that close. Its chill caressed my aching heart, inviting me to walk in and abandon all the sadness of the living world. Off in the distance, to the north, a horn bellowed. Its haunting echo broke my blank stare once again. I turned to look down the track and watch the bright headlight coming fast out of the night. I winced at the rhythmic tones of the massive, steely horn. WoooWAAAAAAAH! WoooWAAAAAAAH! My mind emptied of thought. My blood chilled. All that existed now were the dark, watching creature behind, the expanse of blissful death ahead, my knobby knees holding me from below—and that oncoming train.

"This should be quick." My eyes filled with tears. My lungs heaved like I'd run a marathon. My heart raced. Some thoughts returned. Unhappy ones. I didn't want to be one of those boys at the restroom. Visions flashed of Fran's smirk and Daniel slinking out of the kitchen.

"They all know what I am," I quietly muttered. Everyone I'd ever loved had either been removed or had betrayed me by now. I heard Fran's arrogant voice, proudly announcing, "Scott's not your friend! You need to forget about him."

"I have no friends," I mumbled. Sound faded. I imagined Connor's smiling wave goodbye through the cab window. I saw the growing headlamp. It neared. "Goodbye, Connor," I whispered aloud. "Goodbye, Scooter." My legs crouched. The muscles prepared for the jump. I'd thought about this moment for years. There was no reason not to do it now. This wasn't my time to be alive on the earth. A white bird of some kind flew right at me. The horn blew, almost as if the train could see me and was screaming "*NOOOOOOO!*" I looked straight ahead and closed my eyes. It was almost upon us, me and the spirit.

"I give up," I said into the flurry of churning air being pushed out of the way by the approaching locomotive. The monstrous rumbling from its immense size and weight ignited the adrenaline. My left leg lifted, and with my right, I pushed off.

61

Signs

I know all this dream talk sounds crazy, and I can't explain it. But also I can't disbelieve it. Not only have I experienced the phenomenon for myself, but over the years, many different people have told tales of being connected to others through dreams. Stories come along of mothers, or sisters or brothers, becoming violently ill at the very moment a loved one dies in a sudden accident somewhere else on the earth. I'm not telling anyone to believe this stuff, but I'm reporting that an inordinately long string of coincidences continued to happen during that precariously dangerous time in my life.

By Tuck Taylor

On Saturday, at just a little after midnight, I arrived in Duluth, Minnesota, and stopped for my final gas fill-up at the circle J, a small truck stop/restaurant/gas station combination. Back then, everything, including gas stations, closed at night, but this one, which served truck drivers, was open around the clock.

I'd driven the whole trip by truck stops because of their convenience. They were open twenty-four hours, positioned near the highways, and always had gas available. By July of 1974, it had only been four months since the end of the famous Arab Oil Embargo, which we daily drivers called "the gas crisis." Normal gas stations, and their customers, were still recovering from the national trauma of the ten-gallon per fill-up gas ration and the long lines at the pump. Most cars only got about ten to twelve miles to the gallon back then, and had up to thirty-gallon gas tanks. Ten gallons wasn't much, especially for my gas-guzzling muscle car. A lot of drivers were still nervously lining up to top off these massive tanks, making the standard gas station a stressful place I didn't enjoy dealing with. From October of 1973, through March of 1974, truck stops were among the few places allowed to sell more than ten gallons at a time to trucks and travelers. Even though gas was now becoming available everywhere, I guess I just hadn't broken the truck stop habit.

I was also under common road fatigue, which was made worse for me because I hadn't slept well all summer, my car was not air-conditioned, and to help save on gas consumption, President Nixon had recently dropped the national speed limit from 70 to 55 mph. The whole trip took a day longer than it used to. When you're driving roughly thirteen hundred miles, the speed limit change adds about five more frustrating hours of driving time, which adds more food and rest stops. I used to be able to drive it in eighteen hours. This trip took nearly twenty-four hours of driving, which pushed me over a critical edge: At my age I could usually drive eighteen hours straight through, but twenty-four hours, in my condition, was too much. I needed to add another half-day of stopping for food and napping in my bucket seats in roadside rest areas. By midnight Friday night, I was more road-weary than I'd ever been, and emotionally *exhausted.*

Somehow, though, I had the feeling I had made the right choice to come to Duluth. Across the street was the local Railroad Workers' Credit Union. In the window was a sign *We're strong together*—exactly what the dove had been saying to my sister and me in our dreams.

"Jesus Christ. It followed me here."

As I filled my tank, I stood quietly and listened to the beautiful, peaceful splendor of Duluth. In the distance, a train rumbled. The horn blew. I recalled in Texas hearing a train when the crow mimicked, "Save him!" and then—for some totally unknown reason—I got violently sick and threw-up on the side of my car.

62

The Claw

Was I dead? I'd pushed off. I'd timed it perfectly. I had help. A lot of it. The dark spirit, Fran, Andreo, Krieg—they had all helped set me up to make this decision. But I was the genius who would execute it. The engine and I were to meet at exactly the same place at exactly the same time. How it might turn out was up to fate. But how it started was my choice. I had finally given up everything that first gave up on me.

By Kyle Rickett

Out from the darkness, a claw clamped onto my right elbow, anchoring me mid-jump. Then with a rude yank, that claw jerked me backward, twisting me into a spin. Dying hurt as the Grim Reaper yanked the soul from my body. I lost my grip on the suitcase and it left me. I spun sideways in slow motion to fall shoulder-first onto the duffle bag, then roll painfully onto my back, landing face up on the platform. My head hit the concrete with a thud, hurting my teeth like they had been knocked loose. The pain in my head angered me, but it jolted thoughts back to life. It "knocked some sense into me"—or so my dad would have said.

The first engine flew past; then the second or third one scolded me with a single "WoooWAAAAAAAH!" A warm, violent burst of air washed over me like an ocean wave smelling of diesel.

I looked up at a man hovering over me, holding his stupid Minnesota Twins hat on with one hand. He yelled over the rolling boxcar wheels.

"You all right?"

I blinked slowly in acknowledgment.

"It's a God-dammed good thing that woman yelled for me to save you, kid! You're lucky I did! Ya gotta be more careful around trains. Ya hear me?"

Where had he come from? I had thought I was alone. I nodded obediently but closed my eyes and wished I'd successfully jumped.

"Huh!" The man calmed a little and looked around us. "Well, that's odd," he noticed. "I'm sure I heard her yell, '*Save him!*'"

I looked down the platform. There was no one, not even the dark spirit...anywhere...in any direction. Just me and the man, who then asked one last question.

"Just how'd you get here anyway?"

63

You're Already Late

All the dreams were about to bring two lost souls together. I suppose if it isn't a person's time to go, it simply isn't a person's time to go. Many people tell stories of suddenly changing a flight or a travel plan and finding out later they had avoided an accident because of the change. This was one such time. No one knows who yelled "Save him!" or why that stranger had to be where he was at that moment. No one knows why Connor and Tuck were both struck with nausea at the very moment I'd jumped. And no one can explain how it came to be that Tuck Taylor—a profoundly changed Near-Death-Experience (NDE) survivor—would be the first person I'd converse with after my own near-death-experience.

By Tuck Taylor

I'd gotten to Grandpa's at about 1:00 a.m. He was expecting me so the door was unlocked. Actually, it was the Duluth countryside, so the door was *always* unlocked. Grandpa Tucker, whom I was named after, slept through my arrival, but he woke me up at 9:00 to ask a favor.

"I got breakfast on the table for you, young fella."

Face down in the pillow, I rolled over and squinted with one eye.

"Hi, Grandpa."

"You had a good trip I imagine. Lots of time to think?"

"Thirteen hundred miles. Yes. Too much thinking." I shielded my tender eyes with the inside of an elbow. "Don't make me think now."

"Yer outa' luck, boy. Hate to do this to you, but I got a favor to ask."

Grandpa waited until I'd gotten up, peed, showered, and sat down at the breakfast table before instructing me to go to Duluth Union Depot train station, some half hour back by the Circle J, and pick up Louie's grandson.

Grandpa and Louie had been friends for over thirty years. Both their wives had since passed, and they now spent most of their time together working as a team on each other's farms. I call them farms. Wooded acreage is a better term. Grandpa had two horses that he kept for company, but Louie's had since passed, and he felt he was too late in his own life to restart another relationship with another set of horses.

Louie and I went way back. I was five when he taught me to fish. I didn't mind being asked to pick up his grandson for him.

"Thank you, Tuckster." Grandpa patted my shoulder. "Louie wasn't expecting him. One of his twins, Marie, called a few days ago asking for him to visit, but you know it's Railroad Riding Days and Louie was committed."

"Is he playing music?"

"All day. This year he's head organizer, or whatever you call it."

"That's pretty cool."

"Ahh!" He waved a disgusted hand. "He's been griping all summer about it. I'll be glad when it's over."

"That sounds like the old coot." I laughed as I pulled on a pair of stylish cowboy boots, which were a common accessory in 1974.

"The boy's name is Kyle. He's that little white-haired one in the pictures all over Louie's walls."

"Oh, good. I've always wanted to meet him. He looks like a happy kid." I headed toward the door. "This should be a fun morning."

"Oh, one more thing; I forgot to tell you...you're already late. The train's due in at 10:45."

"Oh, gee thanks!" I looked at my watch. 10:15. "I've been up since nine. Why didn't you tell me that before I took a long shower?"

"Slow down, city boy. We're on country time now. No need to be in a hurry. He can't leave the station without you."

"City boy? Phh. Texas isn't exactly a fast pace, Grandpa. Nonetheless, I still don't like to be late." I shook my head teasingly. "Good thing I drive a fast car."

He walked with me to the door. "Well, will you look at that? You're still driving that old, gold GTO."

"Never letting it go, Gramps. Sometimes it's my only friend."

"Now why would a spry buck like you say something like that?"

"Hey, I have friends. They're just not as reliable as the car."

"Well, you just might be in need of a new one."

"A new car?" I asked indignantly.

"A new friend."

64

Arrival in a New Old Place

Now you know the story of how I—a nice-looking, reasonably affluent, likeable, high-energy teen—found myself lying on death's doorstep, not seeing any living way out of my private despair.

To Mom, an ignored problem was a solved problem. Sweeping-under-the-rug was the great Rickett strategy passed down from a dad who wouldn't talk about war days, through a mom who wouldn't address Fran's behaviors, and through angry elder siblings who drank and smoked their unhappiness away. And then there's me—the late life accident who came into the mess after it was in full bloom—whose gut hurt and whose brain actually broke into pieces to hide the jumble into any available crevice.

If we'd have chosen a Rickett family crest, it would have been an ostrich with its head in the sand. Mom had successfully ignored Dad's aloof escapism, Fran's narcissistic attacks, Dr. Krieg's bullying, and my repeated pleas to be let out of Catholic school. And now at this moment, her plot to ignore this summer's family explosion until it was solved was working—but only for her. Back at home, the house was probably quiet since I wasn't sulking where she could see me. Fran could visit all she wanted, Daniel could walk in and out without sneaking and Dad could stay home more because he didn't need to avoid me. It seemed to me that my trip had solved her problems...for now.

But a backfire was about to bang loudly 2,000 miles from anywhere she could hear it. Without her in my line of sight, I was liberated to try a different tactic for dealing with stress. She had ignored me almost to death, and now she wasn't there to finish me off. My "Atomic-Ant"/"Super-Kyle" high tolerance for pain was now stretched beyond its safety zone. On Saturday morning, July 27, a lifetime of patience and obedience, of vomiting and sleeplessness, had edged me past the point of no return, right to the frayed end of my rope—to rock-bottom. My body might not have actually died on that train track, but part of my life had. A part that I had needed to let go of for a long time. Every good story has a turning point, and this was mine.

I was now suicidal, something a chipper fourteen-year-old should never be. But in a way, I was also reborn. In St. Paul, the culmination of monumental despair had nearly killed me. But here and now—and in not a moment too soon—I'd finally become angry!

By Kyle Rickett

"Pa-*thetic*!" I blurted out as I thought about how I'd been a rule-follower my whole childhood. The disobedient St. Paul walkout showed me something new. "Why'd I have to go and ruin it?" Only five minutes into the good feeling, I had returned like an idiot, in a *panic*, to that same family who had been making me miserable all along.

"Stupid." I shook my head. Why did I have to get back on the train that took me from one family member to *another*? For five minutes, I had been set *free* from the whole damned family. "Why do I have to w*ant* them to love me so much? What a stupid, vulnerable weakness!" I was now buried under a heap of confusing, conflicting emotions.

The dark spirit didn't follow me back onto the train, thank goodness for that. But he wasn't the only scary thing I'd never be able to forget from that trip. I had seen two more things in St. Paul that I could never unsee: 1) I could make real money with my blond hair, and 2) I had the balls to jump off a fucking platform.

"Should I have eggs for breakfast today?" My question was loud enough that a young, redheaded man across the aisle looked over to see if I was talking to him. "Which shirt should I wear today?"

He politely shook his head to say he didn't know.

"Oh, and by the way," I turned toward the window to see my reflection in the glass, "should I fucking *kill myself today*?" I sarcastically shook my head and sighed.

"Just one more decision I have to make every day now…. Uhhh!"

Pulling into town

I recognized the buildings as we slowed into Duluth, which comforted me at first, but quickly became irritating. I loved Papa, but I wasn't here to begin a summer vacation with him. *This was my detention.* I'd been sent to my room—the one in Minnesota.

The town was the same, but I was different. I was now "Anti-Kyle." Krieg's attack had shaken loose mysterious memories that wouldn't explain themselves but also wouldn't politely go back—and stay—under their rock. Constant irritation and a new, quick temper were ready to overthrow me. A dam that held back my self-control was about to crumble. My teeth clenched painfully as Duluth Union Depot peeked into view. What bubbled up from my burning gut was more than a bad mood. I was rapidly developing super-villain *rage*.

Looking out at Minnesota was pissing me off, so I turned away from the window, brought my feet up onto the next seat, and leaned back, arms crossed, eyes staring at my knees. I knew, but didn't care, that I now looked like what Fran would call a typical pissed-off teen. I rested my head against the glass to let the rhythmic rumble fill my body.

What had I turned into? The world—my world—had definitely changed. With my eyes closed, visions of the previous night replaced the old reality. I had jumped for real into the mysterious black ocean that I had seen *with my own eyes*. It was *real*. The Reaper was *real*. My jump was *real*. How could a guy ever forget having seen all that?

Maybe that's why everything felt different this day. It had been a near-death-experience sure as any other, and I was a changed soul. I'd crossed another line I couldn't uncross. Nothing could possibly erase the chill from the spirit that tried to take me into death with him that night, could it?

I wondered if the person who'd invented the Grim Reaper character didn't invent him at all, but had merely drawn a picture of what he—*and I*—had seen while standing at the extreme edge of our perilously fragile lives. No sir, I wasn't Marie Rickett's precious little sweetheart any longer. I could never "unsee" the devil's leering eyes, and I now lived every moment, asleep and awake, with his image burned into the forefront of my memory. If I were ever to see him again, I wouldn't be so freaked out. He was familiar now.

The train kept slowing and slowing until, eventually, it slowed all the way into the station. Irritated, I got up and ambled toward the door as the train rattled and braked to a squawking stop. My luggage bumped a seatback or two as I looked through the windows on both sides of the aisle.

Duluth was similar in many ways to Everett—both steeped in industrial odor. Duluth was a smelly ore mining town whereas Everett was built around a stinky pulp-mill. Both were harbor towns.

I let go of an irritated sigh while stepping from the train beneath a white sign with black letters, *Duluth Union Depot*. Like Mom said, the building had been totally renovated since my last visit, but the sign was in the same place. I remembered three times when Papa and Grandma had stood directly below it, welcoming Mom and me with open arms and million-dollar smiles. Grandma was gone now, I knew that—but where the *hell* was Papa?

Super-villain rage

"God damn it, Louie!" I had barely lived through this journey and was now being *stood up by my jailer?* I felt like an idiot, standing there ungreeted like I'd gotten off at the wrong stop. I sure as hell didn't look cool like that rugged boy with the jean jacket and bag of pot.

"How stupid do I look now?" I lifted the child-sized suitcases and glanced down at my mid-length hemmed shorts and a wrinkled, filthy undershirt. "I look like Disneyland threw up on me."

I set the bags down, which annoyed those who now had to step around me. I didn't care. My lifetime of shame had turned to anger that was growing by the minute.

A woman wearing a Minnesota Twins hat came from the left and passed me without so much as a nod.

"I'm fine. Thank you for asking," I mumbled angrily. "*Bitch....*"

She turned to glare, but held her words. The hat reminded me of my unwanted rescue only hours before. I hated her mostly for wearing it. Or maybe she was the idiot who had yelled, "Save him!" and made that guy pull me back into this crappy world.

"I wouldn't fucking be here right now if that asshole had let me jump," I said right into her eyes as if wearing the hat meant she was related to the stranger who had saved me. But she wasn't. She grimaced like she thought I was rude, shook her head, and walked to the train.

I briefly cared what she thought of me. In fact, I wondered what *I* thought of me. What had made me say those things? I didn't give my mouth permission to insult her or to tell her about my jump. The words had fallen out of my mouth unplanned. I *was* rude. My hair was matted. My shirt filthy. None of this was the real me. "Maybe none of this is real at all."

"Maybe I'm dead." I looked toward the floor and commented on what was probably happening. "The devil took my soul." I suddenly made an obvious connection. "Oh, my God! People in Twins hats *are his helpers*!"

I scanned the platform through eyes that were cold and dry. Maybe I really *was* dead. There wasn't an ounce of love in me for anyone. I didn't feel like Kyle anymore. I seemed to be invisible. No one except the evil spirits in Twins hats could see me at all.

"I'm in hell," I muttered. The idling train hummed softly behind. A couple of dozen people stood in groups. Some were greeting travelers, others saying goodbye.

Still no Papa.

The ghost of Kyle Rickett

"Figures Papa would forget about me too," I scoffed. I probably *was* now the walking spirit of Kyle Rickett, but I just didn't know I was dead yet. Maybe I really had jumped and it hadn't been a stranger but the grip of the devil's hand that had pulled my immortal spirit out of my body before the train hit the flesh of stupid little Kyle.

"That explains everything." I now knew why I hadn't seen the man there before the grab. Because h*e wasn't really there.* It also explained Papa's absence. He'd heard I'd been killed, and so he wasn't here to pick me up.

"Maybe I can fly now." I closed my eyes tightly and tried to reappear at Papa's house. I imagined his ugly yellow countertops, and when I was sure I could see him standing in his kitchen, I opened my eyes.

"Shit," I mumbled and looked around. "Train station." I sighed. "Still here."

"Excuse us, young man." A couple appeared from behind with a clump of three small kids. They broke formation to pass around both sides of me.

"No ball caps," I whispered, but didn't flinch. "Guess I'm not dead."

"Maybe he's deaf," remarked the woman loudly enough to teach me a lesson.

"Fuck you," I mumbled to the final kid trailing behind. As the little girl passed, her big brown eyes looked upward into mine. I didn't smile at her the way I normally would have. Instead, I sneered. She broke her glance and sped to her sister's hand. My heart sank only for a second at the thought that I might have hurt her feelings. But—and this is so unlike the normal me—that stupid look of childlike innocence in her face pissed me off.

Aha! The big picture

With a loud angry sigh, I picked up my bags and wobbled indifferently into the terminal. It smelled of diesel, cigarettes, and new paint, but with a touch of morning heat and Duluth industrial stink added in for uniqueness. My eyes locked onto the men's room door, twenty feet away, not painted black, but with a similar brass push plate. The waterbed salesman flashed to mind. Then Krieg. Then the blond boy.

"Oh, fuck." My mind was going into its tricks again—just like on Krieg's table.

My face flushed. Spine and shoulders lifted defensively. Anger swelled through my chest and spiked to the highest level yet as my heart thumped and ears rang. A past moment hijacked my mind and put me into Krieg's clinic. His ugly, monster face, his cigarette breath, and his crackled old voice commenting on how much he liked my blond hair wrinkled my nose in disgust. The waterbed salesman, also a smoker, smelled the same way just before disappearing into the men's room with that boy who looked like me. I connected the dots.

"Holy shit." Through the power of a runaway imagination, I felt Krieg's invisible hands in my crotch. Then, and to my own shock, disgust, and confusion, I felt a tiny tinge of arousal. "Oh, God." I casually moved a suitcase to the front in order to hold down an erection if it went that far. My raging anger changed to nausea and fear. I recalled the dark-haired boy fanning his cash. "That's *definitely* what the money was for."

I suddenly knew what I probably should have known all along. But my memory had been trained to forget the individual pieces, never to connect them to see the picture I wanted to ignore. How else could I live in the fantasy that childhood was *only* about homework, bikes, friendship, Hot Wheels, Matchies, and Legos?

"I'm not the only guy that men do this to," I whispered. The nausea worsened as I began to accept the truths that had been right in front of me all my life.

But that wasn't the end of it. My relational thought process drove me into the minds of the two boys I'd seen inviting the men in, one of whom looked more like me each time I remembered him.

"Those guys were *okay* with it." I carried it even a step further, "In fact…they were getting…*paid*."

Embracing reality

That's when the headache and dizzy spell hit. The first of many. Even though the building was renovated, I'd stood in that spot several times over the years, but at this moment, the station was a strange place. Not real. Not Norman Rockwell picturesque. Queasiness slacked my jaw and pushed my tongue out for air.

Rage returned to draw the tongue back in and purse my lips. Life had been a God-*damned* lie. I'd staved off anger my whole life, but on that morning, it was *finally* seizing control of me. I'd been living a lie all along. I'd trusted and valued my beliefs about life being quaint. It enraged my very soul to see how obvious the truth had always been.

How come everyone else didn't know what I now knew? Or did they? Maybe that's why Fran had accused me of doing things with Krieg—because everyone knew that boys routinely did that, but everyone had neglected to explain it to stupid little Connor and me. Or, somehow, all through our young lives we knew, too, but we didn't *want* to, so we chose blindness to avoid its shock. Self-induced plausible deniability. *Voluntary stupidity*!

Eyes wide open

No matter the reason, St. Paul opened *my* eyes to a real-life subculture that Island County people didn't talk about—at least not to me. People *acted as if* they didn't know it was *actually* happening in the pediatrician's clinic and in my bedroom while my own clueless mother drugged me for it. Fran knew. When she blurted it out at my birthday,

Mom chose to gloss it over and change the subject. Twice, that same mom had practically watched it happen and had simply chosen not to react. I wasn't allowed to talk about it afterward. Nobody was. We were all to pretend it wasn't real. How many other people knew but didn't talk about it? Who could I trust?

The dizziness returned, but it didn't replace the anger. Both had control over me now. To avoid puking from spinning or screaming from anger, I focused all attention straight ahead.

"Heh-heh-heh!" I murmured like an angry mad scientist as my eyes locked onto the bathroom door. "I know what that's for!" I glanced about the station looking for seedy characters. But people were different here. It was a bright, sunny morning. Everyone had baggage and no one was working the late night visitors or any of the travelers. "That door's *mine*."

As the station spun, I saw how reality worked. We close our eyes, choose what to believe, and pretend the rest doesn't exist. We don't see the starving people, the prostitutes, the racists, or the pedophiles whom we walk among. We ignore the Vietnam Vets holding the door for us. But still, all these people, with all their needs, are here with us on the earth right now. I now knew there was no separation because, as it turns out, *evil shares each moment with good*. We just choose which one to look at. A respected island doctor shakes Dad's hand while in his pocket, six inches away, are photos of us Island Voyager Scouts with no clothes on. Some part of Dad knows those photos are there. But he doesn't want to believe it, *so he chooses not to*. After all, Krieg is Dad's friend. A reasonable man. No reasonable man would ever really do something so icky. Would he?

Well, would he?

Of course he would.

So would plenty of other icky people.

So then why would there not be human transactions made at night in this nicely renovated Minnesota train station? And if there weren't, well maybe it was because there just weren't enough blond boys to hit every train station in America. I knew the customers were here because I suddenly believed they were everywhere.

Why couldn't I start the transactions myself...before someone else did? After all, no one was picking me up, and there had been a *lot* of money in that kid's hand.

65

Anticipating a Good Time

It's funny how we humans think we know someone based on what we know about ourselves. Clinically, the practice is called projection. We project our own personalities, values, likes, and dislikes onto the people we interact with. That's why we think we know them, and why we feel we can relate to them. Even when we haven't met, stories and photos make us believe we know a person. Tuck was about to discover that he was not at all prepared to meet me, because on that particular morning, I was the exact opposite of what he thought he was headed to.

By Tuck Taylor

The drive to the station was another uncomfortable half-hour after nearly two long days in a driver's seat that had shaped itself to my ass. I was five minutes from the station and had not seen the train fly by me, which told me I was not late and the grandson, Kyle, was probably not looking for me yet. Either that, or the train had already arrived and I was very late.

The drive gave me a few more minutes to try to remember whatever I could about this white-haired grandkid. Louie told stories constantly about all twelve grandkids. Kyle, however, was one of the few that he bragged on the most. Grandpa had just told me that he was from one of the twin daughters who lived on the West Coast. One twin had a set of four boys and the other was Marie, the mother of the infamous antagonist, "Fran," whom I had also heard about. I was pretty sure Kyle was (sadly) from Fran's family. If I had my stories straight, he'd be under driving-age, but definitely old enough to kid around with. Knowing how much Louie liked him, I believed I was in for a fun morning. Louie's event would keep him busy all day, so if I were lucky, Kyle and I could goof off for a while. Maybe I could buy him a burger and we could throw a Frisbee around for a bit. If he really was the comedian Louie said he was, then the day was going to be very entertaining. I hadn't wanted to admit it in front of him, but Grandpa was right that morning. I did need a new friend. I desperately needed to laugh with someone.

"This is going to be fun."

66

The Beginning

Anger can be a positive force when it stops injustice, rights wrongs, or empowers one to lift a car off a child. The problem with being angry for the first time in a man's life is that he may not know how to handle it. Anger is a powerful tool when justified and skillfully handled with finesse. Unfortunately, I'd never been taught any anger management skills, so I felt completely out of my element. My anger may have been justified, but with no skills for managing it, I just looked like a fool.

By Kyle Rickett

"All aboard!" resounded through the station.

"Fuck off," I muttered.

The conductor's voice irritated me. In fact, as my frustration grew, every sound, every movement, every stranger's glance irritated my every cell. I nearly jumped out of my skin when the engineer blasted the horn twice to signal a closing of the doors.

Since the bike accident, my distress had continued to build, but it was now reaching the point where it couldn't go on much longer. A summer of bad sleep wasn't helping either. I didn't *want* to think about that day, but it kept flashing before my eyes, pestering and prodding any chance at peace. Every time I tried to fall asleep, I'd fret about waking up in Krieg's office and I'd obsess over wondering how real or imaginary all those new memories of being with him were. But the worst of it was that I couldn't stop worrying about how to defend myself at school if Andreo were to catch wind of what Krieg and I had done.

Why did *any* of this have to happen?

One last short blast warned that I had one last chance to bolt for the train, return to Washington, hug my dad, and beg him to love me again.

But I froze.

Then the engine's tone deepened and the hitches between cars clanked one behind the other. My chest heaved with an anxious blend of fear and hatred. *How did everything go so wrong?* My back stayed to the train and I didn't run for it. I closed my eyes and listened to it leave. I didn't know what to do. I couldn't decide anything. The whole place rumbled, then hushed as the clanking cars trailed off.

Old Kyle and new Kyle fought in my head. I stood paralyzed by the sudden sense of abandon as the small town station restfully emptied of travelers. The large black-and-white clock above the men's room door said ten after ten. Ten after eight back home where Dad was getting dressed for work. I was supposed to have spent this summer in the shop, changing oil unsupervised, like the real mechanic he had proudly taught me to become. But apparently I wasn't that worker anymore. Here I stood instead, a lost boy. Hands quivering, I squeezed the luggage handles hard in hopes of puncturing and bleeding again like I had in my room the night of Krieg's first assault.

"I want things to be *normal*!" My jaw trembled. Nobody was close enough to hear, "If only I hadn't reached for Connor's *bike*! Why did this have to happen to *me*? *Why*? I just want my *life back*! Why do I have to be so *stupid*? Fran's right. I'm a clumsy *idiot!*" I fought back tears and began panting deeply to keep from crying. *How long has my life been so crazy?*

They all knew!

In an attempt to find where things had gone wrong, I inventoried my closest relationships. Daniel's pot-smoking and living mostly alone in a Kenworth came to mind, and suddenly made more sense.

"He knew it all along...."

Fran's excessive drinking and getting fired from jobs flashed next; then Mom's nervous habit of keeping Dad calm at any cost. Who *were* these people?

"They *all* knew life sucked.... They never *fucking* told me.... Nothing was ever *real!*" Still aware of the missing train behind me, I suddenly felt as if I'd been abandoned a long, long time ago—but I had been too *stupid* to see it until now. "They let me believe it like a *dumbshit!*" As I imagined a chasm growing between me and my family, I added volume to my words, losing control of my angry whisper. Fortunately, no one was standing within earshot because once I'd begun, my private outburst took on a life of its own.

"Well, I don't have to pretend anymore *either!*" I shook my head in disgust.

"Do I? Huh? *Do I?* They're all liars. They should have *said* something!"

"And they can all go to *hell!*" I fixed my attention on the restroom door—and that's when it happened.

Sexualizing the distress

It's hard to explain this experience through logic—it was more a *feeling* that washed through me like a dangerous drug that felt good going in. Like with Krieg's tranquilizers, my personality—and values—changed with the feeling. The irritation in my veins calmed. What a *relief.*

My focus intensified on the bathroom door as the only important object in existence. It represented my grand defiance. I loved Fran, but she was the one who'd told Mom that I liked what Krieg and I had done and then had accused me of doing it with other men in the library parking lot. She could be mean, but at that time in my life, I had been tricked into believing she was smart. In a way, she'd predicted that bathroom door to be my inescapable destiny—and look at this: She was right again.

"That's *my* door!" A relaxed but cynical grin crossed my cooling cheeks. Relief tangled with arousal as I recalled how Krieg's left hand had hurt my face while his right hand excited me.

"That would feel good right now."

Years later, I would learn that children who've been sexualized too early *can* sometimes grow up prone to over-sexualizing moments of distress. But back then, all I knew to think was: "I *need* money.... I *like* sex.... I guess I could have some real fun with this." I looked around for anyone who might have already staked claim on the door. Only a few passengers and a man with a broom remained, but no one was for sale. "Yesss! If I wait for another train, someone with 'extra cash' will come along."

I recalled my seventh grade religion teacher, Sister Catherine, once asking the class what it meant to surrender, which then opened up a firestorm of "deep meaningful answers" from two or three of the more dramatic girls, but Sister Catherine cooled the poetic clucking when she revealed the simple truth. "All it means is to move over to the winning team."

How simple. That's what I wanted—to give up on my convoluted past and just *join the winning team*. Family and friends didn't want me anymore—but horny old men did. I recalled detecting a certain inexplicable craving in the eyes of that waterbed salesman when he looked down at my legs and back up at my mouth. I didn't want to wrestle my old life any longer. In fact, it felt deliciously rebellious— even exciting—to think about shattering the rules of decency and surrendering to the next desire-filled man who "had a little cash" on him and liked the way I looked.

"Damn!" My sarcasm flowed freely, almost lightheartedly. "I should have asked that kid in St. Paul if I was supposed to get paid before or after." I looked down at myself. "Uh, oh," I said. "I can't make money looking like an *ass* now, can I?" With the twenty-eight dollars I had left, I needed to score some rugged second-hand jeans and a faded jacket.

"I need to look *bad*...not stupid."

Which half of my brain do I live in?

"Whoa." Another dizzying headache was probably caused by cute little Kyle, who was still alive in my body, asking if I knew what the *hell* I was doing. I relocated to a support pillar in the center of the lobby so I could lean against it. Who was I going to leave this station as? Cute little Kyle, or the next blond boy for sale? I couldn't really be both—or *could* I? The pressure of this decision was tearing my brain in half. I had to choose a side to move all my attention into. Should I wait a little longer? Use the payphone to call Papa? Or should I head out to buy tough-boy clothes?

"God damn it, Papa; where *are* you?" Still abandoned, the absurd life of a street hustler looked imminent, making it up to me to find a way to deal with it.

"Pot!" I blurted out. "It always makes Daniel forget." If it worked so well for him, perhaps it would help me forget what I was about to do too. I'd never gotten over missing the Daniel who would wrestle with me when I was little. He was fourteen—my age—when he started smoking pot, and also stopped hugging me. It was like he'd one day just *pulled away* from the whole family. Maybe fourteen was my time to pull away too.

I wrapped my right arm, duffle bag in hand, around the pillar and pretended it returned the friendship. I hadn't been hugged by *anyone* in days—actually *weeks*. That childlike part of me apparently wasn't gone yet. How tough was I *really*? I still wanted someone to touch me, squeeze me, bury my head into their chest and promise to take me *home* and make everything okay.

Go time!

A tear fell from my eye. I quickly wiped it with a shoulder, causing the duffle bag to slap the post.

"Shit."

The confusion had to stop. No one was going to hug me. It was time to be strong. Nothing could change what was about to happen. It was time to embrace my destiny, and to man up without letting conscience, or a stupid childish desire to be *hugged*, pester me. I would never have to go back to St. Tiberius's if I moved forward with this. I believed that the condemning voices in my head would fade now that Fran and Andreo would be out of the picture forever. This was a new beginning, with no one to torture me with my own secrets. I would never have to keep another secret. Just let people see me for who I am. I had no enemies here.

In the years since Andreo had turned the school against me, I had learned to master wallflower-like invisibility by focusing on the floor. Back on the island, making eye contact could start unwanted fights. But I wasn't *on* the island any longer. So my determined gaze shot straight forward, scanning for customers. I wasn't my cowering self, suffocating from worry about what my peers thought. True, the burning emptiness of losing my family and friends was complicating things, *but only if I let myself think about it.* It was time to break the old rules. I needed money. I needed to survive. And I suddenly wanted *sex*.

As my dizzying headache subsided, my future seemed clear and the Duluth station became more surreal than ever. The janitor's dustpan clanked more. The surfaces were harder, the echoes louder. I used to love the previous building's old-world charm, and they had done a good job of capturing that charm in this new remodel, but on this day, I didn't care. It had changed into another pointless scene in the dream I couldn't wake up from. I was getting so lost in thought and confused by my own inner argument that I almost believed I was a character in a movie.

And that's when I saw him.

First impressions

Over by the street entrance, a young man had entered and was staring at me. He looked too old to be a teen, but not by much. Again, I sensed the hollowness of the missing train that would have connected me to my old life. I tried not to attract his attention, but I was a fairly obvious target, hugging a post in the center of a nearly empty lobby, and when our eyes met, he moved toward me. My blood chilled. *Oh shit, here we go.* I stepped away from the supportive pillar and nervously attempted a comfortable stance. The dream was now a nightmare. I felt freakishly aroused, but then tree vines grew around my wrists.

"Shit!" I whispered. "I forgot about the goddamned *tree vines*!" Old childhood details were surfacing fast, but I had to deal with them one-by-one. *Am I ready for this?* I didn't have the time to decide, but it was too late to back down. I had to say *something*. My past was gone and destiny was walking toward me.

It was time to survive. Time to fill my chest with courage and step up. My heart throbbed. My mouth dried. *No more thinking about it. I'm really going to do this.* Dr. Krieg's words, "You're going to be a big star," rang through my head. I wanted to make a final desperate cry out for Mom, but she was gone for good. One last sweep of the area proved Papa was still a no-show, and it was time to stop looking for him. I was a man now, not a boy. I was completely on my own and about to go into business for myself. *Ready or not...here he comes.*

My muscles tightened. My throat numbed. Thoughts came too fast to organize. I squeezed my suitcase handle even harder. This was going to happen. I wondered where I should put the bags if we went into the bathroom—but I refused to think about what we might do in there.

My heart pounded. I looked for a positive angle. *I can buy a steak dinner with the money.* I didn't know for sure how long it would take, or what response I'd give. I guessed it would depend on what opening line the creep would use. I hoped he didn't taste like a smoker. I hoped he was as gentle as he looked. I needed him to respect and like me enough not to tie me down. Maybe I could nod like I was cool and glad to see him. I could open with a smile and a "Hey, man!"

He got halfway across the room. *Oh shit! How much should I charge?* I thought. *He can't know I'm new at this.* Steak dinners cost about five or six bucks, so I needed at least that much. I didn't know how much pot cost, but I'd best pad my price so I could afford some.

My first customer approached. His eyes connected straight into mine. He gave his line but almost too softly to be heard over the throbbing in my ears.

"Excuse me."

I nodded as cool as I could.

"You're Kyle Rickett, aren't you?"

Second impression

"Hey, man...." Then my eyes burst open. "Wait...." I shook my head. "*What?*"

He laughed like I was intentionally being funny for him.

A single nervous chuckle then fell from my mouth, which felt odd because I hadn't so much as smiled in almost a week, but that was the last line I'd expected to hear, and it surprised the hell out of me. All the anxiety of the morning unleashed through nervous humor. "Um...." I laughed a second time, which heated and moistened my dry eyes. "Yes?"

"Hi, Kyle. Tuck Taylor. Your grandpa sent me. Very glad to meet you." He offered me his right hand and awkwardly leaned forward, politely meeting my shortness. "Is...something funny?"

"No..." I stammered. "I mean...Hello." I laughed a third time, but as normal-Kyle would have, set down the duffle bag, and shyly extended my arm. "I'm sorry...I didn't...expect...."

His grip was firm but not rough. His oddly warm hand sent a wave of calmness to my elbow. It wasn't a hug, but it *was* especially nice. Like I'd known him my whole life. I didn't normally notice eye color, but his eyes were blue, like mine, and the friendliest I'd looked into in days.

"Can I have my hand back?" He tugged.

"Oh!" I blushed. "Sorry."

"It's all right." He retrieved his arm and shined a warm smile. "I'm staying next door to you. My grandfather is Tucker Johnson, Louie's best friend."

"So...where's my grandpa then?" I took a handkerchief from my pocket to wipe my forehead. My entire body warmed and chilled simultaneously. I shivered for a few seconds as muscles instantly relaxed. My focus left the bathroom door. I was Kyle Rickett again— and suddenly able to register the sweltering summer heat. My emotions wanted to force me to start bawling from the relief of the stress. But I was a young man now, so I forced myself to keep it together.

"He couldn't be here. Sorry I'm a couple minutes late."

"It's okay…" I meekly forgave him. "I haven't been here long."

"Oh, good. Then I'm right on time." He nodded and warmly smiled. "Let's get you home."

"Home?" My heart swelled. My right arm was still soaking in the warm sensations from his hand on mine. This time I couldn't stop from turning even more pink and pushing out some tears. I lowered the handkerchief to my chest and envisioned Papa's open arms waiting for me on his front porch. I could barely choke out words. "You're really here to bring me…*home*?"

Acknowledgments

My clients. My compassion was shaped in part by countless clients during the years I worked in crisis intervention, answering crisis hotlines and responding to law enforcement and hospital calls so I could stand with real-life crime victims during the most confusing and chaotic moments of their lives. In the support groups I hosted, many adult survivors of abuse and childhood bullying educated me on how fearful and alone their entire lives had become as a result of such an unruly beginning. These isolated individuals openly shared private stories in ways that enlightened me to the numbers of people who *feel* utterly alone in our crowded world.

My peers: When I have shared personal stories of my own fear and loneliness, my peers have opened up in return to share theirs. I've learned through open, heartfelt interactions that life is difficult for a lot of us— not just me. The more alone we feel, the more we don't see how many people all around us are just as alone. I wrote this series because I now know that we are all alone together.

Angela: My little sister was a well-loved and popular woman. No one, absolutely no one, noticed she was fading away until we discovered she was suddenly gone. Still haunted by her tragic and lonely passing, I now grasp the urgency of my message about recognizing when an isolated person needs rescue—*even from their own family*.

About the Author

James F. Johnson is the author of the Bullies & Allies series, consisting of *Disaster Island*, *The Goat Driver*, and *The Puzzled*, and is a contributor to the Richer Fuller Life project. He has spent years working with people in crisis, most commonly, adult survivors of childhood sexual abuse. He's worked on crisis intervention hotlines, and worked with law enforcement and hospital emergency room staffs to advocate for victims of sexual assault. He has been hosted as guest speaker in various community outreach programs, colleges, and professional development seminars, and is a former amateur standup comedian. In his writing, James expertly captures the experiences from his own life, and from the lives he's shared in with his many clients and peers who have helped him to understand the feelings and pitfalls of living with the lifelong emotional effects of childhood trauma.

James's studies have led him through years of research on PTSD, Complex-PTSD, gaslighting, and sociopathy. He readily shares his knowledge and insight into these topics in his public presentations, private conversations, novels, blog articles, and at his website, www.jamesfjohnson.com. He posts suggested reading lists, showing others how to find the same research that has enlightened him to how to identify and stand up against the many sociopaths who cross our paths. James believes that by teaching others how to identify and handle sociopaths, people have a chance of becoming free from their grips and power, and ultimately, of turning our society into a better, safer place for all of us.

NEXT IN THE SERIES:

BULLIES & ALLIES

Be sure to read the whole series

Be sure to read the whole Bullies & Allies series, to experience Kyle's further adventures as he learns about the sociopaths in his life, and that Post Traumatic Stress Disorder (PTSD) can be managed, trust can be learned, friendships can be made, and a long, happy life can still be lived, even when the traumas of childhood remain hidden in the background.

The Bullies & Allies story is told in the 1970s. Now, forty-plus years later, our hairstyles have changed and our cars, phones, and electronics have advanced in ways we could not have predicted. Our social and human challenges, however, remain unmoved. Bullying, abuse, isolation, PTSD, withdrawal, even suicide, are still prevalent in far too many lives. These problems not only cause the same grief as before, but they are also driven by the same reasons they were then.

In *Disaster Island*, the first book, we traveled down the road into Kyle's isolation with him. In the second book, *The Goat Driver*, we'll see the amazing and glorious healing power of friendship and trust. In the third book, *The Puzzled*, Kyle will learn that the effects of trauma can be challenging and far-reaching, but that there is always a productive future worth living for, and while he will always be an adult survivor of childhood abuse, his capacity for true happiness will be far greater than it would have been had his childhood been easier. Kyle will learn that plenty can be done to thoroughly enjoy an otherwise broken life.

Bullies & Allies Book 2: The Goat Driver.

Now distant from his family's dysfunction in Washington, Kyle arrives in Minnesota to spend the summer with his grandfather, Papa Louie. But Louie sees withdrawn vacancy in Kyle's eyes, and after having lost a friend named Maurey to suicide, Louie comes to believe his grandson is following the same path. When Kyle won't talk to him, Louie rallies the support of his young neighbor, Tuck Taylor, to intervene. Tuck, a trustworthy, but somewhat lost soul, quickly takes a liking to the boy and then makes a promise to Louie that he'll never let Kyle jump like Maurey did. Through Tuck, Kyle is able to learn, for the first time, how to trust someone. What happens over those few weeks surprises even Tuck when, by the end of the summer, he discovers and experiences the great power of benevolence, and that by saving Kyle, he has brought meaning to his own life. By saving another, he has saved himself.

Bullies & Allies Book 3: The Puzzled

Fourteen-year-old Kyle returns to Torano Island to resume the path he once struggled to survive, but this time not alone. He has a long distance alliance with Tuck in the shadows as his secret mentor. Things improve when Dr. Krieg's pedophilic attacks are stopped once and for all, and a change of schools gives a whole new start to a social life. Kyle now seems to have what he needs to survive the last four years of childhood. Or does he?

Unfortunately, trauma lingers and Kyle's traumas have left invisible scars and triggers, which act as dangerously hidden emotional booby-traps. His life is now a complicated puzzle with too many pieces to name. When a key member of the family dies and cousin Scooter vanishes and is presumed dead, Tuck's long-distance advice isn't enough, and best friend Connor becomes the only stable grip to remain in Kyle's life. But Connor is just a boy, and even he becomes frustrated by Kyle's self-destructive episodes.

Kyle has survived his enemies, but now he must learn to survive himself. Before Kyle turns eighteen, the final blow comes when his secret friendship with Tuck, his knowledge of Scooter's whereabouts, and his past sexual abuse at the hands of Dr. Krieg are all exposed once and for all. His family isn't equipped to know how to handle him, so Kyle feels more alone than ever before and unsure how to survive his personal shame or his family's dysfunction. Some say God never gives a person more than he can handle, but Kyle discovers that is not true.

Here's a sneak peek at Bullies & Allies, Book 2: *The Goat Driver*, by James F. Johnson: Expected release date is early 2018. You can check release dates for this, and all James's books by going to www.jamesfjohnson.com.

1

Rescue for a Rescue

My name is Kyle Rickett. I was fourteen when I met and befriended Tuck Taylor. He was twenty-one. We became inseparable after only a few, somewhat rocky days. We soon learned that to explain our intense bond and our age difference, we were wise to introduce ourselves as brothers.

Officer Schuman, now retired, has never forgotten the day he met the two of us brothers in August of 1974. He proudly wrote chapter one for me.

By Minnesota State Police Officer, Rick Schuman

God-damned hotrod

My lazy Friday afternoon patrol was ruined by another punk kid in another fast car. For nearly a year, most chases had been with slower, smaller cars, but now that the 1973-1974 oil crisis was over, some surviving old, big, fast hotrods were coming out of mothballs with a vengeance.

"God damn it!" I blurted out. The old GTO flew past me like Highway 6 was an airport runway. "Goddamned kids!"

I spun the patrol car around with a nasty screech of rubber on road, hit the gas and sirens, and called it in, "Beth, this is Schuman. I'm in pursuit of a mid-1960s Pontiac GTO, gold in color. He's flying fast and low northbound on Highway 6, about fifteen miles north of Deer River."

"Roger that, Rick. Do you need backup?"

"Nah. I got it. Looks like Texas plates, but I can't read them yet. I'll call it in when I catch up...if he doesn't kill himself first!"

"Good luck. Sounds like a fast car."

"Don't you worry, young lady. I can catch this one. There's nowhere for him to go on this stretch of highway."

The chase turned out to be a snoozer. Once I got up to about ninety, the driver gave up. My favorite kind of chase. My guess was that it was a kid. The way they gave up quick, I figured there'd be no trouble.

White-haired boy

I coasted to a stop behind the now quiet hotrod.

"Beth, this is Schuman...." I gave her the license plate and the exact mile marker where we'd stopped. She told me my deputy, Anders was heading in my direction and that she would let him know where I was.

I looked toward the car to see the driver doing something I hated. He or she was getting out of the car. That's when my adrenaline started pumping. I jumped out of mine as fast as I could with one hand up and the other hovering over my holster.

"Just stay in the car!"

The driver's hands went up quick. He or she was tiny. Shorter than the roof of the car, and with the whitest hair I'd ever seen. Was it a little old man? A short-haired, bleached-blonde woman? He or she was wearing a filthy white tank top, yellow gym shorts and some kind of hiking boots. "Jesus!" I questioned. "Is that a little *kid*?"

"Help!" he screamed, not getting back in the car like I had told him to. "Please help! Officer, it's an emergency. Can you help us find a hospital *please*?"

Knowing this could be a trick, I unsnapped my gun holster.

"Just step away from the car and keep your hands up, young man."

The kid's voice hadn't changed yet. No way should he have been driving that car. He followed my orders better now, but at the same time, I saw no other head through the back window. So, who was "us," why was he so covered in dirt and leaves, but driving such a nicely kept hotrod, and why were "they" going in the opposite direction from a hospital? Unless this was a kid who stole his neighbor's car, nothing was adding up yet, so I carefully walked toward him, maintaining my always important authoritative swagger.

"My brother's hurt."

"Is he in the car?"

The boy nodded politely and pointed through the open driver's door.

"How did he get hurt?"

"A tree fell on him." He pointed again, but more frantically into the car. His polite voice began to rise in panic. "We were cutting wood for our grandpa. Please hurry."

I finally made it to the driver's door with one eye on him and another on the passenger's seat. I wasn't ready for what I saw.

"Oh, Mother of *God*," I gasped.

One hell of a lot of blood

In the passenger's seat lay a young man, early twenties maybe, passed out cold—or dead. His thick light brown hair definitely looked like it had been professionally styled before it got messed up. That told me he wasn't a backwoods hick or a 1970s hippy. His jeans were torn at the knee, and his right leg was covered in blood from waist to boot. His white tank top was spattered with a blend of blood, mud, and more tree pieces.

"When did this happen?" I bellowed.

"About an hour ago. He isn't bleeding as bad as it looks; it's just soaked into his pants."

I glanced disbelievingly back at the boy, then at his injured brother. Obviously, reality wasn't setting in with this kid at the moment.

"I'd say he's bleeding pretty bad, son." I should have been less blunt with the poor kid. "This is as God-damned *serious* as it gets!"

The boy was so small. I don't know how he'd driven that big car as fast as he had. The top of his head barely reached my chin. He looked more panicked after I said what I said. I snagged his elbow before he could pass out.

"What's your name, son?"

"Kyle...Taylor." He tried holding it together and politely answering the questions he knew I had for him next. "That's my brother, Tuck. It's his car." He burst into bawling. "He can't die! He can't die! Please, don't let him die! He's all I have left!"

"Shh-shh-shh. I'll do everything I can, Kyle. Come with me." I pulled him by his shoulders toward the back of his car to get him off the highway before someone ran him over. I'd been a cop for two decades and had cleaned up plenty of roadside bloodbaths, but this kid was choking me up. His voice had a sadness to it I would never be able to forget. "Will you stay right here for me, Kyle?"

The kid nodded, but I wasn't sure how coherently.

"I'm calling for an ambulance. Okay? Don't move from that spot!"

"I was trying to get him to a hospital!" He nodded more frantically and kept craning his neck toward his brother in the car. "Please hurry!"

"Deer River Hospital's the other way, son!" I shouted back while running to my car.

He snapped his head toward both directions like he was trying to figure out where he was, but his eyes were glossing over. His expression, though panicked, was also turning vacant. He'd held it together pretty well to get his brother this far, but now that I was here to help, I think he was starting to fall apart. I've seen it before in bloody accidents. Shock. But this Kyle kid went into it deeper and quicker than any kid that age had done before. I think the poor youngster was dropping into his own private hell just then.

"Beth, get me an ambulance as fast as you can."

"Roger that Rick. I'll get Anders there also. What's going on?"

"The passenger's been hurt. His little brother, looks to be no more than twelve, was trying to drive him to a hospital It looks bad, Beth. Some sort of an accident in the woods. Get someone here fast." I looked up at Kyle again. He was starting to shiver and turn gray. He was becoming more and more frazzled by the second. "Beth, I think the driver's going into a bad case of shock, and I can't deal with both these boys. Call a second ambulance. And Anders needs to get here *now*!"

"He's three minutes out."

"Tell him to *speed it up*! I need him *now*!" I threw the mike onto the seat and ran back to the car to see if I could stop any bleeding while we waited for backup and an ambulance, which I knew would be a while. Kyle had handled himself well, but he was headed fast in the wrong direction.